Victor I. Vieth, JD, BS
Bette L. Bottoms, PhD
Alison R. Perona, JD, MA, BS
Editors

Ending Child Abuse: New Efforts in Prevention, Investigation, and Training

Ending Child Abuse: New Efforts in Prevention, Investigation, and Training has been co-published simultaneously as *Journal of Aggression, Maltreatment & Trauma*, Volume 12, Numbers 3/4, 2006.

Pre-publication REVIEWS, COMMENTARIES, EVALUATIONS . . .

"**P**ROVIDES SPECIFIC GUIDING PRINCIPLES that are based on scholarly findings. . . . ANYONE CONSIDERING THE FIELD OF CHILD PROTECTION SERVICES WOULD BENEFIT FROM THIS CLEAR PRESENTATION OF THE IMPORTANT ISSUES facing those in the field, including an informative overview of findings from leading experts in prevention, interviewing, and training. The authors point out what mistakes were made in the past and what changes were implemented to create significant improvements in the system. Forensic interviewers will learn age-appropriate interview techniques that will lead to accurate, complete reports; educators will learn about the most effective curriculum to prepare their students for the child protection field, and policymakers can learn models of prevention programs shown to be effective in reducing the overall prevalence of this all-too-common problem."

Beth M. Schwartz, PhD
Professor of Psychology
Randolph-Macon Woman's College

"**M**UCH-NEEDED . . . Fills a gap in the prevention literature. This collection ties together various disciplines into a single, comprehensive plan for the future. The authors not only present an overall direction, they also present very practical tools to use. WHETHER YOU ARE IN EDUCATION, LAW ENFORCEMENT, MEDICINE, OR SOCIAL WORK, THE IDEAS PRESENTED ARE GEMS. This text should be on the shelf of anyone who is serious about child advocacy. The material is wonderfully written and meticulously researched."

Christopher S. Greeley, MD
Medical Director
Child Abuse and Neglect Program
Vanderbilt Children's Hospital
Nashville, Tennessee

HMTP

The Haworth Maltreatment & Trauma Press®
An Imprint of The Haworth Press, Inc.

New York • London • Victoria (AU)
www.HaworthPress.com

Ending Child Abuse:
New Efforts in Prevention,
Investigation, and Training

Ending Child Abuse: New Efforts in Prevention, Investigation, and Training has been co-published simultaneously as *Journal of Aggression, Maltreatment & Trauma*, Volume 12, Numbers 3/4, 2006.

Monographic Separates from the *Journal of Aggression, Maltreatment & Trauma*[TM]

For additional information on these and other Haworth Press titles, including descriptions, tables of contents, reviews, and prices, use the QuickSearch catalog at http://www.HaworthPress.com.

Ending Child Abuse: New Efforts in Prevention, Investigation, and Training, edited by Victor I. Vieth, JD, BS, Bette L. Bottoms, PhD, Alison R. Perona, JD, MA, BS (Vol. 12, No. 3/4, 2006). *A collection of innovative approaches and aggressive strategies to end or significantly reduce child abuse in every community.*

Trauma Treatment Techniques: Innovative Trends, edited by Jacueline Garrick, CSW, ACSW, BCETS, and Mary Beth Williams, PhD, LSW, CTS (Vol. 12, No 1/2, 2006). *"This collection SIGNIFICANTLY BROADENS THE UNDERSTANDING OF INNOVATIVE TECHNIQUES for the treatment of PTSD and associated conditions." (John P. Wilson, Co-founder and Past President, International Society for Traumatic Stress Studies, Co-director, International Institute on Psychotraumatology)*

Ethical and Legal Issues for Mental Health Professionals: A Comprehensive Handbook of Principles and Standards, edited by Steven F. Bucky, Joanne E. Callan, and George Stricker (Vol. 11, No. 1/2 and 3, 2005). *"It is safe to say that every psychotherapist will be confronted with ethical and legal problems in the course of his or her career. THIS BOOK SHOULD BE RETAINED ON THE SHELF OF EVERY MENTAL HEALTH PRACTITIONER. This is an exhaustive compendium written by a distinguished battery of attorneys and psychotherapists, each of whom is an expert in his or her field. . . . It should be used as a resource guide when problems arise in the course of one's practice." (Martin Fleishman, MD, PhD, Active Staff, St. Francis Memorial Hospital, San Francisco; Author of "The Casebook of Residential Care Psychiatrist")*

The Trauma of Terrorism: Sharing Knowledge and Shared Care, An International Handbook, edited by Yael Danieli, PhD, Danny Brom, PhD, and Joe Sills, MA, (Vol. 9, No. 1/2 and 3/4, 2004 and Vol. 10, No. 1/2 and 3/4, 2005. *"This book pulls together key programs that enable society to cope with ongoing terrorism, and is thus a rich resource for both policymakers and those who aid terrorism's victims directly. It demonstrates the invaluable collaboration between government and private initiative in the development of a resilient society." (Danny Naveh, Minister of Health, Government of Israel)*

The Victimization of Children: Emerging Issues, edited by Janet L. Mullings, PhD, James W. Marquart, PhD, and Deborah J. Hartley, MS (Vol. 8, No. 1/2 [#15/16] and 3 [#17], 2003). *"A fascinating, illuminating, and often troubling collection of research on child victimization, abuse, and neglect. This book . . . is timely, thought-provoking, and an important contribution to the literature. No other book on the market today provides such an authoritative overview of the complex issues involved in child victimization." (Craig Hemmens, JD, PhD, Chair and Associate Professor, Department of Criminal Justice Administration, Boise State University)*

Intimate Violence: Contemporary Treatment Innovations, edited by Donald Dutton, PhD, and Daniel J. Sonkin, PhD (Vol. 7, No. 1/2 [#13/14], 2003). *"Excellent. . . . Represents 'outside the box' thinking. I highly recommend this book for everyone working in the field of domestic violence who wants to stay fresh. Readers will be stimulated and in most cases very valuably informed." (David B. Wexter, PhD, Executive Director, Relationship Training Institute, San Diego, CA)*

Trauma and Juvenile Delinquency: Theory, Research, and Interventions, edited by Ricky Greenwald, PsyD (Vol. 6, No. 1 [#11], 2002). *"Timely, concise, compassionate, and stimulating. . . . An impressive array of authors deals with various aspects of the problem in depth. This book will be of considerable interest to clinicians, teachers, and researchers in the mental health field, as well as administrators and juvenile justice personnel handling juvenile delinquents. I highly commend Dr. Greenwald on a job well done." (Hans Steiner, MD, Professor of Psychiatry and Behavioral Sciences, Stanford University School of Medicine)*

Domestic Violence Offenders: Current Interventions, Research, and Implications for Policies and Standards, edited by Robert Geffner, PhD, and Alan Rosenbaum, PhD (Vol. 5, No. 2 [#10], 2001).

The Shaken Baby Syndrome: A Multidisciplinary Approach, edited by Stephen Lazoritz, MD, and Vincent J. Palusci, MD (Vol. 5, No. 1 [#9], 2001). *The first book to cover the full spectrum of Shaken Baby Syndrome (SBS). Offers expert information and advice on every aspect of prevention, diagnosis, treatment, and follow-up.*

Trauma and Cognitive Science: A Meeting of Minds, Science, and Human Experience, edited by Jennifer J. Freyd, PhD, and Anne P. DePrince, MS (Vol. 4, No. 2 [#8] 2001). *"A fine collection of scholarly works that address key questions about memory for childhood and adult traumas from a variety of disciplines and empirical approaches. A must-read volume for anyone wishing to understand traumatic memory." (Kathryn Quina, PhD, Professor of Psychology & Women's Studies, University of Rhode Island)*

Program Evaluation and Family Violence Research, edited by Sally K. Ward, PhD, and David Finkelhor, PhD (Vol. 4, No. 1 [#7], 2000). *"Offers wise advice to evaluators and others interested in understanding the impact of their work. I learned a lot from reading this book." (Jeffrey L. Edleson, PhD, Professor, University of Minnesota, St. Paul)*

Sexual Abuse Litigation: A Practical Resource for Attorneys, Clinicians, and Advocates, edited by Rebecca Rix, MALS (Vol. 3, No. 2 [#6], 2000). *"An interesting and well developed treatment of the complex subject of child sexual abuse trauma. The merger of the legal, psychological, scientific and historical expertise of the authors provides a unique, in-depth analysis of delayed discovery in CSA litigation. This book, including the extremely useful appendices, is a must for the attorney or expert witness who is involved in the representation of survivors of sexual abuse." (Leonard Karp, JD, and Cheryl L. Karp, PhD, co-authors, Domestic Torts: Family Violence, Conflict and Sexual Abuse)*

Children Exposed to Domestic Violence: Current Issues in Research, Intervention, Prevention, and Policy Development, edited by Robert A. Geffner, PhD, Peter G. Jaffe, PhD, and Marlies Sudermann, PhD (Vol. 3, No. 1 [#5], 2000). *"A welcome addition to the resource library of every professional whose career encompasses issues of children's mental health, well-being, and best interest . . . I strongly recommend this helpful and stimulating text." (The Honorable Justice Grant A. Campbell, Justice of the Ontario Superior Court of Justice, Family Court, London, Canada)*

Maltreatment in Early Childhood: Tools for Research-Based Intervention, edited by Kathleen Coulborn Faller, PhD (Vol. 2, No. 2 [#4], 1999). *"This important book takes an international and cross-cultural look at child abuse and maltreatment. Discussing the history of abuse in the United States, exploring psychological trauma, and containing interviews with sexual abuse victims,* Maltreatment in Early Childhood *provides counselors and mental health practitioners with research that may help prevent child abuse or reveal the mistreatment some children endure."*

Multiple Victimization of Children: Conceptual, Developmental, Research, and Treatment Issues, edited by B. B. Robbie Rossman, PhD, and Mindy S. Rosenberg, PhD (Vol. 2, No. 1 [#3], 1998). *"This book takes on a large challenge and meets it with stunning success. It fills a glaring gap in the literature . . . " (Edward P. Mulvey, PhD, Associate Professor of Child Psychiatry, Western Psychiatric Institute and Clinic, University of Pittsburgh School of Medicine)*

Violence Issues for Health Care Educators and Providers, edited by L. Kevin Hamberger, PhD, Sandra K. Burge, PhD, Antonnette V. Graham, PhD, and Anthony J. Costa, MD (Vol. 1, No. 2 [#2], 1997). *"A superb book that contains invaluable hands-on advice for medical educators and health care professionals alike . . . " (Richard L. Holloways, PhD, Professor and Vice Chair, Department of Family and Community Medicine, and Associate Dean for Student Affairs, Medical College of Wisconsin)*

Violence and Sexual Abuse at Home: Current Issues in Spousal Battering and Child Maltreatment, edited by Robert Geffner, PhD, Susan B. Sorenson, PhD, and Paula K. Lundberg-Love, PhD (Vol. 1, No. 1 [#1], 1997). *"The Editors have distilled the important questions at the cutting edge of the field of violence studies, and have brought rigor, balance and moral fortitude to the search for answers." (Virginia Goldner, PhD, Co-Director, Gender and Violence Project, Senior Faculty, Ackerman Institute for Family Therapy)*

Ending Child Abuse:
New Efforts in Prevention,
Investigation, and Training

Victor I. Vieth, JD, BS
Bette L. Bottoms, PhD
Alison R. Perona, JD, MA, BS
Editors

Ending Child Abuse: New Efforts in Prevention, Investigation, and Training has been co-published simultaneously as *Journal of Aggression, Maltreatment & Trauma*, Volume 12, Numbers 3/4, 2006.

HMTP

The Haworth Maltreatment & Trauma Press®
An Imprint of The Haworth Press, Inc.

New York • London • Victoria (AU)
www.HaworthPress.com

Published by

The Haworth Maltreatment & Trauma Press, 10 Alice Street, Binghamton, NY 13904-1580 USA

The Haworth Maltreatment & Trauma Press is an imprint of The Haworth Press, Inc., 10 Alice Street, Binghamton, NY 13904-1580 USA.

Ending Child Abuse: New Efforts in Prevention, Investigation, and Training has been co-published simultaneously as *Journal of Aggression, Maltreatment & Trauma*, Volume 12, Numbers 3/4 2006.

Cover design by Kerry E. Mack

Library of Congress Cataloging-in-Publication Data

Ending Child Abuse: New Efforts in Prevention, Investigation, and Training/ Victor I. Vieth, Bette L. Bottoms, Alison R. Perona, editors.
     p. cm.
     "Co-published simultaneously as Journal of aggression, maltreatment & trauma, volume 12, numbers 3/4 2006."
     Includes bibliographical references and index.
     ISBN 10: 0-7890-2967-7 (hard cover: alk.paper)
     ISBN 13: 978-0-7890-2967-6 (hard cover: alk.paper)
     ISBN 10: 0-7890-2968-5 (hard cover: alk.paper)
     ISBN 13: 978-0-7890-2968-3 (hard cover: alk.paper)
     1. Child abuse–Investigation–United States. 2. Child abuse–Reporting–United States. 3. Interviewing in child abuse–United States 4. Child abuse–United States–Prevention I. Vieth, Victor I. II. Bottoms, Bette L. III. Perona, Alison R. IV. Journal of aggression, maltreatment & trauma
HV8079. C46E53 2006
362.76′0973–dc22
                                               2006002254

Indexing, Abstracting & Website/Internet Coverage

This section provides you with a list of major indexing & abstracting services and other tools for bibliographic access. That is to say, each service began covering this periodical during the year noted in the right column. Most Websites which are listed below have indicated that they will either post, disseminate, compile, archive, cite or alert their own Website users with research-based content from this work. (This list is as current as the copyright date of this publication.)

(continued)

(continued)

- *Referativnyi Zhurnal (Abstracts Journal of the All-Russian Institute of Scientific and Technical Information–in Russian)* <http://www.viniti.ru> 1998

- *Social Services Abstracts <http://www.csa.com>* .1998

- *Social Work Abstracts <http://www.silverplatter.com/catalog/swab.htm>* . . . 2001

- *Sociological Abstracts (SA) <http://www.csa.com>* 1998

- *Violence and Abuse Abstracts: A Review of Current Literature on Interpersonal Violence (VAA)* 2001

- *Women, Girls & Criminal Justice Newsletter. For subscriptions write: Civic Research Institute, 4490 Rte. 27 Box 585, Kingston, NJ 08528* 2004

Special Bibliographic Notes related to special journal issues (separates) and indexing/abstracting:

- indexing/abstracting services in this list will also cover material in any "separate" that is co-published simultaneously with Haworth's special thematic journal issue or DocuSerial. Indexing/abstracting usually covers material at the article/chapter level.
- monographic co-editions are intended for either non-subscribers or libraries which intend to purchase a second copy for their circulating collections.
- monographic co-editions are reported to all jobbers/wholesalers/approval plans. The source journal is listed as the "series" to assist the prevention of duplicate purchasing in the same manner utilized for books-in-series.
- to facilitate user/access services all indexing/abstracting services are encouraged to utilize the co-indexing entry note indicated at the bottom of the first page of each article/chapter/contribution.
- this is intended to assist a library user of any reference tool (whether print, electronic, online, or CD-ROM) to locate the monographic version if the library has purchased this version but not a subscription to the source journal.
- individual articles/chapters in any Haworth publication are also available through the Haworth Document Delivery Service (HDDS).

ABOUT THE EDITORS

Victor I. Vieth, JD, BS, graduated *magna cum laude* from Winona State University and earned his Juris Doctor from Hamline University School of Law. During law school, Mr. Vieth served as editor-in-chief of the law review and received the American Jurisprudence award for achievement in the study of Constitutional law. From 1988-1997, Mr. Vieth worked as a prosecutor in rural Minnesota where he gained national recognition for his work to address child abuse in small communities. He is a recipient of Distinguished Alumni Awards from both Hamline University School of Law and Winona State University. He has been named to the President's Honor Roll of the American Professional Society on the Abuse of Children. The Young Lawyers Division of the American Bar Association named him one of *"21 Young Lawyers Leading Us Into the 21st Century."* Mr. Vieth is the author of numerous articles pertaining to issues of child abuse and domestic violence. His article *Drying Their Tears* received the Associated Church Press' 1994 Award of Excellence. In 1997, Mr. Vieth joined the staff of the National Center for Prosecution of Child Abuse. From 1997-1999, Mr. Vieth worked as a Senior Attorney with the National Center, providing technical assistance and training to prosecutors around the country. In 1999, Mr. Vieth became Director of the National Center for the Prosecution of Child Abuse. In 2003, APRI appointed Mr. Vieth to serve as the first director of the National Child Protection Training Center on the campus of Winona State University.

Bette L. Bottoms, PhD, is Professor of Psychology at the University of Illinois at Chicago (UIC). She received her BA from Randolph-Macon Woman's College in Virginia, her MA from the University of Denver, and her PhD in Social Psychology from the State University of New York at Buffalo. She is the author of numerous scholarly articles and the co-editor of three books on children's eyewitness testimony, including the recently released *Children, Social Science, and the Law* from Cambridge University Press. She is a recipient of the Saleem Shah Early Career Award for Contributions to Psychology and Law Research (sponsored by the American Psychology-Law Society and the American Academy of Forensic Psychology), and four teaching awards. She is President of the American Psychological Association's Division 37: Child, Youth, and Family Services, and Past-President of Division 37's Section on Child Maltreatment.

Alison R. Perona, JD, MA, BS, is the Inspector General for the Chicago Transit Authority; in this capacity, she is responsible for all internal investigations involving allegations of misconduct, fraud, waste, and/or abuse at this agency. She received her BS from Illinois State University, her MA from the University of Illinois at Chicago, and her JD from DePaul University College of Law. Prior to her appointment as Inspector General, she served as an assistant state's attorney in the Cook County State's Attorney's Office from 1986-2004, where, in addition to trial assignments, she was supervisor of the Mass Molestation Unit, the Child Advocacy and Protection Unit, and supervisor in the Felony Trial Division.

Ending Child Abuse: New Efforts in Prevention, Investigation, and Training

CONTENTS

ABOUT THE CONTRIBUTORS

David L. Chadwick, MD, is Research Professor in the Department of Pediatrics, University of Utah Health Sciences Center. He is also the Director Emeritus of the Chadwick Center for Children and Families at the Children's Hospital San Diego. During his long California career, Dr. Chadwick spent 30 years at the Children's Hospital-San Diego, beginning as the Medical Director of the hospital and eventually launching the Center that now bears his name. His interest in child abuse resulted from early associations with Dr. C. Henry Kempe and Mrs. Helen Boardman, a medical social worker who was another pioneer in child protection. He has been a participant in the development of health care activities to protect children from abuse since the 1960s.

Congressman Robert E. "Bud" Cramer, Jr., has served as the Representative of Alabama's Fifth Congressional District since 1991. He is currently serving his seventh term in the United States House of Representatives. In 1984, while District Attorney, Cramer started the National Children's Advocacy Center (NCAC) in Huntsville in an effort to change forever the way child abuse cases are handled. This revolutionary program was the first of its kind to provide comprehensive support and services for physically and sexually abused children in a child-friendly environment. The Children's Advocacy Center that Cramer started in Huntsville has served as the model for over 600 similar programs in all 50 states, the District of Columbia, and the U.S. Virgin Islands. Last year alone, Children's Advocacy Centers across the country served over 135,000 abused children. To raise awareness of the issue of child abuse among his colleagues in Congress, Cramer has established a group of congressional supporters made up of over 175 members of the House and Senate and their spouses.

Robert D. McCormick, PhD, is the Director of the Center for Child Advocacy and Professor of Psychology at Montclair State University. He has served as a Consultant to the Division of Youth and Family Services (DYFS) and has extensive experience in the field of Forensic Psychology and Child Advocacy. Dr. McCormick maintains a private practice in psychology in Montclair where he has worked for many years with adult survivors of child neglect and abuse. He has published and lectured widely on issues related to the well-being of children.

Sharon G. Portwood, JD, PhD, currently serves as Associate Professor of Psychology at the University of Missouri-Kansas City. Dr. Portwood received her JD from the University of Texas School of Law in 1985, and after more than ten years as a practicing trial attorney, received her PhD in Psychology from the University of Virginia in 1996. Her research reflects an integration of her training and practice in law, community psychology, and developmental psychology applied to a broad spectrum of issues involving social policy, particularly as it impacts children, youth, and families at the systems level.

Erin Sorenson, AM, is currently the executive director of the Chicago Children's Advocacy Center. For the past 20 years, she has specialized in sexual assault and child sexual abuse issues. Ms. Sorenson has interviewed more than 3,000 children regarding sexual abuse allegations and has developed procedures on legally sound techniques to interview child witnesses. Ms. Sorenson has a Master's degree from of the University of Chicago's School of Social Service Administration.

David M. Williams, JD, received his BA from the University of Illinois, an MSc in Politics of the World Economy from the London School of Economics and a JD from Boston College Law School. He is an adjunct professor in the Criminal Justice Department of the University of Illinois at Chicago. He is currently an Assistant State's Attorney in the Gang Crime Unit of the Special Prosecutions Bureau of the Cook County State's Attorney's Office.

Foreword

Congressman Robert E. "Bud" Cramer, Jr.

In reviewing the contents of this book, I was struck by how far we have come as a nation in addressing child abuse and neglect. I was also struck by how much we have left to do.

In my work as a juvenile prosecutor and elected District Attorney, I saw first hand the complex nature of these cases and the need to develop specialized units of investigators and prosecutors to respond to allegations of abuse. As a District Attorney, I had the privilege of starting the nation's first Children's Advocacy Center. Later, as a United States Representative, I championed the cause of children by marshalling congressional support for both my National Children's Advocacy Center in Huntsville, Alabama, and the National Children's Alliance, a coalition of Children's Advocacy Centers (CACs) from across the nation that is headquartered in Washington, DC.

As a result of these reforms, countless children are interviewed sensitively, in child-friendly environments, by professionals skilled in conducting these interviews. As noted in one of the articles of this volume, there is a tremendous amount of research documenting effective interviewing practices. Our nation's Children's Advocacy Centers are dedicated to ensuring that all children are interviewed consistent with the best practices.

The investigation and prosecution of these cases has also improved tremendously in recent decades. This improvement is attributable in no

[Haworth co-indexing entry note]: "Foreword." Cramer, Jr., Robert E. "Bud." Co-published simultaneously in *Journal of Aggression, Maltreatment & Trauma* (The Haworth Maltreatment & Trauma Press, an imprint of The Haworth Press, Inc.) Vol. 12, No. 3/4, 2006; and: *Ending Child Abuse: New Efforts in Prevention, Investigation, and Training* (ed: Victor I. Vieth, Bette L. Bottoms, and Alison R. Perona) The Haworth Maltreatment & Trauma Press, an imprint of The Haworth Press, Inc., 2006. Single or multiple copies of this article are available for a fee from The Haworth Document Delivery Service [1-800-HAWORTH, 9:00 a.m. - 5:00 p.m. (EST). E-mail address: docdelivery@haworthpress.com].

small measure to the work of the National Center for Prosecution of Child Abuse and other programs of the American Prosecutors Research Institute. These and other training initiatives have made a difference on the front lines.

Despite these and other reforms, more remains to be done. We need to improve the mandated reporting system. We need to make forensic interview training available to every front line professional in the United States. We need to improve the training we give child protection professionals at the undergraduate and graduate levels. We need to continue to research prevention initiatives and implement those programs that truly make a difference in the lives of children. We also need to involve the faith community in our prevention efforts. We need to make sure that vertical prosecution is the norm in every community. The need for these and other reforms is also discussed at length in this volume.

This volume's lead article, *Unto the Third Generation*, argues that if our nation commits itself to the task we can virtually eliminate child abuse over the course of three generations. Although I am sure each of us hopes to accomplish this goal more quickly, the timeline is not as important as the goal itself. Simply put, we must, in every community in this country, work ceaselessly toward the end of child abuse.

President Kennedy once told a story of a boy who tossed his hat over a wall so that he would have no choice but to follow. With the publication of this volume, we have tossed our hat over an important wall in the fight against child abuse and we too have no choice but to follow. It is my fondest hope that the reforms proposed in this volume will not only come to pass but that this publication will spur child protection professionals everywhere to engage in a meaningful dialogue that will produce additional ideas for improving our child protection system and speeding the day when child abuse no longer exists.

To this end, let us begin the climb.

INTRODUCTION

Ending Child Abuse:
Introducing a Collection
of New Perspectives
and Practical Techniques

Victor I. Vieth
Bette L. Bottoms
Alison R. Perona

SUMMARY. The editors provide an overview of the obstacles that prevent us from ending child abuse in the United States and briefly summarize the various articles in this volume that address these obstacles from multiple points of view. *[Article copies available for a fee from The Haworth Document Delivery Service: 1-800-HAWORTH. E-mail address: <docdelivery@haworthpress.com> Website: <http://www.HaworthPress.com> ©2006 by The HaworthPress, Inc. All rights reserved.]*

Address correspondence to: Victor I. Vieth, JD, National Child Protection Training Center, Winona State University, 227 Maxwell Hall, Winona, MN 55987.

[Haworth co-indexing entry note]: "Ending Child Abuse: Introducing a Collection of New Perspectives and Practical Techniques." Vieth, Victor I., Bette L. Bottoms, and Alison R. Perona. Co-published simultaneously in *Journal of Aggression, Maltreatment & Trauma* (The Haworth Maltreatment & Trauma Press, an imprint of The Haworth Press, Inc.) Vol. 12, No. 3/4, 2006; and: *Ending Child Abuse: New Efforts in Prevention, Investigation, and Training* (ed: Victor I. Vieth, Bette L. Bottoms, and Alison R. Perona) The Haworth Maltreatment & Trauma Press, an imprint of The Haworth Press, Inc., 2006. Single or multiple copies of this article are available for a fee from The Haworth Document Delivery Service [1-800-HAWORTH, 9:00 a.m. - 5:00 p.m. (EST). E-mail address: docdelivery@haworthpress.com].

Available online at http://www.haworthpress.com/web/JAMT
© 2006 by The Haworth Press, Inc. All rights reserved.
doi:10.1300/J146v12n03_01

1

KEYWORDS. Mandated reporting, model curricula, forensic interviewing, prevention, child abuse

There is, in the United States today, a culture permitting child abuse to thrive. As a result,

- Victims do not feel empowered to report their abuses.
- Mandated reporters often fail to report abuse, no matter how clear the evidence.
- Allegations that are reported are often screened out with little or no investigation.
- When investigations are conducted, many of the front line responders are inadequately trained and/or inexperienced in handling maltreatment cases, and abuse is therefore not well documented or successfully prosecuted.
- When child abuse is eventually documented, the victims are typically older and have needlessly endured years of abuse.
- Child abuse prevention efforts are woefully under-funded and are not present in any meaningful sense in most communities in our country.

In the lead article to this volume, Victor I. Vieth proposes to end this culture by implementing model curricula in every undergraduate and graduate institution in our nation. These curricula will reduce on-the-job training needed by the law enforcement officers, social workers, doctors, nurses, veterinarians, psychologists, clergy, prosecutors, and others who will enter mandated reporting or child protection professions. He also proposes ongoing instruction for child protection professionals that will include forensic interview training for everyone who must speak to children about abuse. Finally, he calls for massive education of America's child protection professionals in the art and science of developing and funding prevention programs at the community level.

These and other proposals are not pie in the sky, but are in fact unfolding at some level across the country. As a case in point, Montclair State University in New Jersey has revamped both its undergraduate and graduate curriculum in the hope of better preparing professionals who advocate for children. The reforms at Montclair State University are detailed in an article by Robert D. McCormick.

Alison R. Perona, Bette L. Bottoms, and Erin Sorenson argue that forensic interviews should be informed by sound research. They provide important, practical recommendations for interviewing children, and they support each recommendation with research and experience. They also review the best practices for conducting a legally defensible forensic interview utilizing a structured protocol, and offer practical advice for professionals seeking to access the social science literature related to children's eyewitness abilities.

To assist communities in developing effective prevention programs, Sharon G. Portwood examines our current knowledge about stopping abuse before it begins. She discusses the strengths and limitations of child empowerment and parent education models for prevention, and she advocates for broader social and system-level reforms.

Although investigators and prosecutors have made great strides in the past 20 years in improving their response to allegations of child abuse, concepts such as vertical prosecution are not yet in place in every jurisdiction. This concept is just as important in responding to allegations of physically abused and murdered children as it those victimized sexually. In his article, David M. Williams outlines the vertical prosecution in such cases, and details a model for its operation.

This volume concludes with an essay from David L. Chadwick, who considers these proposals in their historical context and offers some additional thoughts for building on these proposals and speeding toward the end of child maltreatment.

Thus, our volume is a timely and important collection of papers from an impressive array of social scientists and legal scholars. All contributions are grounded in scholarly work but written for a broad audience, and all place primary emphasis on practical implications. As such, this collection should be of interest to a wide readership, from practitioners, researchers, and students, to mental health, social service, medical, and legal professionals concerned with child abuse and children's welfare.

We wish to thank the many people who made this endeavor possible, including the authors of each contribution, who worked diligently to help us produce this high quality collection, and Bob Geffner and his staff who provided support ranging from encouragement to copy editing. We now invite you to a much needed forum for information exchange among a distinguished group of scholars and professionals. We hope that you, and eventually children nationally, will benefit from it.

ARTICLES

Unto the Third Generation:
A Call to End Child Abuse in the United States
Within 120 Years

Victor I. Vieth

SUMMARY. It is possible to significantly reduce, even eliminate child abuse if we address five obstacles: (1) many mandated reporters fail to comply with the law; (2) most child abuse reports are not investigated; (3) frontline child protection professionals are inadequately trained; (4) we do not address child abuse at the youngest ages; and (5) maltreated

Address correspondence to: Victor I. Vieth, JD, The National Child Protection Training Center, Winona State University, 227 Maxwell Hall, Winona, MN 55987.

The author would like to thank Grant Bauer, Barbara Boat, Jeff Brickman, Allison DeFelice, Robin Delany-Shabazz, Mark Ells, Tom Fallon, Norm Gahn, Joe Gow, Lori Holmes, Todd Kosovich, Nancy Lamb, Jim Luttrull, Christine Mennen, Sarah Murphy, John Myers, Charles Phipps, Bob Reece, George Ross, John Stirling, Rick Trunfio, Anne Graffam Walker, Mary Wennen, Dawn Doran Wilsey, and Debra Whitcomb for research, editing and substantive review. The author is equally indebted to the more than 5,000 front line child protection professionals from all 50 states who have heard this paper delivered as a keynote address and who have offered their valuable input.

[Haworth co-indexing entry note]: "Unto the Third Generation: A Call to End Child Abuse in the United States Within 120 Years." Vieth, Victor I. Co-published simultaneously in *Journal of Aggression, Maltreatment & Trauma* (The Haworth Maltreatment & Trauma Press, an imprint of The Haworth Press, Inc.) Vol. 12, No. 3/4, 2006; and: *Ending Child Abuse: New Efforts in Prevention, Investigation, and Training* (ed: Victor I. Vieth, Bette L. Bottoms, and Alison R. Perona) The Haworth Maltreatment & Trauma Press, an imprint of The Haworth Press, Inc., 2006. Single or multiple copies of this article are available for a fee from The Haworth Document Delivery Service [1-800-HAWORTH, 9:00 a.m. - 5:00 p.m. (EST). E-mail address: docdelivery@haworthpress.com].

children receive an inadequate share of financial resources. Accordingly, we must reform our higher education system to ensure that all child protection professionals have the skills necessary to recognize and respond to abuse. We must provide ongoing training to professionals in the field, have at least one forensic interview-training program in each state, develop prevention programs at the local level, and teach frontline professionals to advocate for children. Finally, we must recruit a second generation that will build on these successes and continue to improve our response until child abuse no longer exists. *[Article copies available for a fee from The Haworth Document Delivery Service: 1-800-HAWORTH. E-mail address: <docdelivery@haworthpress.com> Website: <http://www.HaworthPress. com> © 2006 by The Haworth Press, Inc. All rights reserved.]*

KEYWORDS. Mandated reports, forensic interviews, child protection curriculums, child abuse prevention

> *Take heart. Suffering when it climbs*
> *highest lasts but a little time.*

–Aeschylus[1]

The thought had been in my head for some time but I had never said it aloud much less in a setting quite as public as this one.[2] And yet, there I was sitting as part of a panel discussion in front of 200 Mississippi child protection professionals and faced with the question of predicting the future for child abuse victims in our country. I could have played it safe and offered thoughts on likely challenges and reforms we will see in the years ahead. Instead, I said what I really thought and I will say it again now.

I believe we can end child abuse[3] in the United States within three generations. If we start the clock ticking from this moment, this gives us 120 years to get the job done.[4] Please do not misunderstand me. This statement is not the sort of platitude offered by those seeking votes every other November. I am not carelessly joining the throng of those who speak wistfully but insincerely about ending this nightmare. I really mean it. We can end child abuse and we can do so within the lifetimes of our great grandchildren.

When I say "end" child abuse I mean we can achieve the sort of victory we have in the fight against polio. There will be re-occurrences and I can think of no means to prevent rage, mental illness or other factors from always contributing at some level to the abuse and neglect of children. We can, though, end cyclical child abuse and reduce from millions to thousands the number of children victimized over the course of any decade.

In saying this, I am echoing the voice of many leaders in the child protection field. Although Dr. David Chadwick contends that a significant reduction, much less elimination of child abuse cannot be achieved in less than a century, he does believe victory is possible.[5] According to Chadwick, this victory will "require keepers of a plan who will devote many decades of their lives to the effort. The keepers will keep the message alive. It will take sweat and tears. These keepers must recruit successors with similar dedication. Who, among you, are the keepers? Who will be willing to step forward and work tirelessly to keep the message alive?"[6]

Anne Cohn Donnelly also sees the potential for a very different America a century or so from now but she warns that truly ending child abuse will require "adopting a far longer view than we have historically held, such as planning out our efforts over decades, not years, and likewise measuring their success over decades not years. This new approach would require flexibility and a great deal of patience. But in my own view, it is possible. Not that we will ever totally eradicate child maltreatment, but rather that we do have it within us to bring about very significant reductions in maltreatment over the long haul."[7]

While there may be, then, a consensus that the near eradication of child abuse is possible over the course of a century, there remains the question of who will be the keepers of this plan and what, exactly, will the plan entail? The keepers, I suggest, are the universities that train front line professionals and, in turn, the front line professionals who serve children in need. As for the plan, many specifics will have to be developed between university professors and front line professionals as we strive to bring academia into the street. Having said this, I believe a meaningful blueprint for action is emerging across America. Unlike so many social epidemics, the changes now unfolding in our land are being driven from the bottom up. The mobilization on the front lines means there is every reason to expect success. This is because only when those closest to the front speak with a common, if not altogether united, voice will child maltreatment end. That day is approaching.

THE HISTORY OF THE FIGHT AGAINST CHILD ABUSE

In American history, we can find skirmishes against the social ill of child abuse but, to a great extent, we have abandoned children to the mercy of those who harm them. In 1865, the Society to Prevent Cruelty to Animals was founded but it wasn't until 1874 that the Society to Prevent Cruelty to Children was founded. It wasn't until the 1930s with the passage of the Social Security Act that the federal government recognized an interest in protecting children from abuse. It wasn't until 1962 when C. Henry Kempe authored the Battered Child Syndrome that physicians recognized child abuse as an independent diagnosis. It wasn't until 1967 that all 50 states passed mandated reporting laws. It wasn't until the 1970s that these laws were expanded to include within their purview protecting children victimized sexually. Even then, though, the primary purpose of the laws was to intervene solely with social services. Although the prosecution of child abusers was not new,[8] the 1980s produced a dramatic increase in the number of cases brought to court.[9] Unfortunately, child abuse cases are so complex and so different from other crimes that the investigators and prosecutors courageous enough to pursue these cases often did so incompetently. As a result, there was a backlash[10] and many prosecutors simply chose not to pursue child abuse cases unless there was clear medical evidence or a confession. For all practical purposes, this means that many parts of the country did not, and still do not, prosecute child abusers.

The handling of child abuse cases on the front lines reflects the view of child victims contained in academic literature. As noted by one commentator, prior to the mid-1970s, the "legal, mental health, and medical literature contributed to a legacy of skepticism about allegations of rape and child sexual abuse."[11] Although there continue to be "serious" academic articles perpetuating ancient myths about child victims,[12] the shift in scholarship in the mid-1970s was the forerunner of reforms on the front lines.

In 1985, the National District Attorneys Association took action to improve the quality of investigations and prosecutions by creating the National Center for Prosecution of Child Abuse with funding support from the United States Congress. The organization quickly became and still remains the premiere trainer of child abuse investigators and prosecutors in the United States. In the past three years, for example, NCPCA has traveled to every part of this country and trained over 30,000 police officers, social workers and prosecutors.

In addition to NCPCA, other national organizations began to seek reforms in the handling of child abuse cases. As a result, most states today require that child abuse cases be handled by a multi-disciplinary team (MDT).[13] There is also a clear consensus that children should be interviewed in child friendly environments such as child advocacy centers (CAC). Today there are literally hundreds of CACs that can be found in 48 states and several U.S. territories.[14]

As a nation, we have done more to address child abuse in the past 30 years than occurred in the first 200 years of our history. Unfortunately, the obstacles that remain are nothing less than mountains.

THE PRESENT STATE OF THE CONFLICT: THE FIVE OBSTACLES TO ENDING CHILD ABUSE

Many children suspected of being abused are not reported into the system. A 1990 study found that only 40% of maltreatment cases and 35% of the most serious cases known to professionals mandated to report were in fact reported or otherwise getting into the child protection system (CPS).[15] A study published one decade later found that 65% of social workers, 53% of physicians and 58% of physician assistants were not reporting all cases of suspected abuse.[16]

In a survey of 197 teachers, these educators were given two hypothetical cases of abuse. In the first hypothetical, the teachers were asked if they would make a report when a student tells them a stepfather has been touching their genitals. In the second hypothetical, the teachers were asked if they would make a report when a student tells them that another teacher was touching their genitals. Only 26% of the teachers said they would report the first instance to the authorities and only 11% said they would report the second incident to the authorities.[17]

There are several reasons why mandated reporters do not report. Insufficient evidence, lack of certainty that abuse has occurred, the belief a report will cause additional harm, and the need to maintain a good relationship with patients and clients are some of the reasons cited by reporters who fail to comply with the law.[18] Ambiguity in some mandated reporting statutes also contributes to underreporting. A survey of mandated reporters in Iowa revealed difficulty in determining whether a given injury was reportable under the Iowa law.[19]

Even when the law is clear, ignorance of its provisions may prevent a report from being made. For instance, I once handled a case where a physician was frustrated that he could not report a pregnant mother's use of cocaine. In fact, Minnesota law required him to make such a report.[20]

A lack of training may explain the ignorance of some mandated reporters about their obligations. In a 1989 survey of 480 elementary school teachers, 50% said they had not received any in-service training on mandated reporting and most of the teachers were not fully aware of their school's policies as to the handling of child abuse cases.[21] One decade later, inadequate training of reporters persists. In a 1999 survey of 382 master's level social workers, pediatricians, physicians, and physician assistants, researchers found that 57% of the respondents had received less than ten hours of training on their obligations as mandated reporters.[22] In a 2001 survey of 197 teachers, 74% said they received "minimal" or "inadequate" preparation in college to prepare them for the work of being a mandated reporter and 58% said they were receiving minimal or inadequate training on child abuse once they entered the field.[23]

Even if a reporter is not ignorant about his obligations, other factors come into play. Physicians often worry about the effects of an unfounded report on their private practice.[24] In small towns, patients may be reluctant to visit a physician who has previously reported abuse, particularly if the report is viewed as frivolous.[25] Although the identity of a reporter is to be handled in confidence, small-town life is such that the identity of the reporter can often be detected.[26]

Some skilled reporters recognize that child protection investigators must prioritize the reports received and may be able to respond to only the most serious. Recognizing this, some reporters may not call in a suspicion of abuse because it is believed no action can be taken.[27]

Even when reports come into the system, most children will never have their cases investigated. In 1999, there were 3.244 million children reported as abused and neglected.[28] Most of these cases will never be investigated. According to the Third National Incidence Study of Child Abuse and Neglect (NIS-3), only 28-33 percent of America's maltreated children have their cases investigated by CPS.[29] The report found "especially remarkable the finding that CPS investigation extended to only slightly more than one-fourth of the children who were seriously harmed or injured by abuse and neglect." The gloomy conclusion of NIS-3 is that "as the total number of maltreated children has risen, it means that a larger percentage of these children have not had access to CPS investigation of their maltreatment. This picture suggests that the CPS system has reached its capacity to respond to the maltreated child population."[30]

Seven years after this disheartening conclusion, researchers continue to document that the large volume of children whose allegations are either not investigated or that result in a CPS finding of "unsubstantiated" are just as likely to be victims of abuse as are those children whose allegations are substantiated. As one recent study documents, the "high level of recidivism among unsubstantiated cases show unambiguously that such cases are at high risk for subsequent maltreatment and show clearly that these cases are not simply erroneous reports made against families unlikely to engage in child maltreatment."[31]

In Missouri, for example, approximately 80% of child maltreatment reports were not substantiated and yet this "large number of initially unsubstantiated victims comprises more than three quarters of the victims that later return to the attention of the child welfare system."[32]

In summarizing twenty years of work with child molesters, famed psychologist Dr. Anna Salter laments:

> In the interviews I have done, they (the perpetrators) have admitted to roughly 10 to 1,250 victims. What was truly frightening was that *all* the offenders had been reported before by children, and the reports had been ignored (emphasis added). [33]

Even when cases are investigated, the investigators and other front line responders are often inadequately trained and inexperienced. Undergraduate, graduate and law schools seldom prepare students for the reality of child protection. Reporter Anna Quindlen describes a social worker's obstacles as follows:

> Their training is inadequate, and the number of workers is too small for the number of families in trouble. Some of the cases would require a battalion of cops, doctors, and social workers to handle; instead there are two kids fresh out of college with good intentions and a handful of forms.[34]

Commenting on his lack of training, social worker Marc Parent said he received "two weeks of solemn discussion on child protective issues, but little on getting a drug dealer to let you into an abandoned building or talking a restless police officer into sticking around until you get through with a case and back into your car."[35]

Part of the problem may be the standards promulgated by the Council on Social Work Education (CSWE) for accreditation of social work undergraduate programs. Although CSWE recognizes the "purposes of

social work education are to prepare competent and effective professionals,"[36] some of the accreditation standards limit the ability of universities to adopt curricula that will produce competent child protection
workers. Specifically, the accreditation standards state that "baccalau-
reate social work education programs prepare graduates for *generalist*
professional practice" and that only "master's social work education
programs prepare graduates for advanced professional practice in an
area of concentration"[37] (emphasis added).

The problem with the CSWE standards is that when it comes to the
work of child protection, there simply is no room at the inn for general-
ists. From day one, front line child protection workers must be able to
interview child victims, conduct assessments or investigations, collect
evidence for child protection proceedings, develop case plans with a realistic hope of preventing the re-occurrence of abuse and, in some cases,
to advocate for termination of parental rights. When CPS workers lack
these and other essential skills, children continue to be abused and, in
some cases, they die.

The problem extends to graduate schools as well. A recently published study of American Psychological Association (APA) accredited
graduate programs found that many of the programs "fall far short" of
guidelines proposed by the APA for minimal levels of competence in
handling child maltreatment cases.[38] The study finds the lack of graduate training for psychology students "contradicts the rapidly expanding
literature on responding to maltreatment and the demands of this interdisciplinary, professional endeavor."[39]

Discussing her educational background, psychologist Anna Salter
writes:

> In the two years I spent at Tufts getting a Masters degree in Child
> Study and the five years I spent at Harvard getting a PhD in Psy-
> chology and Public Practice, there was virtually nothing on child
> sexual and physical abuse in any course I took. I had one lecture on
> the victims of child abuse, but not a single lecture anywhere on of-
> fenders. Ironically, many of the lectures were on maladies so rare
> I've yet to see them in twenty years of practice.[40]

The training we provide to medical professionals is similarly inadequate. When it comes to medical schools, the reality is that "more than 40
years after the diagnosis of battered child syndrome entered the literature,
our pediatric residency programs do not have a significant education requirement for preventing, recognizing, or managing child abuse."[41] As a

result, egregious errors occur. In one study, for example, researchers found that 31% of shaken baby cases were not recognized by the physicians who first evaluated these victims.[42]

When universities and other institutions of higher education fail to teach practical information to the child abuse professionals of tomorrow, it means these professionals must learn on the job with the lives of children hanging in the balance. As a result, children are often not protected or even die and child protection workers lose their idealism and add themselves to the list of burned out workers.

Even when an investigation successfully substantiates abuse and gets a victim into the system, the child is typically older and it is more difficult to address the physical, emotional and other hardships caused by the abuse. The inability of many investigators to interview and otherwise work with young children means that we fail to address child abuse at the outset.[43] As a result, it is primarily older victims who are accepted into the system. The average age of victims who come to court is 10 and the median age is 13.[44] In many cases, older victims come into the system as delinquents, runaways, and prostitutes.[45] If, as a nation, we are ever going to break the cycle of child abuse we must intervene in the lives of these children when they are much younger. At the present time, the cost of dealing with child abuse primarily when its victims are older or have reached adulthood is staggering. Each year, we spend approximately 100 billion dollars in dealing with the aftermath of child abuse.[46] Many of these costs could be avoided if we can get more kids into the system at younger ages and address the child abuse in its earliest stages.

Because the child protection community lacks a unified voice in communicating the needs of maltreated children, these victims receive an inadequate share of our country's financial resources. Although child abuse and neglect has been appropriately termed a "public health epidemic," our nation has not invested money in addressing this ill to the extent we have other epidemics. For example, a study of federal research commitment found we invest one nickel for every 100 dollars of societal cost associated with child abuse whereas we invest two dollars for every 100 dollars of societal cost associated with cancer.[47] This is so even though the rate of child abuse is ten times greater than the rate of cancer.[48] In the words of Dr. Chadwick and colleagues, "(w)ithout the appropriate investment, it will be difficult to successfully achieve a systematic, coordinated national effort to ameliorate child abuse and neglect."[49]

In a paper discussing the modern political history of child abuse and neglect, Dr. Richard Krugman, Dean of the University of Colorado School of Medicine, offers this analysis of the problem:

> Effective policy making requires an "iron triangle": an effective lobbying organization, several congressional "champions," and inside help from a supportive bureaucracy. In contrast to the many instances of effective political efforts in health and defense, for example, the child protection system is ineffective. There are few notable Congressional advocates, a weak lobby, and an even weaker bureaucracy.[50]

Arguably the most effective voice for children is the front line professionals closest to the problem. Unfortunately, the turnover rate for social workers and other professionals is so high that it results in those closest to the situation never mastering the art of handling their assigned caseloads much less learn how to communicate to governmental leaders what does and does not work in addressing child abuse and neglect.

THE BATTLE PLAN FOR ENDING CHILD ABUSE

Stated in its simplest terms, three things must happen if we are to significantly reduce and eventually end child abuse. First, abused children must be reported into the system and those reports must be of a high quality. Second, the system must conduct a competent investigation of every child abuse case that comes to its attention and, when abuse is substantiated, appropriate civil and criminal actions must be competently pursued. Third, we must teach police officers, prosecutors and social workers to be community leaders in the prevention of child abuse. As part of this responsibility, front line child protection professionals must effectively communicate to governmental and other leaders the needs of maltreated children and the means most effective in addressing these needs.

Abused children must be reported into the system and those reports must be of a high quality. Teachers, day care providers, foster parents, doctors and others who work daily with young children are on the front lines of the child protection system. If these professionals are ignorant in the detection of abuse or, even if knowledgeable of their obligations, are unwilling to report, most victims will be left unprotected. If the vast majority of these cases are not reported,[51] we are leaving most child victims to fend for themselves. To correct this problem, two things must happen.

Every university must teach students entering mandated reporting professions the necessary skills to competently perform this task. The United States must end on-the-job training for mandated reporters. To this end, every graduate of every American university that declares a major in a field where they will likely be mandated reporters must receive comprehensive training that equips them for this task. Moreover, the training must be tailored to the professions the students will be entering. We should not, for example, teach future teachers how to do an autopsy but we should teach them about unusual sexual behaviors or bruising patterns that indicate abuse.

We must also teach ethics to tomorrow's mandated reporters. What should a teacher do, for example, if she suspects abuse and alerts her principal but the principal tells her not to report? We must teach these students to make the report for the sake of the child and to comply with the law. Even if the student takes a position in a state such as Virginia, where simply alerting the principal is sufficient,[52] we must encourage future teachers to go the extra mile and make the report themselves. They, after all, will have the best and most direct knowledge of the child and the basis for their suspicions.

This is not a pie in the sky proposal. The American Prosecutors Research Institute (APRI) is partnering with a prestigious university in Minnesota interested in becoming the first institution to adopt this plan.[53] Several other universities have approached us to assist them in developing something similar. Once developed, we believe that graduates of these programs will make a higher percentage of substantiated reports than others in their profession who have not received this training. It is our hope that we can demonstrate this with research and persuade hundreds of universities to follow suit.

Mandated reporters in the field must receive annual training on the detection of abuse and their obligations to report. For those mandated reporters already in the field, child protection professionals should take the lead in their communities to ensure reporters are adequately trained on an annual basis. This was the practice in Cottonwood County, Minnesota, where I served as a child protection attorney and child abuse prosecutor for several years.[54] This practice was based on the simple theory that if abused children are not reported, society will be unable to stop the abuse and repair the child's family.

Child protection workers and law enforcement officers must conduct a competent investigation of every child abuse case that comes to their attention and, when abuse is substantiated, pursue appropriate civil and criminal actions. Children reported as victims or witnesses to an act of child abuse must be interviewed by a social worker, police officer or other professional trained in the science and art of speaking to children.

Develop state of the art forensic interviewing courses such as APRI/CornerHouse's Finding Words. Front line interviewers must have basic training on child development, linguistics, memory and suggestibility and other issues impacting on the child interview. Interviewers must have a thorough understanding of how the dynamics of abuse will impact the interview. An older child, for example, may not view herself as a victim or may have guilt over her "compliance" with the act.[55] Irrespective of their age, children should be interviewed as part of a forensic interviewing protocol that is supported by research.[56]

There are a number of national and state organizations that offer quality forensic interview training including the American Professional Society on the Abuse of Children (APSAC),[57] the National CAC Academy in Huntsville,[58] CornerHouse,[59] the Cincinnati Children's Hospital Medical Center,[60] and First Witness.[61]

In 1998, APRI's National Center for Prosecution of Child Abuse partnered with CornerHouse, a child sexual abuse evaluation and training center in Minnesota, to present a forensic interview training program entitled *Finding Words*.[62] One of the unique features of this program is that *Finding Words* trains teams as opposed to individuals and insists that prosecutors be part of the team. Since an investigative interview may need to be defended in court, the prosecutor must have the same base of knowledge as the investigator. Equally important, the prosecutor who may call a child as a witness must be well versed in asking questions the child can understand.

Finding Words not only teaches the students pertinent research in child development, linguistics, memory, and suggestibility but also requires students to read much of the literature. Each student interviews a child about a non-abuse event such as a trip to the zoo and then is critiqued.

The heart of the course is the final two days when the 40 students are divided into four groups of ten. The students then receive ten fictitious reports of child sexual abuse. Working with their teams, they chart out a game plan of how a particular interview will unfold. Developmentally, what is the child's likely attention span? What cultural barriers or blocks should I be on the lookout for? What alternative hypothesis will I explore in the interview? Then, each student gets a chance to do a 30 minute videotaped interview with a sexual abuse victim. The "victims" are portrayed by adult actors/actresses who themselves have received some child development training. In this way, a student who asks a de-

velopmentally inappropriate question will get the answer he is *not* looking for. If, for example, the student asks the actor if "daddy's pee-pee
was hard or soft," the student is trying to find out if the alleged perpetrator had an erection. If the actor, though, is playing the role of a
4-year-old child he will respond "soft" because, at that age, the child is
likely thinking in terms of texture.

When the student completes the interview, he or she receives cri-
tiques from each of his nine peers. The reason we require the students to
critique one another is that we are trying to build into each community
the idea of ongoing peer review. We are trying to drive home to the students the idea that when it comes to protecting children, there is no room
for egos. The final critique would be from the professional interviewer
assigned to the room.

The last part of the course is an essay examination to measure the students' grasp of the materials. As of this writing, we have had over 300
graduates of *Finding Words* and all but a handful of students have successfully completed the course.

Each state must have a forensic interviewing course of the quality of
Finding Words that is locally run and taught. Quality forensic interview
training programs must provide hands-on instruction in which students
can practice their skills. Unfortunately, this necessary approach limits
the number of students and creates a demand for training that no national course can provide. In the case of *Finding Words,* for example,
the demand for admittance into the course was so great that APRI was
turning away as many as 90% of the investigators and prosecutors who
applied.[63] As a result, APRI concluded that the future of forensic interview training lay in establishing state and local training courses that up-
hold national standards.

To establish state-run forensic interview training courses, APRI
launched a program entitled *Half a Nation by 2010.* By the end of the
decade, we will establish in at least 25 states their own version of *Find-*
ing Words that will be locally run and taught. The genesis of the project
comes from Minnesota where our partner, CornerHouse, has trained police officers, social workers and prosecutors in 85 of Minnesota's 87
counties.

The *Half a Nation* project was successfully launched in South
Carolina and, as of this writing, teams of students from more than 50
percent of the counties in that state have received the training. The project has also been completed in the states of Indiana, Mississippi, New
Jersey, Georgia and Missouri. In 2004, the project will be completed in
the states of West Virginia, Maryland and Illinois. In 2005, Kansas and

Ohio will complete the project. In total, representatives from over 40 states have expressed interest in the project.

If APRI reaches its goal of completing the project in 25 states by the end of the decade, hundreds of thousands of children victimized by abuse or neglect will be empowered to share their experiences at a much younger age because the system will be better able to address their needs.

There may be states that choose not be part of the *Half a Nation* project. Within the states that do become part of the project, there may be some jurisdictions that choose an alternative training program for its forensic interviewers. This is perfectly acceptable. What is not acceptable, however, is for any state or local jurisdiction to maintain a status quo that puts thousands of abused children into the hands of inadequately trained, even incompetent forensic interviewers.

In addition to quality forensic interviews, there must be in place a system to assist children that do not respond well to an investigative interview. Finding Words employs a child first doctrine that acknowledges that not every child will respond well to a forensic or investigative interview. Pre-school aged children, for example, may lack the verbal skills to participate in such a model.[64] Some children may have the verbal skills to participate in a forensic interview but, for any number of reasons, will require a more extended forensic evaluation to determine whether or not they have been maltreated.[65] Some children may respond better to a medical model of forensic interviewing in which a physician or nurse is the primary interviewer.[66] Accordingly, MDTs must be prepared to employ alternative approaches when necessary to meet the needs of each victim who comes into the system. Simply educating front line professionals about these alternative models and where to locate professionals and facilities using these alternative approaches may be sufficient to reduce the chance of leaving any child unprotected.

Child protection workers called on to investigate and repair families damaged by abuse must be competent to perform these tasks. Each year, I train thousands of child protection professionals, many of whom are front line social workers. I have asked hundreds of these workers if college taught them anything of value to their jobs. In response, these workers tell me that although college may instruct them as to the prevalence of child abuse, various dynamics that contribute to child abuse, and even offer various theories to address the problem both from inside and from outside the system, that very little instruction is given on the mechanics of investigating a report of abuse and working with a given family to end the maltreatment once and for all. Although well-intentioned and filled with idealism, untrained social workers are ill-equipped to handle the stress and complexity of a situation such as entering a crack house to rescue an addicted baby. As noted by one commentator, "few colleges and universities . . . provide training that specifically targets workers who deliver direct services to children and families. As a result, agencies must hire workers who are woefully unprepared for these critical positions and responsibilities."[67]

The failure of colleges to provide adequate training leaves many workers disillusioned. Burnout is so common that it is unlikely that any CPS system in the country has a truly knowledgeable, experienced team of investigators.[68] Although many measures can be taken to address the ongoing stress of working in the field,[69] we must end the practice of on-the-job training as the primary source of education for child protection professionals. No child's life should be placed in the hands of someone who is inadequately prepared for the task.

The proposed curriculum detailed below constitutes the minimum level of skills front line child protection professionals must have. Hopefully, universities will go even further than this outline in designing curricula that will dramatically improve our nation's ability to protect abused children.[70]

Every university must teach child protection professionals necessary investigative skills. In addition to teaching mandated reporters to competently fulfill their responsibilities, universities must provide rigorous, hands on instruction to tomorrow's police officers and social workers. As a starting point, universities should, in a full semester course, teach students to competently conduct a multi-disciplinary investigation of a report of child abuse.

On the first day of this semester course, students could be presented with a realistic, complex report of child abuse. This hypothetical case can be referred to repeatedly as students learn from the ground up how to build a meaningful investigative response to child abuse allegations. Students should learn about infamous child abuse cases where failed investigations left alleged perpetrators and victims in limbo and ruined the lives of many, including the investigators. Students should learn to create a multi-disciplinary team by exploring different approaches and then drafting an investigative protocol for their hypothetical community. Students should then learn the art of investigating a child abuse report as part of an MDT. Instruction should include interviewing the suspect, interviewing the non-offending parent, and interviewing the children alleged to be abused or who dwell in an abusive environment.

Students should learn the importance of corroborating evidence and how to find it.

As the course progresses, students should be teamed up as part of a fictitious MDT that will be called on to investigate the report of child abuse. Near the end of the semester, the teams of students should enter a house to conduct an investigation. The students should interview professional actors/actresses posing as the child abuse suspect, non-offending parent, and several children who may have been victimized or exposed to the victimization of siblings.[71] Students should search the house for evidence and document their findings with photographs, videotapes, etc.

Once the investigation is complete, students should present their evidence in a mock trial. Students should work with a real prosecutor in presenting the evidence and then be cross-examined by a defense attorney. Students should be critiqued on their performances.

Every university must teach child protection professionals to work meaningfully with families impacted by abuse. Once students learn to competently investigate these cases, they must learn the art of repairing troubled homes. To this end, the child protection workers of tomorrow should complete another semester long course that exposes them to the aftermath of a proven case of child abuse. Taking the case investigated in the previous course, students should be called on to develop a case plan to address the needs of the family in the hopes of healing wounds, building parenting skills, dealing with the mental health needs of the victims and, perhaps, reunification with the perpetrator. Students should also learn approaches to developing programs or otherwise reforming child protection systems that are inadequate to respond to the needs of families impacted by abuse.

Students should also be exposed to alternative responses to reports of maltreatment. According to a study of the U.S. Department of Health and Human Services, alternative response is defined as a "formal response" by a CPS agency that "assesses the need of the child or family without requiring a determination that maltreatment has occurred or that the child is at risk of maltreatment."[72] Alternative response approaches are available in 20 states with 11 states implementing the practice statewide.[73] This approach may be appropriate for many neglect reports or other less "serious" allegations.[74] In cases such as these, an alternative response may prevent mild maltreatment from becoming severe. State policies do not permit alternative responses for maltreatment cases involving criminal offenses, sexual abuse, or cases involving physical injury or endangerment.[75]

A curriculum along these lines should produce child protection workers who will remain on the job longer, will have higher job satisfaction and will perform their jobs better than those CPS workers who receive only on-the-job training. If this logical hypothesis proves to be true, model child protection curriculums may become the norm for every American university undertaking the task of preparing child protection workers for the most difficult, and important, of jobs.

GRADUATE SCHOOLS MUST ADEQUATELY PREPARE PROFESSIONALS TO WORK WITH CHILD VICTIMS

Although there is no substitute for adequate undergraduate training, a number of graduate schools also train professionals who almost certainly will encounter child abuse victims. Consider the following examples

Law Schools. Although law students interested in becoming prosecutors or public defenders are the best candidates to interact with abused children before or during court, tomorrow's civil attorneys will also encounter child witnesses in divorce/custody cases, civil child protection proceedings, and in other instances involving civil litigation. Future judges must also deal with child witnesses.[76]

To this end, law schools should introduce tomorrow's trial attorneys and judges to the concept of court schools[77] and the art of preparing children for court.[78] Law students should understand the research on conducting developmentally appropriate oaths.[79] Most importantly, tomorrow's trial attorneys and judges must be introduced to the concept of questioning children in a manner they can understand.[80] Just as we would oppose questioning in English a child who could only speak Spanish, we must oppose the practice of questioning children in a manner they cannot comprehend. According to one study, 2/3 of public defenders and 1/3 of prosecutors admitted questioning children in a manner designed to confuse the child.[81] Law schools must take the lead in teaching the attorneys and judges of tomorrow that questioning designed to take advantage of a child's vulnerabilities is unethical.

Medical Schools. The role of physicians in ending child abuse cannot be over-stated. A significant portion of child abuse and neglect reports comes from medical providers. Accordingly, the early detection of child abuse and neglect in doctor's offices, emergency rooms, dental and community health offices is essential if we are to address abuse at an age where society is best able to respond effectively. Even when children do not come into the system as a result of a report from a medical provider, many of these children will nonetheless come into contact with a doctor once they enter the system. This is because medical evaluations are an essential part of not only making the case against the perpetrator but also ensuring the child that his or her body is healthy. Accordingly, it is essential that medical students have rigorous training in the recognition, intervention and prevention of child abuse.

In designing a medical school curriculum, it is helpful to remember that child abuse is not always easily detectable.[82] Accordingly, medical schools must give the medical professionals of tomorrow a thorough understanding of taking a history/interviewing a child, conducting a physical examination of a possible victim of abuse, the collection of appropriate laboratory data, diagnostic considerations, proper record keeping not only for assisting the patient but in preparation for court, long term treatment of the child, and various legal issues (hearsay, mandated reporting, etc.).[83] Beginning in medical school, physicians must learn to identify and respond to the physical and psychological neglect of children[84] and continue to receive training on these complex issues. Just as social workers, police officers and other child protection professionals must learn how to conduct themselves in court and, for the welfare of the child victims, present their findings in a convincing way, it is important to instruct medical professionals in the art of testifying.[85] Intervention, of course, is only one piece of the puzzle. As with all professions involved in child abuse, doctors should receive courses on the prevention of abuse and their role in giving parents anticipatory guidance.

Residency training may be the best place to provide this education so long as the training is not only for those desiring to be child abuse specialists. This is because specialists "practice in academic centers," thus making the distribution of these specialists "somewhat limited."[86] Instead, the "complete education of primary care physicians in the evaluation of child abuse and neglect is mandatory in order to reach most pediatric patients with quality evaluation services."[87]

As with all professionals, the training must not end in medical school. In some states, child abuse continuing education is a condition of continued license. This requirement should be expanded to all states. Moreover, it is time that specialists in child abuse and neglect receive subspecialty status in the profession and be certified through examination, provision of fellowships, and a career track in this subspecialty.

Other Graduate Schools. All graduate schools that teach students who will inevitably encounter child abuse victims must adequately prepare these men and women for the challenges they will encounter.

Graduate schools that train tomorrow's psychologists,[88] dentists,[89] journalists, clergy-persons and veterinarians[90] are but some of the professionals that come to mind.

Once in the field, civil child protection professionals must have access to ongoing training and technical assistance. In addition to the aforementioned undergraduate and graduate courses, front line child protection workers must never be left alone in the field. These workers must be able to access ongoing training, technical assistance and publications. A social worker or child protection attorney should receive monthly newsletters to keep themselves current, should be able to attend trainings from nationally renowned presenters, and should have a national program they can call for advice or other technical support on individual cases.

To this end, there are already efforts underway. In February of 2003, Congress appropriated approximately one million dollars to create a National Child Protection Training Center on the campus of Winona State University. The program is up and running, provides precisely the services discussed above, and is modeled after the National Center for Prosecution of Child Abuse's efforts on behalf of prosecutors.[91] If we can achieve on the civil side what we have accomplished on the criminal side, namely training thousands of professionals in the field, we will dramatically improve the quality of work on the civil side of child protection, the side that is necessary to end the cycle of abuse family by family.

PROSECUTORS MUST BE ADEQUATELY TRAINED TO PROSECUTE EGREGIOUS CHILD ABUSERS

Child abuse was, to a large extent, ignored by our criminal justice system until the 1980s. Unfortunately, the criminal justice system was ill equipped to handle these cases and, in a number of instances, did so incompetently. As a result, there was a backlash that deterred many from prosecuting these cases.[92] As I travel around the country, the impact of the backlash remains real and rampant. In some states, for example, prosecutors hold fast to the idea that they will not prosecute a child sexual abuse case unless there is clear, unmistakable medical evidence. Because such evidence is rare,[93] this means that most children will never have their perpetrators brought to justice.

There are some who maintain the criminal justice system is more of a hindrance than help in addressing the horror of child abuse. Hubert

Humphrey, for example, once advocated reducing child abuse crimes to nothing more than a misdemeanor in the hope of encouraging more reports.[94] Though well meaning, such an argument relegates children to the back of the bus of our criminal justice system. We would never suggest that those who beat or rape ourselves or other adults should receive relatively meaningless consequences or that such cases should be handled by unskilled prosecutors. To say that a different standard should apply when the victim is a child is to designate the most helpless part of our population to the status of second-class citizen. The criminal justice system defines our deepest beliefs as to what is right and wrong, moral and immoral. If we fail to say as a society that beating, burning, binding, raping and murdering children is worthy of consequences then we forfeit the right to call ourselves civilized.

Moreover, prosecution is an essential part of prevention. According to one study, 561 non-incarcerated sex offenders accounted for the sexual abuse of 195,000 victims.[95] From studies and personal experience we know that many offenders will accumulate hundreds of victims unless and until they are caught. For every apprehended offender, dozens, even hundreds of other victims can be spared.

Improving the quality of prosecution can only be done through education. Since law schools do not presently teach future prosecutors the intricacies of successfully handling these cases, the training must come elsewhere, must be comprehensive, and must be consistent throughout the nation.

In 1985, the National District Attorneys Association secured from congress funding of 1.5 million dollars to create the National Center for Prosecution of Child Abuse. The purpose of NCPCA is to provide training, technical assistance and publications for front line investigators and prosecutors. NCPCA stands today as the premiere trainer of front line professionals. In 2001, for example, we trained over 14,000 investigators and prosecutors in over 30 states in every region of the nation. In 2002, we again traveled to over 30 states and trained over 12,000 child protection professionals and, in 2003, we continued at this level.[96]

Unfortunately, Congress has not increased NCPCA's funding and the program has been forced to do more and more with less. United States Senator Paul Wellstone examined the program's funding and wrote a letter to the Senate Appropriations Committee asking the funding be tripled to 4.5 million dollars so that, in real dollars, the program has the same operating capacity that it did in 1985. With a relatively small increase in its budget, NCPCA could reach thousands of additional professionals annually.

We must teach police officers, social workers, prosecutors and other child protection professionals to be community leaders in the prevention of child abuse and this training must begin in college and continue once these professionals are in the field. This training must begin in college and continue once these professionals are in the field. Universities must not only equip future social workers and police officers to competently investigate cases of abuse but must teach them to be community leaders who proactively seek to prevent child abuse. Students should be taught interpersonal skills that will be necessary to move entrenched child protection systems. If, for example, a new graduate comes into a community with a poorly defined MDT, how does he or she convince a long-standing and popular sheriff to make the needed reforms? As individual or class projects, students should be given true to life community projects and be asked to develop prevention efforts. If, for example, a community has a significant problem with poor parents not being able to afford infant car seats, is there an alternative to filing neglect petitions or writing citations? The solution could be as simple as giving the offending parent 48 hours to visit the local CPS center and pick up a free car seat donated by community members and organizations. Universities must require students to think meaningfully in both a micro and macro approach to combating child abuse.

In teaching students the art of prevention, a sea of front line professionals will be able not only to initiate new reforms but to complement existing and promising practices such as home based services aimed at preventing abuse in at-risk families.[97]

The idea of teaching college students to be community leaders on a given topic, as opposed to simply passing on ideas to those who are already community leaders, is not necessarily new but it does challenge the status quo in a way that may make some uncomfortable.[98] What was once perceived as novel, though, must become the norm if child abuse is to end. We simply must produce, beginning in college, an army of front line workers well equipped to organize all the players in their local communities for the betterment of children. We must teach child protection workers not only how to organize their communities in efforts that address child abuse, we must teach them the skill of communicating the needs of child abuse victims to governmental leaders. The child protection system is woefully under-funded simply because children cannot communicate their needs to the powers that be.[99]

There is a very compelling reason why the future of children depends on turning front line child protection workers into community leaders. It is because these are the professionals who work directly in our community with children in need. These are the professionals who, in the words of Theodore Roosevelt, are "in the arena"[100] as the brave-hearted souls undertaking to remove bleeding boys and girls from the jaws of the beast. Because experience instills her lessons in a way no other teacher can, these are the professionals most likely equipped to identify necessary programs and services that will prevent abuse.

In my former community, for example, our social workers believed a Parent's Anonymous program would be helpful in preventing egregious acts of abuse. Working with other community leaders, we developed and implemented the program within a year.[101] Just as "all politics is local,"[102] so must be all child abuse prevention efforts. What is needed and what will work in a rural community in Minnesota may be very different from what will work in an apartment complex in New York. The future role of child protection workers must include an assessment of what is needed at the local level to get the job done. The job of policy makers must be to listen to those on the front lines and to adequately fund meaningful efforts.

Prosecutors must also think outside the box and become well versed in the art of community prosecution. Under this approach, prosecutors are proactive in preventing crime. APRI has developed an entire program on the subject of community prosecution and this concept is part of many of our child abuse trainings. We must, though, accelerate the numbers trained in these programs from hundreds to thousands.

IN THEIR ROLE AS COMMUNITY LEADERS, CHILD PROTECTION PROFESSIONALS MUST ENLIST THE SUPPORT OF THE FAITH-BASED COMMUNITY

When police officers, social workers and prosecutors become community leaders proactive in preventing child abuse they learn the art of reaching out to other community leaders who are often hostile to the government's handling of child abuse. Specifically, it is essential that child protection leaders develop bridges with America's faith communities. There are two reasons for this.

First, the work of child protection necessarily involves the social worker or police officer in the religion of families in need. What, for example, does the front line worker do when he or she contends an act of corporal punishment is child abuse but a parent contends the corporal punishment is a fundamental teaching of their church?[103] What does a front line worker do if a parent is healing a child through prayer or other spiritual means as opposed to traditional medical care?[104] What if a child needs a blood transfusion but the child refuses because, as a Jehovah's Witness she believes the transfusion would violate the tenets of her faith?[105] What if a child is to participate in a snake handling ritual as a testament to the child's faith?[106] In conducting an investigation, does the religion or culture of a child make a difference in terms of the tools we use when we interview the victim or investigate the case? Dr. Erna Olafson from the University of Cincinnati, for example, has raised a very important question of whether it would be wise to use anatomical diagrams or dolls with an Amish child who may be particularly sensitive to such tools.[107] It may, of course, be that if an Amish child is particularly sensitive to discussing alleged sexual abuse that the anatomical diagrams or dolls may be even *more important*. The point is that although we can make a plausible argument on both sides of this debate, there is little research to support either position. What, then, should a child protection worker do? What does a child protection worker do when the *child victim* raises a question of religion? For example, many child protection workers have been in the situation of a victim asking questions such as "am I still a virgin in God's eyes?" These are not only spiritual questions, they are mental health issues that would be cruel to ignore.

Child protection workers must confront the religion of families not only when investigating a case of abuse but also when selecting and administering services. Indeed, the law requires us to be sensitive to the culture and religion of families.[108] What does a child protection worker do, for example, if a parent or child needs counseling but the family objects to secular counseling and insists that the counselor be a member of their faith? It may be an easy question if the "religious" counselor is equal in all other respects to the secular counselor. But what if the family's chosen therapist is lacking fundamental knowledge of a given subject that needs to be addressed? When can a child protection worker, and our courts, compel services that a given family considers insensitive to their culture?

These and myriad other issues have been present from the moment the very first child protection case came into the system. Unfortunately, little is being done to prepare social workers and other players in the system to address these issues. As a result, the conflict between child protection and faith communities continues to rise. The casualties in this conflict are not the faith or child protection communities so much as the children both communities care about.

Second, we must reach out to diverse faiths because this community can play an important role in protecting children. In every great social reform, there is a moral backbone driving the effort. In many cases, the religious community provides this moral compass. Although religion is responsible for crusades, bigotries, and an assortment of other evils, religion has also played an important role in social movements such as the abolition of slavery and social reforms such as hospice care and Habitat for Humanity.[109] Mahatma Ghandi in India, Martin Luther King, Jr., in America, and Dietrich Bonhoeffer in Germany are examples of men who used religion to galvanize others to combat bigotries and hatreds and build a better life in this world.[110]

Dr. King, for example, believed religion provided the "necessary foundation" for the civil rights movement,[111] and contended the "thing that we need in the world today is a group of men and women who will stand up for right and be opposed to wrong, wherever it is."[112] In his famous letter from a Birmingham jail, King recognized the importance of awakening the religious community to speak out against the evil of segregation. King lamented that "(s)o often the contemporary church is a weak, ineffectual voice with an uncertain sound. So often it is an arch defender of the status quo. Far from being disturbed by the presence of the church, the power structure of the average community is consoled by the church's silent, and often even vocal, sanction of things as they are."[113]

Just as Dr. King recognized the essential role the church would play in ending segregation, we must likewise awaken the faith community to end its silence and, in some quarters, its vocal support of child abuse.[114] To this end, APRI has already developed some workshops and has written a paper with concrete proposals for crossing the divide between these communities.[115] We are also in the process of creating a working group of faith and child protection leaders to develop further solutions to this problem. One possibility is to design a model curriculum for seminaries on the issues surrounding child abuse. When the cause is protecting children, liberals and conservatives alike should be able to find room at the table for the nation's faith communities.[116]

PREVENTION EFFORTS MUST BE LOCALLY RUN AND TAILORED TO LOCAL NEEDS

There are many factors that contribute to child maltreatment. Caregivers engaging in substance abuse or who themselves had poor parental role models are at greater risk to offend against their children.[117] Parental age, stress levels, unemployment, poverty, and child characteristics such as disabilities are additional factors that increase the chances of maltreatment.[118] These and other factors, however, may not be present in every community. For example, poverty may contribute to child abuse and yet not every community has measurable rates of poverty. Even factors that may be present in each community, such as substance abuse, may exist at different levels or take different forms. One community may have a significant problem with cocaine while another deals primarily with alcoholism.

In many communities, widespread ignorance about child sexual abuse increases pedophiles' success rate of abusing children undetected. If prevention efforts can create a well educated populace that understands child molesters can be the local softball coach as well as the community flasher, parents will be less likely to give a potential abuser unbridled access to their child.[119]

Given the numerous factors that contribute to maltreatment, and the different levels of these factors in each community in this country, we can never launch effective prevention programs unless these programs are designed at the local level by those closest to the situation and unless these programs are tailored to the dynamics unique to each community.

Deborah Daro and Anne Cohn Donnelly evaluated the history of child abuse prevention efforts in America and found six factors contributing to the shortcomings of these efforts.[120] When the shortcomings of past prevention efforts are compared to the overall structure of the *Unto the Third Generation* proposal, there is reason to believe this approach will be more successful.

First, Daro and Donnelly accuse prevention proponents of "oversimplifying things" and promoting "singular solutions."[121] Prevention as envisioned by *Unto the Third Generation* will be just the opposite. Recognizing that prevention is complex and will differ from community to community, this proposal puts the responsibility of prevention in the hands of front line child protection workers, police officers and prosecutors who are closest to the situation. The nation's communities will serve as mini-laboratories testing myriad prevention efforts until we finally get it right.

Second, Daro and Donnelly accuse prevention proponents of overstating "prevention's potential, allowing rhetoric to outpace research and empirical support."[122] According to these authors, "prevention efforts are framed as offering the potential for success in all cases, an impossible standard to achieve."[123] The *Unto the Third Generation* proposal realizes that prevention will not succeed in all cases and thus advocates competent investigators and full funding for training programs that will assist in the prosecution of egregious child abusers and in providing competent child protective services in those cases where family preservation is a realistic goal.

The third and fourth factors are related. Daro and Donnelly allege that prevention advocates "continue to misrepresent the pool of families they can successfully attract and retain in voluntary prevention services" and that these advocates have "failed to establish a significant partnership with their local child protective services."[124] Recognizing that many, if not most, abusive families will not seek or stay in services, the *Unto the Third Generation* proposal places the primary responsibility of these efforts in the hands of child protection workers and allied professionals. When generic prevention efforts come up short, the well trained child protection workers of tomorrow will be able to competently investigate abuse reports and get more of these hurting children into a system better prepared to receive them.

Fifth, Daro and Donnelly contend that prevention efforts have focused more on breadth than depth and there has been too much emphasis "on increasing the number of program sites before it fully understood what it would take to make these programs sustainable and effective."[125] Because the *Unto the Third Generation* proposal decentralizes prevention efforts, making them the responsibility of local professionals, these professionals will not implement prevention programs as if they were a franchise in a fast food chain. Instead, they will take ownership of their efforts and tailor them to local needs. This ownership will give these programs depth and, through the work of the National Child Protection Training Center, the very best approaches will be shared with other communities interested in applying hopeful practices.

Sixth, Daro and Donnelly contend the "field has failed to establish the public will and the political clout to bring to fruition the policies and programmatic reforms needed to prevent child abuse."[126] Again, the *Unto the Third Generation* proposal advocates teaching child protection professionals beginning in college that they have a responsibility to prevent abuse and develop all necessary services from the ground up. This responsibility includes organizing their community and effectively communicating the needs of child abuse victims to local, state and national leaders. As these model university programs sweep across the land, we will eventually have thousands of child protection workers serving as public advocates for the children so often left out of public policy considerations. The world will change, and it will change in relatively quick order.

EVERYONE ENGAGED IN THE CAMPAIGN
AGAINST CHILD ABUSE
MUST UNDERSTAND THEIR ROLE IN HISTORY
AND ACT ACCORDINGLY

Whether we are dealing with divergent faiths or divergent members of our multi-disciplinary teams, we must understand that we have within our means the ability to significantly reduce if not eliminate child abuse within several generations. To this end, our conduct will eventually be judged by those who come after us.

At the national level, this means that organizations competing for limited resources must put children first and work with any ally in the fight against child abuse. When I became director of NCPCA, I developed a set of seven principles that would serve as the ethical core of our program.[127] One of those principles requires us to "collaborate with other organizations that can assist us in our primary mission of helping prosecutors help the children whose lives depend on us. We are not in competition with other child abuse organizations. We are in competition with child abusers for the futures of a sea of children. As long as children and prosecutors are being served, it doesn't matter who gets the job done and it matters even less who gets the credit."[128]

The founders of our nation were acutely aware of their role in history and this no doubt enabled them to put significant differences, even hatreds aside for the good and glory of their cause.[129]

THE TIMELINE FOR ENDING CHILD ABUSE
WITHIN 120 YEARS

The First 40 Years: 2001-2040

We must within the next 40 years achieve six goals. Although each goal will require a great deal of effort and some financial resources, the effort and money pales in comparison to the time and money we currently spend on dealing with child abuse. Unless we believe the status quo is the best we can do, a new course must be set. Efforts are already under way to achieve each of these goals within the suggested time frame.

Every suspected case of child abuse will be reported and every report will be of a high quality. We must complete and perfect in one or more universities a comprehensive training program that provides everyone entering a mandated reporting profession the skills necessary to perform this task. We must then replicate the program in every university in our nation. If this can be achieved by 2040, we will have gone a long way in ensuring that children suspected of being abused will be reported as required by law and that those reports are of a high quality.

Every child reported into the system will be interviewed by someone who can competently interview a child about abuse and the investigation of all child abuse allegations will likewise be competently completed. we must, by 2010, complete the project *Half a Nation* in 25 states and complete the project in the remainder of our country by 2020. In each state, the local leaders must work diligently to make sure that, by the year 2040, every child reported to be abused or neglected will be interviewed by someone trained to competently interview children.

Every substantiated case of egregious child abuse must be prosecuted by a child abuse prosecutor skilled at handling these complex, special cases. We must as a society draw a line in the sand and say that just as those who beat, rape and murder adults are subject to prosecution, those who commit egregious acts of child abuse will also be held accountable in our criminal courts. This sends a message to the perpetrators and to society that this conduct is intolerable. To do this, we must give state and local prosecutors ready and stable access to high-quality training, technical assistance and publications. Simply put, we must ensure that every child abuse prosecutor competently handles these cases.

Every CPS worker will be competent to investigate and work with child abuse victims and their families from day one. We must implement in one or more universities the type of comprehensive training outlined in this paper and make sure that, within 40 years, every university that undertakes to train child protection workers gives them the necessary skills to investigate these cases, defend their actions in court and, equally important, the skills to address the myriad problems child abuse brings to a family in the hopes of breaking forever the cycle of abuse in each of these homes.

Every CPS worker will be a community leader skilled in the art of prevention. We must ensure that every university teaches social workers to be community leaders who can assess the needs of the children and families they interact with and develop those programs necessary to prevent abuse.

Every child protection worker and attorney will have access to national trainings, publications and technical assistance. The work of child protection is an ever-changing field. As we improve our ability to work with child abuse victims and their families, this information must be shared quickly and effectively with those on the front lines. Accordingly, we need a national program that can annually train thousands of child protection professionals at the state and local level regarding new and better practices. We also need a program that those in the field can call when in need of assistance on individual cases. Again, the National Child Protection Training Center at Winona State University is one effort currently being undertaken to achieve this goal.

The Next 80 Years (2040-2120): The Search for a Tipping Point

What if, in the next 40 years, we created an America where every suspected case of abuse was reported and those reports were of a high quality? What if every child reported into the system was interviewed by a child protection professional trained in the art of speaking to children? What if every child abuse case was the subject of a quality investigation? What if every child abuse prosecutor was trained in the art of prosecuting those who commit egregious acts of abuse? What if every CPS worker was well trained to work with families impacted by abuse? What if our CPS workers, those closest to the crisis of child abuse, were trained as community leaders to develop at a local level the resources necessary to prevent abuse and to deal with it when it has occurred?

What if we achieved all of the above within 40 years and then sustained these efforts for another 80 years or an additional two generations? Although only God knows for sure, I suspect we would dramatically reduce, if not eliminate child abuse in our country. This would occur because we would get most of the victims into the system when they were younger and the problems associated with abuse would be easier to address. We would be removing from society the hard-core child abusers who, left unchecked, do immeasurable damage to countless children. We would be developing prevention efforts at the local level by those closest to the problem. And the difficult task of breaking the cycle of abuse in these homes would be placed in the hands of child protection workers well trained from day one in the art of working with these families. We would also be providing the ongoing support and training all of these heroes and heroines so richly deserve. This would reduce burnout and, over time, create a child protection work force that is not only well trained but is experienced.

The Tipping Point

At some point in this process we would find what Malcolm Gladwell calls a "tipping point" that results in a social epidemic of positive change.[130] To create a social epidemic, Gladwell argues that three things are necessary. First, social epidemics are driven by "the efforts of a handful of exceptional people" who are "sociable . . . energetic . . . or knowledgeable or influential among their peers."[131] To some extent, the initial charge of *Unto the Third Generation* will be led by the attorneys and other child protection professionals employed at the National Center for Prosecution of Child Abuse (NCPCA) and the National Child Protection Training Center (NCPTC). NCPCA alone trains thousands of child protection professionals each year. These numbers will expand as the NCPTC begins its training of those handling the civil side of child protection cases. The NCPCA and NCPTC messengers, however, will not be alone. States participating in the *Finding Words/Half a Nation* initiative consist of statewide coalitions of child protection professionals that will also be instrumental in disseminating the message. As Winona State University develops a model undergraduate curriculum, and other universities follow suit, the academic community will also play a critical role in spreading the word. To the extent medical schools, law schools and other graduate schools get on board, these institutions will also fuel this train. Finally, and most importantly, it is the front line professionals who receive this message and who are at the heart of the reformation, who must communicate the message to their peers and to the leaders of local, state, and national governments. All things considered, the conditions are ripe for a social epidemic.

Second, Gladwell says a social epidemic must have a message that possesses a quality he calls "stickiness." According to Gladwell, "(s)tickiness means that a message makes an impact. You can't get it out of your head. It sticks in your memory."[132] The goals of the NCPCA are easily understood by academics and those on the front lines. The goals of our programs are contained in the titles themselves. *Half a Nation by 2010* clearly states the goal of establishing the *Finding Words* course in 25 states by the end of the decade. *Unto the Third Generation* contains a similarly understood goal of ending child abuse within 120 years. More importantly, each of these proposals has an easily understood blueprint for accomplishing these ideals. That blueprint is contained in the pages of this article. The stickiness of this proposal is exemplified in the fact that its supporters have included famous liberals[133] and conservatives.[134]

Third, Gladwell claims a social epidemic is driven by the "power of context." Gladwell contends that when too many people are assigned the task of solving a problem, the problem continues unabated. He argues the "key to getting people to change their behavior, in other words to care about their neighbor in distress, sometimes lies with the smallest details of their immediate situation."[135] This is perhaps the greatest hope that *Unto the Third Generation* will cause a social epidemic that greatly reduces, if not eliminates, child abuse. In the past, the great cause of ending child abuse was the subject of university debate or political banter. *Unto the Third Generation* turns the world upside down by making the front line professionals the army that will win this fight and subordinates politicians and academics to the role of providing these soldiers with the necessary ammunition. By placing the task of ending child abuse on the shoulders of those closest to the front, we will force a massive army to act on behalf of the smallest victims.[136]

When we reach the tipping point, the culture that permits child abuse will be crushed and the numbers will spiral down rapidly. Take, for example, the crime rate in the City of New York. During the 1980s crime was rampant, reaching a high point in 1990 with over 2,000 murders and 600,000 violent felonies. Suddenly, the murder rate was cut by 2/3 and violent felonies were cut in half.[137] Given that New York's economy was stagnant, poor neighborhoods were being negatively impacted by welfare cuts, and the population was getting younger, logic would suggest an increase in crime as opposed to a dramatic reduction.[138]

The crime rate in New York decelerated rapidly because the city, under the leadership of Mayor Rudolph Giuliani,[139] employed the "Broken Windows" theory of criminologists George Kelling and James Q. Wilson.[140] Under this theory, if the city continued to allow broken windows, graffiti, and turnstile jumpers at subway stations, it was conveying the image of chaos and sending to criminals the message that anything goes. Under this theory, the criminal "far from being someone who acts for fundamental, intrinsic reasons and who lives in his own world, is actually someone acutely sensitive to his environment, who is alert to all kinds of cues, and who is prompted to commit crimes based on his perception of the world around him."[141] If this is true, we may not have to undertake the Herculean tasks of ending poverty or social injustice to reduce crime. It may be that our task is as simple as ending the culture that permits the disease.

If the broken windows theory worked in New York and reduced so dramatically the incidence of murders and violent crimes, perhaps the same theory can be applied to the ending of child abuse. The *Unto the Third Generation* proposal will strike at the heart of the culture permitting child abuse. Mandated reporters will learn in college that their first priority is to recognize and report suspected abuse. Police chiefs and social service supervisors will understand that on the job training is no longer acceptable when it comes to handling child abuse cases. Instead, they must hire graduates only from universities who adequately teach these professionals to perform at a high level from day one. Moreover, these professionals will never again be left alone but will have access to ongoing training on both the civil and criminal side of child protection. Most importantly, child protection professionals will be taught beginning in college to be community leaders who, in essence, create a broken windows policy in each town in our country.

At some point, the message will be clear to all offenders. If you fail to respond to the prevention efforts in your community and proceed to beat or rape a child, a mandated reporter will call the authorities, the authorities will respond competently, egregious abusers will be incarcerated, and social services will repair the remaining family by every means necessary to break the cycle of abuse once and for all.[142]

Will ending the culture permitting child abuse really end abuse altogether? Since nothing this sweeping has ever been attempted, no one can be absolutely certain if the ultimate victory will be achieved at all, much less quickly. We can, though, be certain of this much–even if our aiming for the stars falls short we will, three generations from now, land at a better place than we are presently at.

If we can reach the tipping point in the next 40 years, we will have at least two more generations who can analyze the extent of our success and build on what we accomplish. Just as an earlier generation instilled in the child protection community the idea of multi-disciplinary investigations and the importance of child advocacy centers, our present generation can instill in this country the ideas that child protection professionals should receive more than on the job training and that all prevention is local. The task of the second and third generations will be to finish any part of the job that remains once the enormous undertaking set forth in this paper is part of history.

ENDING CHILD ABUSE: OUR LAST FULL MEASURE

History is replete with examples of dreamers who accomplished things as difficult as ending child abuse. Henry A. Wallace, who served as Agriculture Secretary under President Franklin Roosevelt contended that the "highest joy of life is complete dedication to something outside of yourself."[143] One of the tasks that Wallace dedicated himself to was ending world hunger. Wallace's work with hybrid corn and chicken breeding impacted the world.

In 1931, the United States corn yield was 24.1 bushels per acre, largely unchanged since the end of the Civil War.[144] By 1941, the figure rose to 31 bushels an acre and, by 1981, the United States was producing three times as much corn on one-third the acres we had in 1931.[145] The introduction of hybrid maize in this country and around the world saved and continues to save countless lives and the person most deserving of credit is Henry Wallace.[146] Wallace's efforts to produce the "perfect chicken" also met with success. Even a quarter of a century after his death in 1965, one-third of all the eggs eaten in the United States and nearly fifty percent of the eggs consumed in the world were laid by descendents of Wallace's chickens.[147] Orville Freeman said "no single individual contributed more to the abundance we enjoy today than Henry Wallace."[148]

How could one man, in his lifetime, set in motion an agricultural revolution that saved millions around the world from starvation? According to Dr. Paul Mangelsdorf of the Harvard Botanical Museum, "it was Wallace's fate to be often regarded as a 'dreamer' when actually he was only seeing in his own pragmatic realistic way some of the shapes of things to come. . . ." [149]

Although Wallace's pragmatism saved untold lives, world hunger remained because succeeding generations did not pick up the banner and eliminate political and other factors that contribute to malnutrition and starvation. Wallace may have given us the capacity to feed the world but he could not give us worthy successors that would complete the job.

Therein lies the dilemma. Just as Wallace did with world hunger, we can pledge our lives, fortunes and sacred honors to the equally noble task of ending child abuse. Unfortunately, this is not a dream that can be achieved in our lifetimes and, no doubt, there are many stone-throwers eager to argue that ours is a dream that can never be realized, a dream that only fools can harbor. How do we live, and die, for such a cause?

THE LAST FULL MEASURE

What, for me, began as a handful of hesitant comments on a stage in Mississippi culminated on a Pennsylvania battlefield. Until I visited

Gettysburg with my family, I had no response to the critics who contend our quick-fix, fast-food nation will never dedicate itself to a long-term battle against child abuse, a battle that may extend into the next century.

As I walked the hallowed grounds of Gettysburg, though, an idea began to take shape. I was deeply moved by the displays of unbridled courage on both sides of the conflict. Although we didn't have the time to fully absorb every aspect of the battle, I did, as a native Minnesotan, make a special effort to visit the monument commemorating the valor of my home-state heroes. As I read of their sacrifice, I began to understand the sort of faith we must have in the campaign to end child abuse.

In the second day of battle at Gettysburg, Union General Daniel Sickles erred in seeking higher ground to defend. As a result of this error, Sickles' soldiers were subjected to a relentless attack from Confederate General Longstreet and the Union line was in danger of collapsing to advancing rebels. If the line had folded, the battle and likely the war would have been lost.

Union General Winfield Scott Hancock, who had an uncanny ability to appear at the moment of greatest danger, perceived the situation and immediately looked for help. All he found was a Minnesota regiment of 262 soldiers. "My God," asked the general, "are these all the men we have here?" Hancock then ordered the regiment to charge in the hope he could slow the confederate advance for five minutes and get reinforcements.

Upon this order, 262 Minnesotans charged into a field of 1,600 advancing troops. It was, in every sense of the word, a suicide charge in the hope of buying a few minutes time for soldiers who may or may not later appear and secure the victory. With casualties approaching 82% and a death toll of 70%, no regiment gave more at Gettysburg. General Hancock later said, "I saw that in some way five minutes must be gained or we were lost. It was fortunate that I found there so grand a body of men as the First Minnesota. I knew they must lose heavily and it pained me to give the order for them to advance, but I would have done it if I had known every man would be killed. It was a sacrifice that must be made. . . . There is no more gallant deed recorded in history." For their country, and for all that our nation has been and can be, these Minnesotans gave their last full measure.[150]

For our country, and for our children, we too must give our last full measure in the hope that others just as dedicated will come after us and complete what we begin. Someday, somewhere, somebody will write the history of our nation's victory over child abuse. When that history is written, may it be recorded that the beginning of the end occurred in the early part of the 21st century when thousands of child protection professionals from every region of the country joined forces to lead the charge.

If we act now and for the rest of our lives as a testament to the invisible attributes of faith, hope and love, a later generation may one day see with their eyes what our hearts tell us is our nation's destiny.

Child abuse will end.

NOTES

1. Maxwell Kennedy Taylor, Make Gentle the Life of this World 145 (1998).

2. Throughout this paper, I will revert to the first person as I share some personal experiences. I do this because I share with some legal scholars the conviction that "individual experience must be considered more carefully, analyzed more critically, and elevated in importance." Charles Ogletree, *Beyond Justifications: Seeking Motivations to Sustain Public Defenders*, 106 Harv. L. Rev. 1239, 1244 (1993). According to Ogletree, the "formalized, doctrinal style of argument that characterizes much contemporary legal writing can too easily elude the realities of human experience." *Id.*

3. For purposes of this article, the child abuse we seek to end should be construed in the broadest sense possible: physical abuse, sexual abuse, neglect and emotional maltreatment. To do otherwise is to suggest that child abuse at any level is acceptable. As acknowledged in this paper, we may never achieve the complete eradication of child abuse but nothing less than complete victory must be our unequivocal goal. Until we speak of ending child abuse in serious terms, as opposed to expressing this sentiment as a mere platitude, we can never achieve the massive reformation necessary to move us dramatically toward the desired end. It is also important for those on the front lines, those who often devote their entire lives to children, to know this country is seriously working toward the great goal. Just as the "sentiment of the United States brightened up very much" when President Franklin Roosevelt announced our country would battle the Nazi powers until there was an "unconditional surrender" we must likewise comfort front line child protection professionals with a firm commitment to ending the suffering of all of America's maltreated children. For the impact on American soldiers and citizens of Roosevelt's unconditional surrender demand, *see* Justice Robert H. Jackson, That Man 109 (2003). Of course, defeating the Nazis was arguably easier than defeating child abuse. Even if this is true, there is tremendous value in seriously working for a cause as noble as ending child abuse. Martin Luther King, Jr. pointed out that although Woodrow Wilson, Mahatma Gahndi and other historical figures did not obtain world peace, their unyielding efforts toward this end achieved great things. In the words of Dr. King: "(S)o often as you set out to build the temple of peace you are left lonesome; you are left discouraged; you are left bewildered. Well, that is the story of life. And the thing that makes me happy is that I can hear a voice crying through the vista of time, saying 'It may not come today or it may not come tomorrow, but it is well that it is within thine heart. It's well that you are trying.' You may not see it. The dream may not be fulfilled, but it's good that you have a desire to bring it into reality. . . . Thank God this morning that we do have hearts to put something meaningful in." Dr. Martin Luther King, Jr., A Knock At Midnight 192-194 (1998) (Carson & Holloran, Eds).

4. The title for this paper came about this way. The reaction to my Mississippi talk was quite positive with a number of folks urging me to turn these ideas into an article. As I began to outline the article on a subsequent flight to Las Vegas, I was struck with the idea of three generations or 120 years. I recalled the Sunday school lesson of God warning Moses about the dangers of idolatry: "I, the Lord your God, am a jealous God, punishing the children for the sins of the fathers unto the third and fourth generation ... but showing love to a thousand generations of those who love me and keep my commandments." Exodus 20:5 (NIV). Although this story about idolatry has, on its surface, nothing to do with child abuse, I couldn't, and still cannot, get from my head this powerful literary allusion. Because child abuse is so often cyclical, we pass down the consequences of this evil to generation upon generation. I can recall many cases in which police or child protection investigators told me that abuse had been rampant in a given family dating back to a victim's grandfather or even great-grandfather. What if, though, we ended abuse once and for all? Would not a thousand generations be blessed? Stated differently, "families give our destiny its first momentum." Al & Tipper Gore, Joined at the Heart 3 (2002). As president Hoover once observed, "if the United States could have but one generation of properly born, trained, educated and healthy children, a thousand problems of government would vanish overnight. . . . It is not the delinquent child that is at the bar of judgment, but society itself." Herbert Hoover, On Growing Up 6-7 (1990).

5. David L. Chadwick, *The Message*, published as part of *Convening A National Call to Action: Working Toward the Elimination of Child Maltreatment*, 23 Child Abuse & Neglect 957, 959 (1999).

6. *Id.* at 957.

7. Anne Cohn Donnelly, *The Practice*, published as part of *Convening A National Call to Action: Working Toward the Elimination of Child Maltreatment*, 23 Child Abuse & Neglect 987, 993 (1999).

8. As an example of the dramatic increase in prosecuting child abusers in recent years, consider this. In 1996, there was an estimated 1,500 appellate opinions addressing cases of child sexual abuse. From 1900-1950, there was approximately 500 appellate opinions. *See* John E.B. Myers, Susan E. Diedrich, Devon Lee, Kelly Fincher & Rachel M. Stern, *Prosecution of Child Sexual Abuse in the United States*, in Critical Issues in Child Sexual Abuse 27, 47-48 (2002) (J. Conte, Ed).

9. This history of U.S. efforts against child abuse is a summary taken from Victor I. Vieth, *In My Neighbor's House*, 22 Hamline L. Rev. 143, 145-146 (1998). For a much more complete history of child protection in the United States, *see* John. E.B. Myers, A History of Child Protection in America (2004).

10. *See generally*, David Hechler, *The Battle and the Backlash (1988)*.

11. Myers et al., *supra* note 8 at 41. Famed psychologist Dr. Anna Salter put it more bluntly when she wrote:

The history of psychology in the past one hundred years has been filled with theories that deny sexual abuse occurs, that discounts the responsibility of the offender, that blame the mother and/or child when it does occur, and that minimize the impact. It constitutes a sorry chapter in the history of psychology, but it is not only shameful, it is also puzzling. Hostility toward child victims and adult women leaks through the literature. Anna C. Salter, Predators 57 (2003).

12. *See* Salter, *supra* note 11 at 57-61 (2003) (criticizing some contemporary articles and books minimizing sexual abuse and its impact). Consider, for example, a book

published by the University of Minnesota Press in which its author advocates lowering the age of consent to 12. Judith Levine, Harmful to Minors (2002).

13. Jerome R. Kolbo and Edith Strong, *Multidisciplinary Team Approaches to the Investigation and Resolution of Child Abuse and Neglect: A National Survey*, 2 Child Maltreatment 61 (1997).

14. For information on the exact number and location of CACs, visit the website of the National Children's Alliance at www.nca-online.org

15. David Finkelhor, *Is Child Abuse Overreported?* Pub. Welfare, Winter 1990 at 25.

16. Steven Delaronde et al., *Opinions Among Mandated Reporters Toward Child Maltreatment Reporting Policies*, 24 Child Abuse and Neglect 901, 905 (2000).

17. Maureen C. Kenny, *Child Abuse Reporting: Teachers' Perceived Deterrents*, 25 Child Abuse & Neglect 81, 88 (2001). Journalists are echoing the work of scholars by documenting in mainstream media egregious instances of professionals failing to report unequivocal cases of child abuse. *See,* e.g., Annette Foglino, *Teachers who prey on kids: Why they're still going free*, Good Housekeeping (December 2003) p. 61.

18. Kenny, *supra* note 17 at 902.

19. *See* Margaret H. Meriwether, *Child Abuse Reporting Laws: Time for a Change*, 20 Fam. L. Q. 141, 142 (1986).

20. Minn. Stat. Section 626.5561, subd. 1 (2003).

21. *Teachers and Child Abuse*, National Center for Prosecution of Child Abuse UPDATE (American Prosecutors Research Institute, Alexandria, Virginia), October, 1989.

22. Delaronde, *supra* note 16 at 905. Inadequate training leading to a shortage of quality reports is also a problem in the faith community. The pastoral care department of the Children's Hospital Medical Center of Akron, Ohio surveyed 143 clergy of numerous faiths and found that 29% believed that actual evidence of abuse, as opposed to suspicion was necessary before a report could be made. The same study found that only 22% of the respondents were required by their denomination/faith group to receive child abuse training. This study also documented an under-reporting of suspected abuse cases with the most prevalent reason being "lack of trust in Children's Services Bureaus." The 143 clergy responding to this survey impact, at some level, the lives of 23,841 children. Daniel H. Grossoehme, *Child Abuse Reporting: Clergy Perceptions*, 7 Child Abuse & Neglect 743-747 (1998).

23. Kenny, *supra* note 17 at 88.

24. Martha Bailey, *The Failure of Physicians to Report Child Abuse*, 40 U. Toronto Faculty L. Rev. 49, 55, 57 (1982).

25. *Id.*

26. Victor I. Vieth, *A Strategy for Confronting Child Abuse in Rural Communities*, 28 The Prosecutor 15, 16 (September/October 1994).

27. Gail Zellman, *Reducing Underresponding: Improving System Response to Mandated Reporters*, Journal of Interpersonal Violence 115, 116-117 (March 1991).

28. Prevent Child Abuse America, *The Results of the 1999 Fifty State Survey*, found at www.preventchildabuse.org

29. Andrea J. Sedlak & Diane D. Broadhurst, U.S. Dep't. of Health & Human Servs., Third Nat'l Incidence Study of Child Abuse & Neglect 7-16 (Sept. 1996). A more recent study finds that nearly 2/3 of reports are screened into the CPS system but that investigations result in only 27.5 of the cases as being substantiated for abuse or neglect. In each of the past 5 years, abuse has been substantiated in no more than

29% of the cases accepted for referral. Child Maltreatment 2001 (Published by U.S. Department of Health and Human Services, Administration on Children, Youth and Families, Washington, D.C., U.S. Government Printing Office, 2003). This data suggests that the reporters, investigators or both are performing poorly in locating and assisting abused children. One problem may be the sheer number of reports that must be investigated. The average CPS investigator conducts 69 investigations per year-more than one per week. *Id.* 10. Given that a quality investigation may require interviewing numerous witnesses, searching the premises where the alleged abuse took place, collecting and reviewing data from numerous other agencies, CPS investigators may simply lack the time to conduct competent investigations. This is particularly so when we recall that investigators may have many other duties as well. In rural communities, for example, the investigator is often responsible for providing ongoing services. *Id.*

30. Sedlak, note 29 at 7-16.

31. Brett Drake, Melissa Jonson-Reid, Ineke Way & Sulki Chung, *Substantiation and Recidivism*, 8(4) Child Maltreatment 248, 257 (November 2003).

32. *Id.*

33. Salter, note 11 at 57.

34. Anna Quindlen, *Forward* to Marc Parent, Turning Stones: My Days and Nights with Children at Risk (1996).

35. *Id.*

36. Handbook of Accreditation Standards and Procedures, 5th Ed., standard 1.1, chapter 2 (published by Council on Social Work Education 2003).

37. *Id.* at standard 2.0, chapter 2.

38. Kelly M. Champion, Kimberly Shipman, Barbara L. Bonner, Lisa Hensley, and Allison C. Howe, *Child Maltreatment Training in Doctoral Programs in Clinical, Counseling, and School Psychology: Where Do We Go From Here?* 8 Child Maltreatment 211, 215 (August 2003).

39. *Id.* at 215. To improve graduate training of psychologists, the authors recommended "team-taught classes, visiting instructors, and class visits by outside professionals" as "means by which to increase interdisciplinary training without developing entirely new programs." *Id.*

40. Salter, *supra* note 11 at 2.

41. Ann S. Botash, *From Curriculum to Practice: Implementation of the Child Abuse Curriculum*, 8(4) Child Maltreatment 239 (November 2003).

42. Jenny et al., *Analysis of missed cases of abusive head trauma*, 281 JAMA 621-626 (1999).

43. According to one expert, the "most common age at which sexual abuse begins is three." Gavin de Becker, *Foreword* in Salter, note 12 at x.

44. Thomas D. Lyon, *False Allegations and False Denials in Child Sexual Abuse*, 1 Psychology, Public Policy and Law 429, 433 (1995).

45. *See generally*, Richard Estes, *The Commercial Sexual Exploitation of Children in the U.S., Canada and Mexico*, available online at http://caster.ssw.upenn.edu/~restes/CSEC.htm

46. Prevent Child Abuse America, *Total Estimated Cost of Child Abuse and Neglect in the United States* (2001) found at www.preventchildabuse.org

47. Blair L. Sadler, David L. Chadwick, and Dominique J. Hensler, *The Summary Chapter–The National Call to Action–Moving Ahead*, 23 Child Abuse & Neglect 1011, 1016 (1999).

48. *Id.*

49. *Id.*

50. Richard Krugman, *The Politics*, published in *Convening A National Call to Action: Working Toward the Elimination of Child Maltreatment*, 23 Child Abuse & Neglect 963 (1999). Of course, there are some political figures who have advocated for maltreated children. As noted in the foreword to this volume, U.S. Rep. Robert E. "Bud" Cramer was instrumental in creating the child advocacy center movement. Former United States Senator Walter F. Mondale was the driving force behind the Child Abuse Prevention and Treatment Act (CAPTA) which became law in 1974. CAPTA provided federal funds for numerous child protection initiatives and played a significant role in shaping our modern child protection system. John E.B. Myers, A History of Child Protection in America 299-303 (2004) (Mondale's role in enacting CAPTA is referenced or discussed on pages 289-291, 299, 351-352, and 354 in the Myers book). Other political figures have played a role in establishing some of the reforms discussed in this paper. Ohio Attorney General Jim Petro, for example, has played a key role in establishing the *Finding Words* program in his state.

51. *See* Finkelhor, *supra* note 15 and accompanying text.

52. Va. Code. Ann section 63.2-1509 (2002).

53. The university referenced is Winona State University. For an overview of the extraordinary history of WSU, *See* R.A. Dufresne, Winona State University: A History of One Hundred Twenty-Five Years (1985).

54. Vieth, *supra* note 9 at 177-179.

55. *See* Ken Lanning, *Law Enforcement Perspective on the Compliant Child Victim*, The Apsac Advisor (Spring 2002).

56. *See generally, Alison R. Perona, Bette L. Bottoms, & Erin Sorenson Research-Based Guidelines for Forensic Interviews* (this volume). There are many forensic interviewing protocols in use around the country. Each protocol has strengths and weaknesses and there will never be a perfect model. Nonetheless, most protocols share common features such as the importance of building rapport, incorporating instructions into the interview, using developmentally appropriate questions and aids, and a sensitive closure to the process. Some of the leading protocols are discussed in the Perona et al., article cited above. For a discussion of the protocol used in San Diego, see Deborah Davies et al., *A Model for Conducting Forensic Interviews with Child Victims of Abuse*, 1 Child Maltreatment 189 (1996). For a discussion of the protocol used in the forensic interview training programs of CornerHouse and the American Prosecutors Research Institute, *see* Lori S. Holmes & Victor I. Vieth, *Finding Words/Half a Nation: The Forensic Interview Training Program of CornerHouse and APRI's National Center for Prosecution of Child Abuse*, 15(1) Apsac Advisor 4-8 (Winter 2003).

57. For more information, visit the APSAC web site at http://www.apsac.org/

58. This program offers basic and advanced forensic interview training as well as a course on Spanish speaking forensic interview training. For more information, visit the Academy's website at http://www.nationalcac.org/academy/acad.html

59. For more information, visit the CornerHouse website at: http://www.cornerhousemn.org

60. For more information, visit the Children's Hospital website at: www.cincinnatichildrens.org

61. For more information visit the First Witness website at firstwitness.org

62. For an overview of the history and quality of this program, *see* Holmes & Vieth, *supra* note 56 at 4-8.

63. Victor I. Vieth, *Half a Nation by 2010*, Volume 14(2) Update (2001) (published by APRI's National Center for Prosecution of Child Abuse, Alexandria, VA). *See also*, Holmes & Vieth, *supra* note 56 at 4-8.

64. *See generally*, Sandra K. Hewitt, Assessing Allegations of Sex Abuse in Pre-School Children (1999).

65. Connie Nicholas Carnes, Charles Wilson and Debra Nelson-Gardell, *Extended Forensic Evaluation When Sexual Abuse is Suspected: A Model and Preliminary Data*, 4(3) Child Maltreatment 242-254 (1999).

66. The Midwest Children's Resource Center in Minnesota is an excellent example of this model. For more information about MCRC, contact them at 347 N. Smith, Suite 401, St. Paul, MN 55102.

67. Kristen Kreischer, *Burned Out*, Children's Voice article (July/August 2002) available online at www.cwla.org/articles/cv0207burnedout.htm

68. *Id.*

69. *See*, Victor I. Vieth, *When Days Are Gray: Avoiding Burnout as Child Abuse Professionals*, 14(4) Update (2001) (published by APRI's National Center for Prosecution of Child Abuse, Alexandria, VA)

70. Montclair State University in New Jersey, for example, offers a post BA "certificate in child advocacy" for child protection workers and is developing a Master of Arts in Child Advocacy with an optional concentration in child public welfare. This master's program will provide students with knowledge of mandated reporting laws, investigative techniques including the child interview, and legal issues surrounding these cases. Reflecting the multi-disciplinary nature of child protection work, the faculty is drawn from diverse fields. By addressing the need for practical education of front line child protection workers at both the undergraduate and graduate levels, Montclair State University is well-positioned to be recognized as a true pioneer in child protection education. *See* Robert H. McCormick, *The Master of Arts in Child Advocacy: A Contribution to an Emerging Discipline*, Journal of Aggression, Maltreatment & Trauma (this volume).

71. The use of well-trained actors has been a very successful formula in bringing academia into the street by forcing students to think on their feet and apply the instruction they have been given in realistic settings. CornerHouse uses this approach in their forensic interview training and APRI has adopted this approach in the *Finding Words* curriculum. All actors, however, must be adults including those playing the roles of children. Given the nature of the subject matter, it is unethical to use child performers in such a role. If the adult actor is properly trained in child dynamics, he/she can respond in a realistic way to the fictitious investigation suggested in this paper.

72. National Study of Child Protective Services Systems and Reform Efforts (U.S. Department of Health and Human Services, Washington, D.C., U.S. Government Printing Office, 2003).

73. *Id.* at 5-1.

74. There is research to suggest that various types of child neglect, such as emotional abuse, may increase the risk for poor outcomes in adulthood to a greater extent than other forms of maltreatment. *See*, e.g., Stephanie Hamarman, Kayla H. Pope, & Sally J. Czaja, *Emotional Abuse in Children: Variations in Legal Definitions and Rates Across the United States*, 7(4) Child Maltreatment 303 (2002). Accordingly, we should not say we are putting neglect cases into the alternative response system because this form of maltreatment is less egregious but rather because this form of maltreatment is

better handled in an informal setting without the adversarial nature of a legal proceeding.

75. National Study of Child Protective Services Systems and Reform Efforts, *supra* note 72 at 5-1, 5-2.

76. A recent survey of 2,240 judges found that barely 50% of them had received any child welfare training before hearing child dependency and neglect proceedings. *View from the Bench: Obstacles to Safety & Permanency for Children in Foster Care* (July 2004) (this survey was conducted by the Children & Family Research Center, School of Social Work, University of Illinois, Urbana-Champaign and is available on line at www.fosteringresults.org. Much has been written about the proper credentials for being a trial judge including courage, self-doubt, and a deep and genuine affection for the law. *See* Victor I. Vieth *Selecting Trial and Appellate Judges: Exceptions to the Rules and Rules to Find the Exceptions*, 18 Hamline J. Pub. L. & Pol'y 52 (1996). To this list should be added experience with child witnesses. Indeed, there is literature suggesting that unless a judge is well-versed in linguistics, child development, memory and suggestibility and other issues impacting on the child witness, that he/she is incompetent to serve as a judge in a case involving the testimony of children or in a case where the statements of children is an issue of some sort. *See* Victor I. Vieth, *When Cameras Roll: The Danger of Videotaping Child Abuse Victims Before the Legal System is Competent to Assess Children's Statements*, 7(4) Journal of Child Sexual Abuse 113-121 (1999).

77. For an excellent overview of the concept and use of court schools, *see* Martha J. Finnegan, *Creating and Administering a Kids Court Program*, 13(5) Update (2000) (published by APRI's National Center for Prosecution of Child Abuse, Alexandria, VA).

78. *See* Lynn M. Copen, Preparing Children for Court (2000).

79. *See* Thomas D. Lyon & Karen Saywitz, *Young Mistreated Children's Competence to Take the Oath*, 3(1) Applied Developmental Science 16-27 (1999).

80. *See* Anne Graffam Walker, Handbook of Questioning Children (2d Edition) (1999); *see also* Myers, Goodman, & Saywitz, *Psychological Research on Children as Witnesses: Practical Implications for Forensic Interviews and Courtroom Testimony,* 27 Pacific L. Journal 1 (1996).

81. Michael R. Leippe et al., *The Opinions and Practices of Criminal Attorneys Regarding Child Eyewitnesses: A Survey*, in Ceci et al., Perspectives on Children's Testimony 100, 118 (1989).

82. Munchausen Syndrome by Proxy cases, for example, are extremely complex and since the abusive caretaker often has medical training, the treating physician "will be hard pressed not to be caught up in trying 'too hard' to find the cause of the child's pain (and) the potential for missing that she is standing right next to us at the bedside is great." Herbert Schreier, *Munchausen Syndrome by Proxy Defined*, 110(5) Pediatrics 985, 987-988 (2002).

83. For a more thorough analysis of these issues, *see* American Academy of Pediatrics/Committee on Child Abuse & Neglect, *Guidelines for the Evaluation of Sexual Abuse of Children: Subject Review*, 103 Pediatrics 186-191 (1999).

84. Even in a busy clinic, physicians may be able to identify neglect by "brief screening questions" on issues such as "access to health care and medications, adequacy of food supplies, possible depression, and social supports and coping." Howard Dubowitz et al., *Child Neglect: Outcomes in High-Risk Urban Preschoolers*, 109(6) Pediatrics 1100, 1105 (2002). In terms of screening for psychological neglect, physicians can assess the parent-child interaction and ask questions such as "is the overall

tone of the interaction positive? What is the nature of their affect? It is useful to note the responsivity of parent and child to each other. Do they listen to and consider each other?" *Id.* at 1105.

85. *See* Charles Felzen Johnson, *The Use of Charts and Models to Facilitate a Physician's Testimony in Court*, 4 Child Maltreatment 228 (1999); Victor I. Vieth, *Tips for Medical Professionals Called as Witnesses*, 13(2) Update (2000).

86. Suzanne P. Starling & Stephen Boos, *Core Content for Residency Training in Child Abuse and Neglect*, 8(4) Child maltreatment 242-243 (November 2003).

87. *Id.*

88. For a discussion of the inadequate training of psychologists working with victims of child maltreatment, see notes 38-39 and the accompanying text.

89. Numerous studies document that dentists under-report cases of abuse and neglect because of lack of knowledge as to what injuries are consistent with abuse. For a summary of these studies and a call for continued and increased efforts to educate dentists about child maltreatment, *see* Howard L. Needleman, *Orafacial Trauma in Child Abuse and the Role of the Dental Profession*, 12 Apsac Advisor 10 (Summer 1999).

90. There is a growing body of evidence showing a correlation between animal abuse and child abuse. As a result, some states, such as Ohio, have made veterinarians mandated reporters. For an excellent overview of the research documenting the correlation between animal abuse and child abuse, *see* Allie Phillips, *How the Dynamics Between Animal Abuse and Child Abuse Affect the Forensic Interview Process*, 1(4) reasonable Efforts (Published by APRI's National Child Protection Training Center, Winona, MN).

91. *See* Victor I. Vieth, *The National Child Protection Training Center: A Partnership between APRI and Winona State University*, 38(1) The Prosecutor 33 (January/February 2004).

92. *See generally,* Hechler, *supra* note 10.

93. Adams and Wells, *Normal Versus Abnormal Genital Findings in Children: How Well Do Examiners Agree?* 17 Child Abuse and Neglect 663, 673 (1993).

94. Sheldon D. Engelmayer & Robert J. Wagman, Hubert Humprhey and His Dream 313 (1978).

95. Gene G. Abel et al., *Self-Reported Sex Crimes of Nonincarcerated Paraphiliacs*, 2 J. Interpersonal Violence 3, 17 (1987).

96. NCPCA hosts several national conferences a year. However, most of our training is conducted at the state and local level. A child protection professional asks an NCPCA trainer or trainers to visit their state and teach one or more workshops. Training at the state and local level is oftentimes more effective because it requires the speaker to tailor the training to local laws and dynamics.

97. For an excellent overview of the promising practice of home-based services, *see* John M. Leventhal, *The Prevention of Child Abuse and Neglect: Successfully out of the Blocks*, 25 Child abuse & Neglect 431 (2001). For an additional discussion of home based services and other prevention programs that do and do not work, *see* Sharon Portwood, *What We Know–and Don't Know–About Preventing Child Maltreatment* (this volume).

98. When Paul Wellstone was a political science professor at Carleton College he taught students to bring academia into the street by organizing on behalf of poor people. When his students began collecting data that would be used by and for poor people, the university reacted harshly. The president of Carleton said "(o)ne would think that in good public policy research, there would be a clear set of policy recommendations for

the relevant decision makers." Although university animosity lead to Wellstone's firing, a student revolt resulted in this "radical" professor being tenured at the age of 28. Senator Paul Wellstone, The Conscience of a Liberal 5, 6-7 (2001).

99. According to Hubert Humphrey, "child abuse has been ignored because children have no political muscle, no effective way of articulating their needs to those of us who write the law." Engelmayer and Wagman, *supra* note 94 at 313. In 2001, Senator Wellstone echoed these sentiments when he wrote "(w)hen historians write about American politics over the past several decades, the ultimate indictment will be of ways in which we have abandoned our children and devalued the work of adults who take care of children." Wellstone, *supra* note 98 at 73.

100. Child protection workers who so often are subject to criticism for their action or inaction may be comforted by the words of Theodore Roosevelt: "It is not the critic who counts; not the man who points out how the strong man stumbles, or where the doer of deeds could have done them better. The credit belongs to the man who is actually in the arena, whose face is marred by dust and sweat and blood; who strives valiantly, who errs, and comes short again and again; because there is not effort without error and shortcoming; but who does actually strive to do the deeds; who knows the great enthusiasms, the great devotions; who spends himself in a worthy cause, who at the best knows in the end the triumphs of high achievement and who at the worst, if he fails, at least fails while daring greatly, so that his place shall never be with those cold and timid souls who know neither victory nor defeat." This quote appears on the title page in Richard Nixon, In the Arena (1990).

101. For a discussion of these and other efforts in Cottonwood County, Minnesota *see* Vieth, *supra* note 9.

102. These are the words of former Speaker of the House Tip O'Neill as recorded in Wellstone, *supra* note 98, at 200.

103. *See* Victor I. Vieth, *Corporal Punishment in the United States: A Call for a New Approach to the Prosecution of Disciplinarians*, 15 Journal of Juvenile Law 22, 27-30 (1995).

104. *See generally*, Mary Baker Eddy, Science and Health (2000). *See also*, S.M. Sasser & R. Swan, *Deaths from Religion-motivated Neglect*, 101(4) Pediatrics 625 (1998).

105. *See In Re EG*, 133 Ill. 2d 98, 549 N.E.2d 322 (1989).

106. I once took a technical assistance question from a prosecutor dealing with this very issue. As the prosecutor related the situation to me, the parents were "snake handlers" who believed that, as a sign of their child's faith, the boy should be allowed to handle venomous snakes and to drink poison. The boy was eleven years old at the time.

107. Dr. Erna Olafson of the University of Cincinnati shared this concern with me in her role of advising APRI about our forensic interviewing course, *Finding Words*.

108. In Minnesota, for example, the law provides: "Once a child alleged to be in need of protection or services is under the court's jurisdiction, the court shall ensure that reasonable efforts including *culturally appropriate services* by the social services agency are made . . ." Minn. Stat. Section 260.012(a). The same statute reiterates this several paragraphs later when it provides that in determining whether the government has made reasonable efforts in working with a child in need, the court must consider whether the services offered to the child and his/her family were "culturally appropriate." Minn. Stat. Section 260.012(c)(3). Nebraska requires placing the abused child in a foster family with religious practices similar to the biological family whenever practicable. Neb. Rev. Stat. section 43-29B (2003).

109. Philip Yancey, Soul Survivor 3-4, 8-9 (2001).

110. In writing about his obligation to improve the world, Lutheran theologian Dietrich Bonhoeffer said: "The essence of optimism is not its view of the present, but the fact that it is the inspiration of life and hope when others give in; it enables a man to hold his head high when everything seems to be going wrong; it gives him strength to sustain reverses and yet to claim the future for himself instead of abandoning it to his opponent. It is true that there is a silly, cowardly kind of optimism, which we must condemn. But the optimism that is will for the future should never be despised, even if it is proved wrong a hundred times; it is health and vitality and the sick man has no business to impugn it." Dietrich Bonhoeffer, Letters and Papers from Prison (1997). This optimism led Bonhoeffer to resist Hitler and his reign of terror. The Nazis executed Bonhoeffer in 1945. Sargent Shriver is another example of a man whose religious faith compelled him to develop programs of lasting benefit to humanity. Shriver "inspired, led or created" the Peace Corps, Head Start, VISTA, Job Corps, Community Action, Upward Bound, Foster Grandparents, and the Special Olympics. Scott Stossel, Sarge xi (2004). Bill Moyers described Shriver as "the Christian who comes closest, in my experience, to the imitation of Christ. . . . Shriver has lived his life as a great gamble that what we do to serve, help, and care for our fellow human beings is what ultimately counts." *Id.* Even many of those who reject a spiritual worldview acknowledge the contributions, real or hoped-for, of religion in creating a moral society. For example, Supreme Court Justice Hugo Black was an agnostic who nonetheless used various religious teachings, from diverse faiths, to illustrate moral truths. Hugo Black, Jr., My Father 172-176 (1975).

111. Clayborn Carson & Peter Holloran, Eds, A Knock at Midnight xiv (1998).

112. *Id.* at xii

113. Flip Schulke, Ed, Martin Luther King, Jr. A Documentary. . . . Montgomery to Memphis 217 (1976)

114. In his last sermon before going to jail, Rev. Arthur Allen Jr. removed his belt and waved it behind a 14 year old boy as part of a mock whipping to demonstrate his unwillingness to accept the verdict that his previous whipping of boys who had to be restrained by men constituted cruelty to children. *Pastor Encourages Parish to Whip Children*, Washington Post a28 (Tuesday, October 22, 2002).

115. Victor I. Vieth, *Keeping the Faith: A Call for Collaboration Between the Child Protection and Faith Communities,* to be published in Giardino, Cooper, Vieth, & Kellogg, Medical & Legal Aspects of Child Sexual Exploitation (forthcoming from GW Publishing, 2004).

116. In writing about the need for grassroots efforts to create positive social reform, Senator Paul Wellstone not only saw the importance of the faith community but he felt they were coming into stride. In his last book, Wellstone applauded the part of the religious community that is "finally finding its voice." Wellstone, *supra* note 98 at 212. Although he opposed the involvement of religious leaders in either Democratic or Republican politics, President Richard Nixon believed that religion played an important role in motivating men and women to accomplish noble deeds. According to Nixon, "God's will is expressed by men through their actions toward and on behalf of others . . . the most important step is using the energy and creativity faith gives you to make the world a better place." Richard Nixon, In the Arena 97 (1990).

117. Jill Goldman, Marsha K. Salus, Deborah Wolcott, Kristie Y. Kennedy, A Coordinated Response to Child Abuse and Neglect: The Foundation for Practice 28-29 (U.S. Dep't of Health and Human Services, Washington, DC 2003).

118. *Id.* at 32-33. Some people suggest that we can never significantly reduce child abuse until we significantly reduce poverty in the United States. According to John Myers, "If child maltreatment is a piece of cloth, poverty is the thread that holds it together. Cut the thread and the cloth unravels. Although we will never rid ourselves entirely of maltreatment, we guarantee high rates of suffering as long as we tolerate widespread poverty." John E.B. Myers, A History of Child Protection in America 444 (2004). Although there is no question that reducing poverty would reduce the rate of some forms of maltreatment, this would not, by itself, eliminate child abuse. This is because maltreatment, at some level, exists among all socioeconomic classes. Moreover, it may not be an absolute necessity to reduce poverty before reducing the rate of child abuse among poor people. This is because most poor people do not abuse their children. If we can determine the skills, resources or other factors that prevent most poor families from maltreating their children, and instill these dynamics in poor families where maltreatment does occur, we may be able to limit the role of poverty in contributing to child abuse.

119. *See generally*, Salter note 11.

120. Deborah Daro and Anne Cohn Donnelly, *Charting the Waves of Prevention: Two Steps Forward, One Step Back*, 26 Child Abuse & Neglect 731 (2002).

121. *Id* at 737.

122. *Id* at 737.

123. *Id.*

124. *Id* at 738.

125. *Id* at 738.

126. *Id* at 738.

127. These principles are as follows: (1) Take actions that help children and prosecutors. With respect to every action, NCPCA employees must ask the question "is it good for kids and prosecutors?" If the answer is yes, we should engage in the task. If the answer is no, we should move on to another project. (2) We are not bridge burners, we are bridge builders. We cannot function effectively if we operate in a vacuum. Where possible, we will collaborate with other units of APRI and other organizations who can assist us in our primary mission of helping prosecutors help the children whose lives depend on us. We are not in competition with other child abuse organizations. We are in competition with child abusers for the futures of a sea of children. As long as children and prosecutors are being served, it doesn't matter who gets the job done and it matters even less who gets the credit. (3) Mistakes do not matter, responsibility does. An error is simply evidence of our human nature. In some cases, an error is caused by our creativity and willingness to try new approaches. When things go awry, however, we must take responsibility for our errors and work to correct any problems the error may have caused. (4) We will never settle a score by hurting a child. We work with many of the best and brightest child abuse professionals in the world. On occasion we may have a conflict with one or more of these professionals. All conflicts will be dealt with in a professional manner. Under no circumstance will this office be used to punish a child protection professional who rubs us the wrong way. For instance, being angry with a prosecutor is not justification for denying that prosecutor technical assistance on a case of child abuse. Such conduct merely serves to hurt a child who needs us and will not be tolerated. (5)When on the road, take the time to get to know the students. Before speaking at a conference, NCPCA trainers will walk around the room, shake hands with the students and get a sense of what the audience is looking for in a given lecture. We will not wait for students to come to us with their needs, we will seek out the stu-

dents. (6) Let me know when I'm wrong, inconsistent or adrift. You can count on me to make mistakes and you can count on me to be unaware of some of my errors. Point them out to me. Churchill called critics his friends because the critics allowed him to see his errors and to improve. Be my friend and point out deficiencies I need to work on. (7) Remember Lincoln and Einstein. Lincoln said "determine that the thing can be done and it will be done." We do not have limitless resources and we will face the occasional difficulties that come with being alive. We must, however, be dedicated to overcoming any roadblock that separates children from justice. Einstein said that there are only two ways to look at life. The first way to view life is as if nothing you see is a miracle and the second is as if *everything* you see is a miracle. We agree with Einstein that the latter choice is preferable. When the varied talents and abilities of NCPCA workers come together to serve a higher purpose, we are not only witnesses but participants in a miracle.

128. *Id.*

129. *See* Joseph J. Ellis, Founding fathers 4-5 (2000).

130. Malcolm Gladwell, The Tipping Point (2000).

131. *Id.* at 21.

132. *Id.* at 25.

133. U.S. Senator Paul Wellstone advocated that the appropriation for NCPCA be tripled to 4.5 million dollars and supported full funding for the NCPTC (3 million dollars). At a campus memorial service, Winona State University President Darrell Krueger spoke of a brief walk across campus in which he and Senator Wellstone discussed their plans to develop in Winona the National Child Protection Training Center. Stacy Booth & Theodore Evans, *Memorial Held for Wellstone*, 81(8) Winonan (November 6, 2002). As another example of progressive support for *Unto the Third Generation*, I was honored to deliver the keynote at the 20th anniversary of the Minnesota Justice Foundation in November of 2002. This is a progressive group originally founded by law students seeking to address the needs of the poor. This "liberal" group responded to the *Unto the Third Generation* proposal with a standing ovation. In a letter from MJF president Sharon H. Fischlowitz I was told: "Our audience loved your speech. People found it very moving and have told me it was a very memorable evening. As I mentioned last night, rarely does this audience deliver a standing ovation . . . I know people felt privileged to have heard your insights." *Letter from Sharon H. Fischlowitz*, dated November 7, 2002 (The original is on file with the National Center for Prosecution of Child Abuse).

134. Talk show host Dr. Laura Schlesinger also advocated that NCPCA's budget be tripled and urged her 12 million listeners/readers to write their senators and representatives in support of the NCPTC. Dr. Schlesinger called the *Unto the Third Generation* concept the "best hope for children in crisis in America." She likened NCPCA's call to end child abuse to JFK's challenge to put a man on the moon and urged her listeners/readers not to underestimate "the troops at the National Center for Prosecution of Child Abuse . . . these remarkable public servants will point the way." Dr. Laura Schlesinger, *Child Abuse is Terrorism*, Dr. Laura Perspective 10-13 (January 2003).

135. Gladwell, *supra* note 130, at 29.

136. There is evidence that the UTG proposals are resonating with front line child protection professionals. *See* Maja Beckstrom, St. Paul Pioneer Press 3F (May 23, 2004) (noting the UTG proposals were "met with enthusiasm" at a child abuse conference in the Twin Cities).

137. Gladwell, *supra* note 130 at 135, 137.

138. *Id.* at 140.

139. For a summary of Giuliani's role in reducing New York's crime rate, *see* Rudolph W. Giuliani, Leadership 71-82 (2002).

140. Gladwell, *supra* note 130 at 141.

141. *Id.* at 150.

142. This may require some social service agencies to alter their view of their work. In one survey of social service supervisors, 60% saw the role of their agency simply to identify the problems in abusive or neglectful homes and to offer services as opposed to actually changing the behavior of abusive or neglectful parents. Thomas D. Merton, *Compliance vs. Change*, Commentary (February 2003) (published by the Child Welfare Institute, Duluth, GA).

143. John C. Culver and John Hyde, American Dreamer, A Life of Henry A. Wallace 528 (2000).

144. *Id.* at 149

145. *Id.*

146. *Id.*

147. *Id.*

148. *Id.* at 531.

149. *Id.* at 531

150. For an account of this part of the battle at Gettysburg, *see* Richard Moe, The Last Full Measure (1993).

APPENDIX

Unto the Third Generation:

An Outline for A Call to End Child Abuse in the United States within 120 Years

I.   Introduction

II. The history of the fight against child abuse

III. The present state of the conflict: the five obstacles to ending child abuse

A. Many children suspected of being abused are not reported into the system

B. Even when reports come into the system, most children never have their cases investigated

C. Even when cases are investigated, the investigators and other front line responders are often inadequately trained and inexperienced

D. Even when an investigator successfully substantiates abuse and gets a victim into the system, the child is typically older

APPENDIX (continued)

and it is more difficult to address the physical, emotional and other hardships caused by the abuse

E. Because the child protection community lacks a unified voice in communicating the needs of maltreated children, these victims receive an inadequate share of our country's financial resources

IV. The battle plan for ending child abuse

A. Abused children must be reported into the system and those reports must be of high quality

1. Every university must teach students entering professions where they will be mandated reporters the skills necessary to perform this task
2. Mandated reporters in the field must receive annual training on the detection of abuse and their obligations to report

B. Child protection workers and law enforcement officers must conduct a competent investigation of every child abuse case that comes to their attention and, when abuse is substantiated, pursue appropriate civil and criminal actions

1. Children reported into the system must be interviewed by a social worker, police officer or other professional trained in the art of speaking to children.

a. Develop state of the art forensic interviewing courses such as APRI/CornerHouse's *Finding Words*
b. Each state must have a forensic interview training course of the quality of *Finding Words* that is locally run and taught
c. In addition to quality forensic interviews, there must be in place a system to assist children that do not respond well to an investigative interview

2. Child protection professionals called on to investigate and repair families damaged by abuse must be competent to perform these tasks

     a. Every university must teach child protection profes-
sionals necessary investigative skills

     b. Every university must teach child protection profes-
sionals to work meaningfully with families impacted
by child abuse

     c. Graduate schools must adequately prepare profes-
sionals to work with child victims
1. Law schools
2. Medical schools
3. Other graduate schools

     d. Once in the field, civil child protection professionals
must have access to ongoing training and technical
assistance

   3. Prosecutors must be adequately trained to prosecute
child abusers

C. We must teach police officers, social workers, prosecutors
and other child protection professionals to be community
leaders in the prevention of child abuse

   1. The training must begin in college and continue so long
as these professionals are in the field

   2. In their role as community leaders, these child protection
professionals must enlist the support of the faith based
community

   3. Prevention efforts must be developed and run at the local
level and tailored to meet local needs

   4. Everyone engaged in the campaign against child abuse
must understand their role in history and act accordingly

V. The timeline for ending child abuse within 120 years

A. The first 40 years: 2001-2040

   1. Every suspected case of child abuse will be reported and
every report will be of a high quality

APPENDIX (continued)

2. Every child reported into the system will be interviewed by someone who can competently interview a child about abuse and the investigation of all child abuse allegations will likewise be competently done
3. Every substantiated case of egregious abuse must be prosecuted by a child abuse prosecutor skilled at handling these complex cases
4. Every CPS worker will be competent to work with child abuse victims and their families from day one
5. Every child protection social worker, police officer and prosecutor will be a community leader in preventing child abuse
6. Every child protection worker and attorney will have access to ongoing training, technical assistance and publications to constantly refresh and improve their skills

B. The next 80 years (2040-2120): the search for a tipping point

VI. Ending child abuse: the last full measure

What We Know–
and Don't Know–
About Preventing Child Maltreatment

Sharon G. Portwood

SUMMARY. Although child maltreatment is routinely acknowledged as a serious social problem, it remains widespread, raising questions about how prevention efforts can be improved. Following a review of theory and research relevant to prevention programming, the two dominant models of child abuse prevention–child empowerment and parent education–are examined, emphasizing both those factors that appear to contribute to program success (e.g., early intervention, sufficient time commitments, cultural sensitivity) and weaknesses in current efforts (e.g., poor implementation). Although underutilized, broader social and system-level reforms, including social policy and media initiatives, hold promise for prevention. Ways in which to leverage these tools are explored. Additional research is urged to explore assumptions on which programs are based, as well as to conduct more rigorous evaluation of current programs. The article concludes that a sustained commitment to prevention efforts aimed at child abuse and neglect is required. *[Article copies available for a fee from The Haworth Document Delivery Service:*

Address correspondence to: Sharon G. Portwood, JD, PhD, University of Missouri-Kansas City, Department of Psychology, 5100 Rockhill Road, Kansas City, MO 64110.

[Haworth co-indexing entry note]: "What We Know–and Don't Know–About Preventing Child Maltreatment." Portwood, Sharon G. Co-published simultaneously in *Journal of Aggression, Maltreatment & Trauma* (The Haworth Maltreatment & Trauma Press, an imprint of The Haworth Press, Inc.) Vol. 12, No. 3/4, 2006; and: *Ending Child Abuse: New Efforts in Prevention, Investigation, and Training* (ed: Victor I. Vieth, Bette L. Bottoms, and Alison R. Perona) The Haworth Maltreatment & Trauma Press, an imprint of The Haworth Press, Inc., 2006. Single or multiple copies of this article are available for a fee from The Haworth Document Delivery Service [1-800-HAWORTH, 9:00 a.m. - 5:00 p.m. (EST). E-mail address: docdelivery@haworthpress.com].

doi:10.1300/J146v12n03_03

KEYWORDS. Abuse, neglect, prevention, programs, policy

Much has been written on child abuse prevention since the 1960s, when Kempe and colleagues (Kempe, Silverman, Steele, Droegemuller, & Silver, 1962) first identified "the battered child syndrome." However, taken as a whole, this literature might well leave the reader wondering whether to feel optimistic or discouraged about the current state of child abuse prevention efforts. While some commentators have heralded the progress in prevention efforts, others paint a more dismal picture, emphasizing the limitations of current approaches and the fact that there are still many unanswered questions as to whether these approaches achieve their desired effects.

Whatever success is attributable to current efforts, it is clear that the ultimate goal of preventing child maltreatment is far from a reality. According to the U.S. Administration for Children and Families' National Clearinghouse on Child Abuse and Neglect Information (NCAAN), in 2001, approximately 3 million reports involving 5 million children were made to child protection agencies in the United States. Approximately two-thirds of these reports received additional assessment and/or investigation, resulting in the identification of approximately 903,000 children as victims of child maltreatment. Interestingly, although these most recent figures reflect an increase in the total number of cases reported for investigation, the number of substantiated cases of child abuse and neglect has remained virtually unchanged since 1993. Moreover, more than half of confirmed cases were closed on the day of substantiation. However, it should be noted that during roughly the same period, 1992 to 2000, the number of substantiated cases of *sexual* abuse declined. Jones and Finkelhor (2001) reported a remarkable 40% decrease, from an estimated 150,000 cases to 89,500 cases. Based on an examination of the relevant data, they concluded that this trend was due, at least in part, to an actual decline in the number of child sexual abuse cases (Finkelhor & Jones, 2004).

Perhaps in contrast to popular perceptions of child maltreatment, the vast majority of child victims (57%) suffer from neglect, followed by physical abuse (19%), sexual abuse (10%), psychological or emotional abuse (7%), and medical neglect (2%). Overall, the likelihood of victimization was inversely related to age, with children in the youngest age group (birth to 3) constituting the largest percentage (28%) of identified victims. In 84% of cases, the abuser was a parent or parents (NCCAN, 2003).

Given the continuing severity of the problem of child abuse and neglect, this article aims to review the status of current prevention efforts, using examples of current programs and the relevant research to provide an overview of what we know and do not know about effective prevention. Specific attention will be given to parent education and child empowerment service models, which dominate current programming. The potential of broader solutions, including those that expand their focus beyond a single system within the overall framework of systems (e.g., individual, family, and society) that contribute to the occurrence of child maltreatment, will also be explored.

THE GOAL OF PREVENTION EFFORTS

At the outset, it important to identify exactly what prevention efforts aim to accomplish. Prevention is generally conceptualized according to a three-tiered model. At the broadest level, *primary* (or universal) prevention encompasses interventions that are designed to prevent the target behavior from ever occurring. Such approaches typically focus on reducing risk factors and enhancing protective factors. Examples of primary prevention efforts aimed at child maltreatment include prenatal interventions and universal home visiting programs for all new parents. In contrast, *secondary* (or selected) prevention efforts focus on the early detection and treatment of existing problems, often targeting groups or individuals identified as "at risk." For example, the majority of parent education programs designed to prevent child maltreatment focus on families who meet certain criteria deemed to place them at high risk for abuse and/or neglect. *Tertiary* (or indicated) prevention approaches are designed to reduce the impact of existing problems (i.e., the re-occurrence of abusive behaviors). Thus, tertiary prevention programs focus on families in which abuse has already been identified.

It is important to note that only primary prevention targets the ultimate goal of preventing child abuse and neglect *before* they occur. Nonetheless, the vast majority of current prevention efforts directed at child maltreatment employ secondary or tertiary approaches. For example, some (e.g., Melton, 2002) have criticized current prevention policies and programs for an over-reliance on solutions based in the legal system, which necessarily focus on only that minority of cases that have been, at a minimum, identified and substantiated. Clearly, if we are to achieve a significant reduction in the occurrence of child maltreatment, a broader approach to prevention is needed.

DEVELOPING A CLEAR CONCEPT
OF CHILD MALTREATMENT
AND HOW IT CAN BE PREVENTED

Once prevention goals have been clarified, other essential questions remain. Foremost among these are identifying the target behavior and effective strategies for eliminating and/or reducing that behavior.

Definitions

A logical first step in formulating effective response to child maltreatment is to articulate a clear and accurate picture of the problem. Unfortunately, the field continues to be plagued by a lack of clarity of key terms, both between and within the numerous disciplines at work. For example, there has yet to be a definitive answer to such basic questions as "What specific behaviors constitute abuse?" and considerable disagreement persists regarding whether specific acts (e.g., striking a child, kissing a child) can be deemed abusive (Portwood, 1999).

Prevention efforts have been complicated by this difficulty in reaching a consensual definition of key terms, which include not only *child maltreatment*, but also each of its four standard sub-categories: *physical abuse, psychological abuse, sexual abuse*, and *neglect*. Currently, there is little consensus among the definitions used in law, practice, and/or research. Relevant definitions of child maltreatment are also subject to social, cultural, and historical influences given that child maltreatment is, essentially, a social judgment about appropriate and/or minimal standards of care.

Neglect, in particular, is generally defined as the failure to meet minimal standards of care. Neglect has been subdivided in multiple categories, commonly including physical neglect, educational neglect, emotional neglect, and medical neglect. What each of these typologies has in common is a failure to meet a child's basic needs. Thus, neglect contemplates an act of omission rather than commission. In contrast, *abuse* typically contemplates an intentional act. Many definitions of abuse encompass both a harm standard, requiring some observable injury, and an endangerment standard, under which a child is deemed to be abused if he or she is placed at substantial risk for harm. *Child sexual abuse* has been defined to include contacts or interactions between a child and an adult (or a person under age 18 who is significantly older than the victim or who is in a position of power or control over the child) when the child is being used for the sexual stimulation of the perpetrator or another person.

Clearly, the experiences of maltreated children are extremely diverse. Likewise, research indicates that the origins and consequences of child maltreatment are complex. No single factor accounts for significant amounts of abuse. To the contrary, the impact of perpetrator characteristics, child characteristics, family characteristics, and the broader social context vary by type of abuse. The task of ascertaining the causes of particular sub-types of abuse, and thus the appropriate targets for prevention, is further complicated by the fact that many children experience multiple forms of maltreatment.

Theoretical Foundations for Prevention Efforts

Current prevention efforts have been based on multiple theoretical foundations.

Macro-Level Theories. The broadest of these theories link child mal-treatment to cultural and societal conditions, including poverty, social isolation, racism, sexism, and widespread tolerance of violence and child maltreatment. Within this context of social inequality and injustice, strain theories propose that deviance (e.g., abusive behaviors) is more common among those individuals who experience frustration when they are de-nied equal access to resources while society emphasizes opportunities for success. The frustration-aggression hypothesis further posits that aggres-sion may be focused on an innocent party (e.g., a child) when the direct source of frustration (e.g., "society") is not available as a target for ag-gression. According to these theories, maltreatment would decrease if re-sources and supports for parents were increased and systemic changes were made (e.g., placing high legal and social costs on maltreatment; Daro, 1988). Commentators have also highlighted the role of sexual in-equality in contributing to child maltreatment. For example, Straus and Smith (1990) point out that inequality both within and outside the family contributes to the occurrence of family violence.

Family and Individual Theories. Overall, individual- and family-ori-ented theories underlie most current prevention strategies, including therapy for parents and/or children, parent education, home-visitation, and support groups (Daro, 1988). According to these theories, changes within particular families or individuals will prevent maltreatment; however, the types of change required vary. Many researchers (e.g., Straus & Smith, 1990) believe that the structure of the family creates a likely setting for violence, noting that family members spend a lot of time together, power differences exist, emotional interactions tend to be frequent, relationships between family members are difficult to break, and families are considered a private institution.

Theories involving psychological and behavioral characteristics of offenders, including caregiver psychopathology, have also been proposed. However, the relationship between specific psychological characteristics and child maltreatment is unclear. While much of the literature has focused on perceived deficits, leading to prevention approaches that emphasize "correction," more recent views have also examined protective factors. For example, the National Research Council (1993) encouraged those developing programs aimed at reducing the risk for child maltreatment to consult research findings from the field of child development regarding those factors that contribute to the development of healthy relationships.

The transactional model of child maltreatment views maltreatment as the result of interactions over time between the parent, the child, and the family context (Wolfe, 1993). For example, research on attachment theory supports the assertion that interactions between caregivers and children that involve maltreatment lead to disorganized patterns of attachment (George, 1996). It follows from this transactional model that parent/child interactions are appropriate targets for prevention efforts.

Many have sought to explain child maltreatment, and in particular, child neglect, through low socioeconomic status. Although abuse and neglect occur in all socioeconomic groups, data have consistently evidenced that child maltreatment, with the exception of sexual abuse (Milner, 1998) occurs at a disproportionately high rate among economically disadvantaged families. However, the relationship between SES and child maltreatment is a complex one. Poverty is characterized by many factors, including unemployment, limited education, single parent households, and social isolation, each of which influences child maltreatment. For example, social distancing often characterizes neglectful families. They tend to move frequently, which can contribute to a deficit in social support networks. Distancing may then extend to the parent-child relationship; neglectful parents have been found to interact less and more negatively with their children (Garbarino & Collin, 1999). The sugges-

tion is that of a cycle of neglect, in which the parent is psychologically neglected by others and then becomes psychologically unavailable to the
child. These factors point to the establishment of enduring and productive
social relationships as a key factor in preventing child neglect.

Learning and behavioral theories link child maltreatment to a caregiver's lack of knowledge or childcare skills, thus suggesting that prevention should focus on parent education and training (Daro, 1988). One set
of factors that distinguishes maltreating parents from their non-abusive
counterparts involves the social-cognitive and affective processes tied to
parents' perceptions of their children and the parent-child relationship.
Offending parents often do not understand the emotional complexity of
human relationships, particularly the parent-child relationship. "They
have difficulty seeing things from the child's perspective or understanding behavior in terms of the child's developmental level and the context
or situation" (Erickson & Egeland, 1996, p. 13). Abusive parents may
have high expectations of their children's behavior and/or believe that
this behavior is deviant. Lack of understanding regarding the child's developmental level may lead a parent to make negative attributions regarding the child's behavior or motivations. Parents' own developmental
level, which is a product of their history of care, autonomy, trust, and
level of cognitive functioning, may also impede their ability to provide
for children's needs. Social learning theory is frequently applied to understand the perpetuation of maltreatment within families, positing that
children who experience or witness violence are more likely to become
violent themselves (Widom, 1989).

Recent research suggests that biological factors may also place some
individuals at risk for committing child abuse. For example, perpetrators
of physical abuse have shown hyperresponsive physiological activity to
both negative and positive child stimuli that may influence their physiological responses in stressful situations involving children (Milner &
Chilamkurti, 1991). However, there is a clear need for further research in
regard to potential biological contributions to child maltreatment.

Scientific Research Relevant to Prevention Efforts

The field of child maltreatment research is relatively young; in fact,
almost all relevant research has been conducted since 1970. A significant portion of this research has investigated the causes and consequences of child maltreatment, revealing the complex nature of both
constructs. As previously noted, attempts to delineate the causes of
child maltreatment have produced evidence that no single factor ac-

counts for significant amounts of abuse. Instead, four categories of causal factors (perpetrator characteristics, child characteristics, family characteristics, and the broader social context) must be considered, with an acknowledgment that the impact of these factors varies by type of abuse, specifically, physical abuse and neglect versus sexual abuse.

Physical Abuse and Neglect. Several parent characteristics have been associated with physical abuse and neglect, including substance abuse and lack of involvement in community activities (Brown, Cohen, Johnson, & Salzinger, 1998). Abusive parents also tend to be single and young, to have lower self-esteem, to have inappropriate expectations of their children, and to be less empathetic with their children (Milner, 1998). In general, five areas have been associated with abusive parenting: cognitive disturbances, deficits in parenting skill, problems with impulse control, difficulties with stress management, and social skill problems (Azar & Twentyman, 1986). Each of these deficits, alone or in combination, can play a role in more systemic difficulties that increase the risk of abuse (e.g., a parent's poor social skills may result in a smaller support network). Child characteristics that have been associated with maltreatment include having a disability, a difficult temperament, psychiatric symptoms, and behavioral problems (Brown et al., 1998). However, when examining the behavior of both parents and children, the question of directionality arises (i.e., does negative parenting behavior produce negative behavior from the child or vice versa?).

Family characteristics are also related to the rate of child maltreatment. Situations that contribute to the level of stress within a family, including illness, death of a family member, and larger than average family size, have been established as risk factors for physical abuse (Miller-Perrin & Perrin, 1999). Other family factors associated with child maltreatment include high levels of conflict, the occurrence of partner violence, social isolation, high levels of stress, and a lack of support (Milner, 1998). Parents who abuse their children tend to communicate less frequently with their children, and they demonstrate fewer positive parenting behaviors. Abusive parents also tend to report more violence in their family of origin. However, it is important to note that while "cycle of violence" theories have garnered a great deal of public attention, the majority of individuals abused as children (about 70%) do not grow up to be abusers (Widom, 1989).

Rates of child physical abuse and neglect are higher in communities with a larger proportion of residents living in poverty (Garbarino, Kostelny, & Grady, 1993). Communities with more female-headed households, a higher unemployment rate, a lower percentage of wealthy residents, a lower median education level, more overcrowding, and a higher percentage of new residents also tend to have higher rates of maltreatment. However, it is important to note that violence is by no means typical of all families living in poverty, suggesting that other factors, most notably social bonding/social isolation, are at work. Emery and Laumann-Billings (1998) found that even in low income neighborhoods, child maltreatment rates tend to be low when residents know one another, there is a sense of community pride, people are involved in community organizations, and residents feel that they can ask their neighbors for help.

Sexual Abuse. In regard to sexual abuse, the abuser tends to be male, to have interpersonal problems, and to be antisocial (Milner, 1998). Thus, it is perhaps not surprising that research on characteristics of sexual abusers has focused primarily on men and may not be generalizable to female perpetrators. The majority of this research has also been generated from an assumption that the root cause of sexual abuse lies in the individual psychopathology of male abusers. As noted, there is some evidence to suggest that sexual abusers exhibit some antisocial tendencies, including a disregard for others and lack of impulse control, and/or deficits in heterosocial skills. Other theories center on deviant sexual arousal, which prompts offenders to solicit sexual encounters with children. The as yet undetermined origins of this deviant sexual arousal are believed to be primarily biological. However, this explanation does not appear adequate to explain incest. Instead, family dysfunction models posit that either the family or one of its adult members contributes to a context in which the sexual victimization of children is permitted or even encouraged (Miller-Perrin & Perrin, 1999).

Many early researchers focused on child characteristics in seeking explanations for sexual abuse, examining the victim's role in permitting or even encouraging the abuse. However, little evidence has been produced to support such a stance. While many victims of sexual abuse do exhibit sexualized behavior, most experts believe this to be a consequence rather than a cause of the abuse (Miller-Perrin & Perrin, 1999). In regard to family characteristics, poor parent-child relationships and marital conflict are associated with sexual abuse. Additional risk factors, including the presence of a stepfather and not living with one's natural parents for extended periods of time, attest to the heightened risk of being abused by non-biological family members (Brown et al., 1998; Finkelhor, 1984; Finkelhor, Hotaling, Lewis, & Smith, 1990). At the macrolevel, social and community factors, particularly social attitudes that view women and children as subordinate, no doubt contribute to the prevalence of sexual abuse (Williams, 2003).

PREVENTION PROGRAMMING

Ideally, prevention programs will be based on sound theory and reflect current research knowledge. However, the degree to which particular programs are grounded in theory and empirically-based is highly variable, as an overview of the two most popular program models–child empowerment and parent enhancement–demonstrates.

Prevention of Sexual Abuse: Child Empowerment Models

To date, most "child abuse" prevention efforts have targeted the more restricted category of child sexual abuse, even though this type of abuse accounts for a relatively small proportion of all cases of maltreatment. These programs tend to emphasize "stranger danger," despite clear evidence that the vast majority of abusers are known to the child. One of the most popular models for child sexual abuse prevention, the child empowerment service model, focuses on teaching children to recognize, resist, and report abuse. Among 400 school districts surveyed, Daro (1994) found that 64% had offered a prevention program during the preceding year. Similarly, 67% of children from a nationally representative sample had been exposed to a sexual abuse prevention program; almost all of these programs were school-based and targeted children during the late elementary grades (Finkelhor & Dziuba-Leatherman, 1995). While diverse in format and content, child empowerment program models share the same core assumptions: (a) many children do not know what sexual abuse is; (b) children do not need to tolerate sexual touching; (c) adults want to know about children who experience sexual touching by adults; and (d) disclosure of sexual touching will help to stop it. Clearly, at least some of these assumptions are flawed. For example, when asked how they would respond to a report of abuse from one of their child's playmates, only 14% of parents indicated that they would make an official report (to child protective services or law enforcement) if the alleged abuser was a stranger. This rate increased to a modest 33% for CPS and 25% for police when the perpetrator was a parent (Berrick, 1988).

Key concepts typically incorporated into child empowerment program models include the following: (a) children can control access to their own bodies; (b) there are different types of touches (e.g., good vs.

bad); (c) children can and should tell others about touching; and (d) supportive adults are available for children to tell about problems with touching. It is widely agreed that older children are better able to learn the concepts of sexual abuse prevention than are younger children; however, regardless of age, all children appear to learn best from programs that integrate active behavior skills components (Davis & Gidyez, 2000). Components that allow children to participate physically and behavioral skills training appear to be important program features. However, it remains to be established whether knowledge gains will translate into desired behavioral change when children are confronted with a potential abuser. In fact, research suggests that the self-protection responses that children use most often are not those responses recommended in most prevention programs (Asdigian & Finkelhor, 1995).

Despite support from school administrators, teachers, and parents, most school-based child sexual abuse prevention programs have not been evaluated. In their meta-analysis of 27 studies of such programs, Davis and Gidyez (2000) did find a relatively large effect size for programs, which they interpreted to mean that children's prevention-related knowledge and skills improved as a result of program participation. However, the researchers acknowledged that the largest effect sizes were found in less methodologically sound studies, casting doubt on the validity of study results. Even more troubling was the fact that the large majority of these studies were rated as poor in regard to at least one aspect of their methodology.

Overall, while there is limited evaluation data to suggest that child participants in comprehensive school-based sexual abuse prevention programs demonstrate an increase in knowledge, there is no evidence of a reduction in the actual number of victimizations as a result of participation in these programs (Finkelhor, Asdigian, & Dziuba-Leatherman, 1995). The effectiveness of the child empowerment model as a primary prevention tool is particularly suspect. Although such programs emphasize primary prevention as a goal, in fact, their major emphasis is often on disclosure, which constitutes tertiary prevention (i.e., preventing the re-occurrence of abuse).

Not only is the effectiveness of child empowerment programs subject to debate, but critics (e.g., Reppucci & Haugaard, 1989) have expressed other serious concerns, including (a) the impact of these programs on children's sexual development; (b) confusing curricula (i.e., some concepts may be difficult for children to understand); (c) the danger that such approaches may instill feelings of fear, vulnerability, and anxiety in children, while at the same time giving adults a false sense of security regarding children's safety; and (d) the threat that these programs send the message to children, teachers, parents, and society that children are responsible for preventing their own abuse. Despite the potential for harm, echoes of public support for so-called "child empowerment" can be seen in recent legal precedent, the effect of which is to place a heavy reporting burden on children. In *Stogner vs. California* (2003), the U.S. Supreme Court rejected a California law affording victims additional time to pursue legal action based on previously unreported abuse. The Court's ruling did not acknowledge scientific evidence put forward by the State and the American Psychological Association (in an amicus curiae brief) to the effect that childhood sexual abuse is rarely reported and that there are numerous reasons why victims do not report their abuse.

Prevention of Physical Abuse and Neglect: Parent Education Models

Parent education models target primarily physical abuse and neglect. Increasing support for parent education programs among practitioners, policymakers, and the general public is linked to a belief that lack of knowledge about child development and inadequate parenting skills are fundamental causes of child maltreatment (Cowen, 2001; Wolfe, 1985). Such programs emphasize teaching parents new skills (outside those learned during their own upbringing) that will enhance their resources, coping skills, and parenting competencies (Reppucci, Britner, & Woolard, 1997).

Despite the prevalence of parent education programs, as with child empowerment programs, relatively few have been evaluated in the scientific literature. Even fewer have been examined for their impact, if any, on child maltreatment specifically. While some evaluations of parent support programs demonstrate success, many fail to provide evidence of program effectiveness (Gomby, Culross & Behrman, 1999). It may well be that some programs are better than others; however, little work has focused on identifying those factors that increase a program's likelihood of success.

We do know that, ideally, parent education and support programs are initiated early in the child's life or before birth. Such interventions (a) seek to influence the parent-child relationship early in the child's life, before abuse can occur and before parents have established themselves in their parenting role; and (b) tend to be voluntary and to provide in-home services as well as case management support. However, there are also a number of characteristics that differentiate prevention programs aimed specifically at families with young children. Individual programs vary by the setting in which services are delivered (e.g., home, school, community center, clinic); primary target (e.g., child, parent, family); timing of onset (e.g., prenatal, infant); intensity; duration; and training background of the service provider. Programs also vary in terms of the type and number of services that they offer. Home visiting services, the key feature of many parenting programs, have been identified as the "best documented preventive effort," as well as the most promising form of intervention (Daro, 1996, p. 345). Although most programs do involve some form of home visiting, they may also include group meetings or some other form of center-based support, assistance in meeting basic needs, cognitive behavioral skills training, or training in infant cognitive stimulation. While there are programs that focus on primary prevention, many others target specific groups identified as "at risk."

Today, hundreds of parent education and support programs have been developed; however, two have come to dominate the prevention landscape–the Olds model (Olds, Henderson, Chamberlin & Tatelbaum, 1986) and the Healthy Families Model (Breakey & Pratt, 1991). The first of these is also one of the earliest, most comprehensive, best evaluated, and most cited parenting-focused prevention programs. Developed by Olds and colleagues, the Prenatal/Early Infancy Project was initially evaluated through a randomized clinical trial in Elmira, New York. Data demonstrated that intensive nurse home visitation during pregnancy and through the child's first two years had positive effects on parenting attitudes and behavior, as well as on reports of child maltreatment. The Olds' model was subsequently replicated in Memphis, Tennessee, with a population whose demographic characteristics differed substantially from those in the earlier study. Results in Memphis again demonstrated important program effects: children had fewer injuries and ingestions of hazardous substances before age 2 than did a control group of children who did not participate in the program, and their homes were rated as more supportive of healthy development (Kitzman et al., 1997, 2000). However, these results were less pronounced than in the previous study. In part due to its promising results, the Olds' model has now been extended to well over 100 sites (Leventhal, 2001).

An even greater number of programs have been based on the Healthy Families model, which was launched by Prevent Child Abuse America in partnership with Ronald McDonald House Charities in 1992. The Healthy Families model began through the Hawaii Healthy Start program (Duggan et al., 1999), and today exists in over 420 communities across the United States and Canada (Healthy Families America, 2003). In contrast with the Old's model, the Healthy Families model utilizes a trained paraprofessional home visitor supervised by a social worker and health personnel, rather than a nurse supervised by a social worker. However, as with the competing model, the role of the home visitor is to establish a trusting relationship with parents, to help parents address their needs and connect with resources, and to provide parenting education.

Pilot evaluation data from Hawaii Healthy Start indicated that few reports of child maltreatment were made on participating families during the first three years of the program (Fuddy, 1992). However, the evaluation did not employ a control group, and the follow-up period was short. Initial results have also indicated that the Healthy Families model is rarely implemented as designed. For example, rather than receiving weekly visits for most of the first year as provided in the project design, home visitors averaged 13 contacts per year with parents. Nonetheless, initial results indicate improvements in maternal attitudes and self-reported use of harsh discipline (Duggan et al., 1999).

While both the Olds and the Healthy Families models rely on early and frequent home visits, the provision of care within the context of a therapeutic and supportive relationship, an established curriculum, modeling of effective parenting, and connecting families to appropriate services in the community, Leventhal (2001) noted that there are also several important distinctions between the two models. The primary distinction, as previously noted, relates to the individual providing the intervention. The Olds' model employs nurses, who, as trained health professionals, are practiced at making clinical assessments and offering guidance to clients. In contrast, the Healthy Families model relies on paraprofessionals as the primary change agents. Although less skilled at making assessments and less trained in regard to health and development issues, as community members, these paraprofessionals may nonetheless be better able to establish stronger personal connections with families at risk.

A second distinction between the two models involves the criteria used to identify families for service provision. While both programs target first-time mothers from families perceived as at high risk, the specific criteria, as well as the procedures for determining eligibility, vary. For the Healthy Families program, potential participants are initially selected based on information on various risk factors (e.g., unmarried mother, mother under 19 years of age) obtained through medical records. Qualifying individuals then undergo an interview. Assuming that at least one parent receives a score indicative of high risk, the family is eligible to receive services from Healthy Families. First-time mothers are eligible for the Olds' model if they demonstrate two of three identified risk factors: less than 12 years of education, unmarried, and/or low socioeconomic status (Leventhal, 2001).

As noted, despite the promise of these parent education models, there are notable limitations to the current research. Clearly, well-designed research is both difficult and expensive to conduct (Leventhal, 2001). In addition, it is at least equally difficult to deliver high quality services. Parent education programs continuously face serious challenges from high attrition and staff turnover (Gomby, 2000).

While preliminary data suggest that parent education models can reduce child abuse and neglect, research also illustrates that home visiting is not a "cure-all." For example, Eckenrode et al. (2000) found that where high levels of domestic violence are present, it is difficult to improve parenting through home visiting. Clearly, change at levels beyond the individual are required to prevent child maltreatment. Even well-designed and well-implemented programs are unlikely to lead to substantial change if they are unsupported by their context.

PREVENTION THROUGH SYSTEMS AND SOCIETAL REFORM

Child maltreatment may also be prevented through social and system level reform; however, the development of programs and policies that aim to prevent maltreatment at this level has begun only recently. Despite substantial evidence that community level factors impact child abuse and neglect, examples of community-based child abuse prevention programs are rare. As noted by Garbarino and Collin (1999), an overarching issue is that of the neglectful society; whereas it is important to intervene on behalf of the individual child, the larger issue looms of how whole segments of society (e.g., the poor) are "neglected." Although, as previously noted, one goal of many parent education and support programs is to enhance social support and to connect families to needed resources, these components tend to be under-emphasized.

While efforts to support parents and to provide them with needed education and/or services recognize, to at least some extent, that certain resources are required to parent effectively, the extent of the multiple difficulties (e.g., poverty, limited education) that many individuals face is sometimes overlooked. Currently, there are not many programs that seek to prevent maltreatment by helping families to escape poverty. While there are some programs that encourage teen parents to return to school or to obtain further training, this component is often absent from programs targeting older parents, even though they typically face even more serious economic problems. Recently, some programs have been developed to help parents obtain economic self-sufficiency. Initial evaluations of these programs suggest that they may be helpful in improving the economic situation of poor families; however, they require an intensive and long-term approach (Hay & Jones, 1994). Careful evaluation will also be needed to determine their effect, if any, on preventing child maltreatment.

Provision of high quality care for children can also assist in the prevention of child maltreatment, not only directly, but also indirectly, by reducing parent stress. In the United States, statistics evidence both a large number of mothers employed outside the home and an increasing number of female-headed households; when combined with other policies, such as welfare-to-work, the result is a growing number of women who find themselves with no choice but to find some form of childcare. The lack of any national day care system in America results in what Zigler and Styfco (2000) characterized as "a hodgepodge of childcare centers, family day care homes, baby-sitting by neighbors and relatives, for-profits, nonprofits, regulated and underground services," that results in a "nonsystem of care" in the years before children enter kindergarten–a system that is a frequent source of child neglect (p. 16). Only the implementation of uniform standards for early childcare services holds serious promise for reversing this crisis.

As noted, it is difficult to establish uniform standards of parenting behavior given the diverse ethnic and cultural milieu of American society. One controversial area is corporal punishment and the extent to which abolishing it would serve to prevent child maltreatment. Straus and Smith (1990) believe that the elimination of physical punishment is a crucial step in preventing family violence and urge early training in alternative discipline techniques. They emphasize that such training should occur before individuals are parents, possibly through school-based training. Nonetheless, the use of spanking remains widespread, and ending the use of corporal punishment has been widely omitted from discussions of child abuse prevention (Straus, 2000).

The media is one potentially powerful tool for promoting positive parenting and discouraging maltreatment. Although there are some limited data indicating that such campaigns can be effective, the use of public service announcements to prevent child maltreatment has been limited. For example, in the early 1970s, the doctor who first recognized shaken baby syndrome recommended mass education on the dangers of shaking a baby. Despite support from physicians and researchers, as well as research documenting the lack of public knowledge on shaken baby syndrome, educational campaigns were slow in coming; however, their results have been notable. In an example of public education at the local level, the Mayor's Office for Children and Youth and the Baltimore City Commission for Children and Youth evidenced a reduction in observed incidents of child abuse associated with receiving a bad report card following implementation of a school-related prevention initiative that included televised public service announcements prior to and during the week of report card distribution, along with informational inserts in report cards (Mandell, 2000). On a national level, results from a campaign in the Netherlands aimed at encouraging abused children to disclose their abuse indicated that such societal-level interventions hold considerable promise (Hoefnagels & Baartman, 1997). However, such wide-scaled initiatives require a considerable investment of resources if positive effects are to be maintained over time.

Adult caregivers may also be reached through the health care system. In response to research on attachment and early bonding, many health care facilities have made institutional reforms related to childbirth practices (e.g., preparing parents for childbirth, treating parents as active participants in the process, encouraging parent-child contact directly after delivery, having the baby stay in the mother's room, encouraging visits by family and friends). Although initial evaluation data indicate that the period directly after birth may not be as crucial to the development of a bond between parent and child as was initially believed (National Research Council, 1993), reforming hospital practices to be more family-centered can serve to transform the birth of a child into a social event. Family-centered childbirth may help prevent maltreatment by fostering feelings of social connectedness and social competence in new parents (Garbarino, 1980).

Other opportunities for preventing child maltreatment through health care system reform focus on interactions between hospital staff and parents (Wurtele, 1999). Prenatal visits, perinatal prevention programs, and well-child visits present health care professionals with multiple opportunities to provide education, guidance, and referrals to parents. Potential topics for discussion include child development, handling common problems such as feeding difficulties, how to "child proof" one's home, how to enhance children's development, how to choose child care, how to handle behavior problems, and how to discipline children without using violence. Clearly, health care professionals are in a unique position in that they have access to almost all families at critical time periods.

Although societal and systems-level prevention efforts are currently underutilized, they do provide a promising direction for the future.

PREVENTION THROUGH PUBLIC POLICY

Given the potential of societal and system-level interventions, it follows that public policy could be a powerful tool in the prevention of child maltreatment. A majority of politicians, at all levels of government, purport to place a high value on children; however, child advocates would vigorously dispute whether this proclaimed concern for children is reflected in current policy. As previously noted, Kempe's seminal paper identifying the "battered child syndrome" was published in 1962. However, it was not until 12 years later, in 1974, that Congress enacted the Child Abuse Prevention and Treatment Act (CAPTA). Today, almost 30 years later, CAPTA remains the sole federal program aimed specifically at child abuse prevention.

In its original form, CAPTA defined child abuse and neglect; established the National Center on Child Abuse and Neglect (NCCAN); established basic state grants for prevention and treatment; provided money for demonstration grants to prevent, to identify, and to treat child abuse and neglect; and founded an advisory board to coordinate the federal response to maltreatment. CAPTA has been reauthorized several times since 1974. These reauthorizations have tended toward expanding the law (e.g., broadening the definition of child maltreatment). Notably, the 1996 reauthorization of CAPTA influenced its prevention component by consolidating several small grant programs previously funded under CAPTA into the Community-Based Family Resource and Support (CBFRS) program. CBFRS is the major prevention component of CAPTA, providing funding for various community-based family support programs designed to prevent child maltreatment, including parenting classes, substance abuse treatment, mental health services, respite care, and domestic violence services. Despite its promise, the impact of CAPTA on child abuse prevention efforts has been seriously undermined by a lack of adequate funding.

To see real evidence of commitment at the national level, it is necessary to examine not only legislation, but also the funding put in place to support that legislation. When legislation is passed, funding is *authorized* for various programs; however, in order for a program actually to be funded, Congress has to *appropriate* money to the program by including program funds in an appropriations bill. Actual funding appropriated for CAPTA has *always* fallen far short of the amount authorized. For example, in 2003, CAPTA was authorized at $120 million; however, basic grants (to help states improve their child protection systems) and discretionary grants (i.e., research and demonstrations grants that could help to advance knowledge about addressing child maltreatment) received appropriations of only $56 million. Appropriations for Community-Based Family Resource and Support Grants, which support proven prevention programs and strategies designed at the local level to meet individual family and community needs, totaled only $33.4 million of the $80 million authorized. While even these numbers may seem large, it is important to recognize that when considering a federal budget in excess of $2 trillion, the financial investment in protecting children is quite insubstantial.

Other federal policies may impact child maltreatment. For example, health care reform focused on making health care affordable and accessible to all families could prevent infant mortality and medical neglect. The development of welfare policy that seeks to keep children out of poverty and ensures the availability of affordable, quality childcare could also help to reduce maltreatment (Hay & Jones, 1994). However, the lack of specific provisions dedicated to the protection of children makes it clear that the actual federal role in the prevention of child maltreatment is limited. In contrast with other countries, such as Sweden, which have had considerable success with national initiatives that strengthen families and thus serve to protect children, the United States has instead diluted accountability by shifting legislative responsibility back and forth from the national to the state level. At present, there is a trend toward increasing responsibility for child-related programs at the state level, despite the fact that the majority of states are experiencing severe financial problems that have resulted in the reduction of social programs. Arguably, if child abuse and neglect is a "societal" problem, it cannot be addressed effectively unless solutions are implemented at the broader societal level.

CONCLUSIONS AND RECOMMENDATIONS

What We Know

Current research supports several promising approaches to child abuse prevention. Foremost among these are parent education programs that contain a home visiting component. These programs, which primarily target physical abuse and neglect, are particularly critical to efforts to reduce the incidence of child maltreatment since almost three quarters of identified cases involve these two forms of abuse. We also know a great deal about the factors that make these programs successful, specifically: initiation of services before or as close to the birth of the first child as possible; services that focus on the child's particular developmental level; opportunities for parents to model the behaviors being promoted; sufficient time commitments (i.e., more than 6 months); an emphasis on social supports and the skill needed to access these supports; a balance of home- and group-based alternatives; and recognition of cultural differences in family functioning and the nature of parent-child interactions (Daro, 1996). Conversely, unsuccessful programs tend to be implemented poorly, lack intensity, are of short duration, and/or are insufficiently comprehensive (Guterman, 1997).

Overall, the primary problem in regard to the effectiveness of current child abuse prevention programs appears to be not with the approach, per se, but with its application to a particular subpopulation (Daro, 1988). Although hundreds of parent education and support programs have been developed, few have been focused on specific subpopulations, thus limiting their effectiveness. For example, the literature suggests that existing parent training programs are less effective with disadvantaged parents and low-income single mothers in particular (Webster-Stratton, 1998).

We also know that in order to have maximum impact, child abuse prevention efforts must focus on potential perpetrators who are known to the child. For example, sexual abuse prevention programs, particularly those based on a child empowerment model, typically promote strategies that are more effective with strangers (Ko & Cosden, 2001). Clearly, when the perpetrator is known to the child, there are fewer adults to whom to report, and alternatives may appear more limited. In addition, there has been no evidence that programs that attempt to teach children to protect themselves from abuse lead to a decline in actual victimization. In fact, such programs threaten to promote the message that children are capable of protecting themselves and thus bear some responsibility for their own abuse.

Finally, we know that multiple systems factors (e.g., characteristics of individuals, the family, and society) combine to cause child maltreatment. It follows that multiple levels of intervention are required to address this complex issue, including changes at the broader societal level.

What We Don't Know

Even those who are optimistic about current prevention efforts typically recognize that these approaches are limited. Inadequate research and evaluation is pervasive, and the failure to integrate multiple levels of intervention is a serious weakness. Many studies fail to adhere to appropriate methodology, and there is a critical need to identify appropriate outcome measures. At present, published evaluations of programs tend to provide little information about specific program content and even less information regarding the process by which the program achieved or failed to achieve its desired effects. For example, there is very little data on the effectiveness of specific components of prevention curriculums for children (Reppucci, Land, & Haugaard, 1998). Other potentially promising strategies have yet to be explored. For example, although several good arguments have been put forth encouraging parents' involvement in sexual abuse prevention programming, only a few such programs have actually been implemented (Reppucci, Jones, & Cook, 1994). These parent-focused programs have experienced serious difficulty in recruiting parents to participate (Hebert, Lavoie, & Parent, 2002). Effective responses to this challenge have yet to be explored.

As noted by Melton (2002), child protection policy is based largely on untested assumptions. At the most fundamental level, since most cases of child maltreatment are not identified, it is not at all clear whether those cases that are identified, and upon which current scientific and clinical knowledge is based, are representative of the population of all cases of abuse and neglect. A more integrated and well-supported approach to research, such as that encouraged through recent initiatives by the National Institutes of Health (e.g., increased research on child neglect and a focus on definitional issues around child maltreatment) are required to fill in these critical knowledge gaps.

Directions for the Future

In 1984, the McMartin preschool case, in which the owner of the day care center and six of her employees were accused of sexually abusing 125 children over a 10-year period, brought child sexual abuse to the forefront of the American consciousness. By 1988, the McMartin case, which was still being prosecuted, had cost $7.5 million, prompting Judge Pounders to dub it the most expensive case in American history. Pounders nonetheless believed the expense to be justified since "The case has benefited society as a whole . . . because people have become aware of a social problem that may not have been spoken about" (quoted in Reppucci & Haugaard, 1989, p. 1266). Public opinion surveys from the 1980s showed that over 90% of the public were aware of the problem, understood that there were different forms of child maltreatment, that the causes of child maltreatment were diverse, and that they would need to act in order to resolve the problem (Daro & Donnelly, 2002). Now, roughly 20 years later, it is clear that increased awareness, without a sustained commitment to action, is insufficient. Given the prevailing political rhetoric, it stands to reason that many, if not a majority, of citizens assume that lawmakers are putting measures in place that protect children. Lawmakers may themselves assume that issues are being addressed at other levels of government. In any event, little pressure is exerted for change, with child advocacy left, in large part, to small, under-funded groups with little political power.

As others (Daro & Donnelly, 2002; Leventhal, 1996; Vieth, this volume) have noted, child abuse and neglect *can* be prevented, if not totally eliminated. There is a great deal that we know about what works in preventing child maltreatment; however, programs are admittedly difficult and expensive to provide. At present, the majority of public funds dedicated to child maltreatment are directed to treatment, despite evidence that prevention efforts for children are cost-effective. For example, Weikart and Schweinhart (1997) demonstrated that for each dollar invested, the High Scope/Perry Preschool Program saved $7.16.

In order to prevent child maltreatment, pervasive and active public support must be amassed. Public opinion favors government funding of prevention programs, particularly home visitation for families with young children (Melton, 2002). However, we have yet to mobilize public opinion to ensure that these services are provided to all families, or even to those most in need. For better or for worse, any issue that impacts society is political (Conte & Savage, 2003). Children are not in a position to advocate for themselves within a complex, politically-charged environment. Accordingly, child abuse prevention is not the responsibility of children; it is the responsibility of all adults.

REFERENCES

Asdigian, N. L., & Finkelhor, D. (1995). What works for children in resisting assaults? *Journal of Interpersonal Violence, 10*, 402-418.

Azar, S. T., & Twentyman, C. T. (1986). Cognitive behavioral perspectives on the assessment and treatment of child abuse. In P. C. Kendall (Ed.), *Advances in cognitive behavioral research and therapy* (Vol. 5, pp. 237-267). New York: Academic Press.

Berrick, J. D. (1988). Parental involvement in child abuse prevention training: What do they learn? *Child Abuse & Neglect, 12,* 543-553.

Breakey, G., & Pratt, B. (1991). Healthy growth for Hawaii's "Healthy Start": Toward a statewide approach to the prevention of child abuse and neglect. *Zero to Three, 11,* 16-22.

Brown, J., Cohen, P., Johnson, J., & Salzinger, S. (1998). A longitudinal analysis of risk factors for child maltreatment. *Child Abuse & Neglect, 22,* 1065-1078.

Child Abuse Prevention and Treatment Act, Pub. L. No. 93-247 (1974).

Conte, J. R., & Savage, S. B. (2003). Concluding observations. *Journal of Interpersonal Violence, 18,* 452-468.

Cowen, P. S. (2001). Effectiveness of a parent education intervention for at-risk families. *Journal of the Society of Pediatric Nurses, 6,* 73-82.

Daro, D. (1988). *Confronting child abuse: Research for effective program design.* New York: The Free Press.

Daro, D. (1994). Prevention of child sexual abuse. *The Future of Children, 4,* 198-223.

Daro, D. (1996). Preventing child abuse and neglect. In J. Briere, L. Berliner, J. A. Bulkley, C. Jenny, & T. Reid (Eds.), *The APSAC handbook on child maltreatment* (pp. 343-358). Thousand Oaks, CA: Sage.

Daro, D., & Donnelly, A. (2002). Charting the waves of prevention: Two steps forward, one step back. *Child Abuse & Neglect, 26,* 731-742.

Davis, M. K., & Gidyez, C. A. (2000). Child sexual abuse prevention programs: A meta-analysis. *Journal of Clinical Child Psychology, 29,* 257-269.

Duggan, A., McFarlane, E., Windham, A., Rohde, C., Salkever, D., Fuddy, L. et al. (1999). Evaluation of Hawaii's Healthy Start program. *The Future of Children, 9,* 66-90.

Eckenrode, J., Ganzel, B., Henderson, C. R., Smith, E., Olds, D. L., Powers, J. et al. (2000). Preventing child abuse and neglect with a program of nurse home visitation: The limiting effects of domestic violence. *Journal of American Medical Association, 284,* 1385-1391.

Emery, R. E., & Laumann-Billings, L. (1998). An overview of the nature, causes, and consequences of abusive family relationships: Toward differentiating maltreatment and violence. *American Psychologist, 44,* 121-135.

Erickson, M. F., & Egeland, B. (1996). Child neglect. In J. Briere, L. Berliner, J. A. Bulkley, C. Jenny, & T. Reid (Eds.), *The APSAC handbook on child maltreatment* (pp. 4-20). Thousand Oaks, CA: Sage.

Finkelhor, D. (1984). *Child sexual abuse: New theory and research.* New York: Freedom Press.

Finkelhor, D., Asdigian, N., & Dziuba-Leatherman, J. (1995). The effectiveness of victimization prevention instruction: An evaluation of children's responses to actual threats and assaults. *Child Abuse & Neglect, 19,* 141-153.

Finkelhor, D., & Dziuba-Leatherman, J. (1995). Victimization prevention programs: A national survey of children's exposure and reactions. *Child Abuse & Neglect, 19*, 129-139.

Finkelhor, D., Hotaling, F., Lewis, I. A., & Smith, C. (1990). Sexual abuse in a national survey of adult men and women: Prevalence, characteristics and risk factors. *Child Abuse & Neglect, 14*, 19-28.

Finkelhor, D., & Jones, L. M. (2004). *Explanations for the decline in child sexual abuse cases.* Bulletin. Washington, DC: U.S. Department of Justice, Office of Justice Programs, Office of Juvenile Justice and Delinquency Prevention.

Fuddy, L. (1992, September). *Hawaii's Healthy Start success.* Paper presented at the Ninth International Congress on Child Abuse and Neglect, Chicago, IL.

Garbarino, J. (1980). Changing hospital childbirth practices: A developmental perspective on prevention of child maltreatment. *American Journal of Orthopsychiatry, 50*, 588-597.

Garbarino, J., & Collin, C. C. (1999). Child neglect: The family with a hole in the middle. In H. Dubowitz (Ed.), *Neglected children: Research, practice, and policy* (pp. 1-23). Thousand Oaks, CA: Sage.

Garbarino, J., Kostelny, K., & Grady, J. (1993). Children in dangerous environments: Child maltreatment in the context of community violence. In D. Cicchetti & S. Toth (Eds.), *Child abuse, child development, and social policy* (pp. 167-189). Norwood, NJ: Ablex Publishing.

George, C. (1996). A representational perspective of child abuse and prevention. *Child Abuse & Neglect, 20*, 411-424.

Gomby, D., Culross, P., & Behrman, R. (1999). Home visiting: Recent program evaluations–analysis and recommendations. *The Future of Children, 9*, 4-26.

Gomby, D. S. (2000). Promise and limitations of home visitation. *Journal of the American Medical Association, 284*, 1430-1431.

Guterman, N. (1997). Early prevention of physical child abuse and neglect: Existing evidence and future directions. *Child Maltreatment, 2*, 12-34.

Hay, T., & Jones, L. (1994). Societal interventions to prevent child abuse and neglect. *Child Welfare, 73*, 379-403.

Healthy Families America. (2003). *Vision and overview. Prevent Child Abuse America.* Retrieved July 24, 2003, from http://www.healthyfamiliesamerca.org/about_hfa/index.html

Hebert, M., Lavoie, F., & Parent, N. (2002). An assessment of outcomes following parents' participation in a child abuse prevention program. *Violence and Victims, 17*, 355-372.

Hoefnagels, C., & Baartman, H. E. M. (1997). On the threshold of disclosure–The effects of a mass media field experiment. *Child Abuse & Neglect, 18*, 349-356.

Jones, L. M., & Finkelhor, D. (2001). *The decline in child sexual abuse cases.* Bulletin. Washington, DC: U.S. Department of Justice, Office of Justice Programs, Office of Juvenile Justice and Delinquency Prevention.

Kempe, C. H., Silverman, F., Steele, B., Droegemueller, W., & Silver, H. (1962). The battered child syndrome. *Journal of the American Medical Association, 181*, 17-24.

Kitzman, H., Olds, D. L., Henderson, C. R., Hanks, C., Cole, R., Tatelbaum, R. et al. (1997). Effect of prenatal and infancy home visitations by nurses on pregnancy outcomes, childhood injuries, and repeated child bearing: A randomized controlled trial. *Journal of the American Medical Association, 278,* 644-652.

Kitzman, H., Olds, D. L., Sidora, K., Henderson, C. R., Hanks, C., Cole, R. et al. (2000). Enduring effects of nurse home visitation on maternal life course: A 3-year follow-up of a randomized trial. *Journal of American Medical Association, 283,* 1983-1989.

Ko, S. F., & Cosden, M. A. (2001). Do elementary school-based child abuse prevention programs work? A high school follow-up. *Psychology in the Schools, 38,* 57-66.

Leventhal, J. M. (1996). Twenty years later: We do know how to prevent child abuse and neglect. *Child Abuse & Neglect, 20,* 647-653.

Leventhal, J. M. (2001). The prevention of child abuse and neglect: Successfully out of the blocks. *Child Abuse & Neglect, 25,* 431-439.

Mandell, S. (2000). Child abuse prevention at report card time. *Journal of Community Psychology, 28,* 687-690.

Melton, G. B. (2002). Chronic neglect of family violence: More than a decade of reports to guide U.S. policy. *Child Abuse & Neglect, 26,* 569-586.

Miller-Perrin, C., & Perrin, R. (1999). *Child maltreatment: An introduction.* Thousand Oaks, CA: Sage Publications.

Milner, J. (1998). Individual and family characteristics associated with intrafamilial child physical and sexual abuse. In P. Trickett & C. Schellenbach (Eds.), *Violence against children in the family and the community* (pp.141-170). Washington, DC: American Psychological Association.

Milner, J. S., & Chilamkurti, C. (1991). Physical child abuse perpetrator characteristic: A review of the literature. *Journal of Interpersonal Violence, 6,* 336-344.

National Clearinghouse on Child Abuse and Neglect Information. (2003). *Child maltreatment 2001: Summary of Key findings.* U.S. Department of Health and Human Services. Retrieved June 20, 2003, from http://www.calib.com/nccanch/pubs/factsheets/can stats.cfm

National Research Council. (1993). *Understanding child abuse and neglect.* Washington DC: National Academy Press.

Olds, D. L., Henderson, C. R., Chamberlin, R., & Tatelbaum, R. (1986). Preventing child abuse and neglect: A randomized trial of home nurse visitation. *Pediatrics, 78,* 65-78.

Portwood, S. G. (1999). Coming to terms with a consensual definition of child maltreatment. *Child Maltreatment, 4,* 56-68.

Reppucci, N. D., Britner, P. A., & Woolard, J. L. (1997). *Preventing child abuse and neglect through parent education.* Baltimore, MD: Paul H. Brooks.

Reppucci, N. D., & Haugaard, J. J. (1989). Prevention of child sexual abuse. *American Psychologist, 44,* 1266-1275.

Reppucci, N. D., Jones, L. M., & Cook, S. L. (1994). Involving parents in child sexual abuse prevention programs. *Journal of Child & Family Studies, 3,* 137-142.

Reppucci, N. D., Land, D., & Haugaard, J. J. (1998). Child sexual abuse prevention programs that target young children. In P. K. Trickett & C. J. Schellenbach (Eds.), *Violence against children in the family and the community* (pp. 317-337). Washington, DC: American Psychological Association.

Stogner vs. California, Slip Opinion No. 01-1757. U. S. Supreme Court (June 26, 2003).

Straus, M. A. (2000). Corporal punishment and primary prevention of physical abuse. *Child Abuse & Neglect, 24,* 1109-1114.

Straus, M. A., & Smith, C. (1990). *Physical violence in American families: Risk factors and adaptations to violence in 8,145 families.* New Brunswick, NJ: Transaction Publishers.

Vieth, V. (2006). Unto the third generation: A call to end child abuse in the United States within 120 years. *Journal of Aggression, Maltreatment & Trauma, 12*(3/4).

Webster-Stratton, C. (1998). Parent training in low-income families: Promoting parental engagement through a collaborative approach. In J. R. Lutzker (Ed.), *Handbook of child abuse research and treatment* (pp. 183-210). New York: Plenum.

Weikart, D. P., & Schweinhart, L. J. (1997). High Scope/Perry Preschool Program. In G. W. Albee & T. P. Gullotta (Eds.), *Primary prevention works* (pp. 146-166). London: Sage.

Widom, C. S. (1989). Does violence beget violence? A critical examination of the literature. *Psychological Bulletin, 106,* 3-28.

Williams, L. M. (2003). Understanding child abuse and violence against women: A life course perspective. *Journal of Interpersonal Violence, 18,* 441-451.

Wolfe, D. (1985). Child-abusive parents: An empirical review and analysis. *Psychological Bulletin, 97,* 462-482.

Wolfe, D. (1993). Prevention of child neglect: Emerging issues. *Criminal Justice and Behavior, 20,* 90-111.

Wurtele, S. K. (1999). Preventing child maltreatment: Multiple windows of opportunity in the health care system. *Children's Health Care, 28,* 151-165.

Zigler, E., & Styfco, S. J. (2000). Preventing child abuse through quality early care and education: A plea for policymakers to act. *UMKC Law Review, 69,* 15-24.

Research-Based Guidelines
for Child Forensic Interviews

Alison R. Perona
Bette L. Bottoms
Erin Sorenson

SUMMARY. We present important considerations for conducting forensic interviews with children who are witnesses to or alleged victims of crime. Specifically, we (a) present the basic principles of the forensic interview and review some of the best structured forensic protocols currently available; (b) provide a detailed, practical blueprint for conducting a structured forensic interview and emphasize how the components of the interview are based upon empirical research; and (c) discuss special con-

Address correspondence to: Bette L. Bottoms, PhD, Department of Psychology (MC 285), University of Illinois at Chicago, 1007 West Harrison Street, Chicago, IL 60607-7137 (E-mail: bbottoms@uic.edu).

The authors would like to thank Aaron Rudnicki and Danielle Lemon for research assistance. They also thank the members of the Cook County (Illinois) Task Force on Intake and Interviewing, a multidisciplinary task force responsible for a manual that preceded and influenced this paper.

The foundation of this paper was laid in the authors' book *Intake and Forensic Interviewing in the Children's Advocacy Center Setting: A Handbook* (published by National Network of Children's Advocacy Centers, 1997), which was made possible by grants from the Office of Juvenile Justice and Delinquency Prevention and the National Children's Alliance (formerly the National Network of Children's Advocacy Centers).

[Haworth co-indexing entry note]: "Research-Based Guidelines for Child Forensic Interviews." Perona, Alison R., Bette L. Bottoms, and Erin Sorenson. Co-published simultaneously in *Journal of Aggression, Maltreatment & Trauma* (The Haworth Maltreatment & Trauma Press, an imprint of The Haworth Press, Inc.) Vol. 12, No. 3/4, 2006; and: *Ending Child Abuse: New Efforts in Prevention, Investigation, and Training* (ed: Victor I. Vieth, Bette L. Bottoms, and Alison R. Perona) The Haworth Maltreatment & Trauma Press, an imprint of The Haworth Press, Inc., 2006. Single or multiple copies of this article are available for a fee from The Haworth Document Delivery Service [1-800-HAWORTH, 9:00 a.m. - 5:00 p.m. (EST). E-mail address: docdelivery@haworthpress.com].

siderations for interviews with children of different age groups and children who have special needs or circumstances, and interviews involving various crime circumstances. We end with suggestions to assist legal and social service professionals in accessing the social science research literature that should inform forensic interview techniques. *[Article copies available for a fee from The Haworth Document Delivery Service: 1-800-HAWORTH. E-mail address: <docdelivery@haworthpress.com> Website: <http:// www.HaworthPress.com> © 2006 by The Haworth Press, Inc. All rights reserved.]*

KEYWORDS. Child forensic interview, child abuse, child sexual abuse, child witnesses, children's eyewitness testimony, interview techniques

The societal recognition of child maltreatment, particularly child sexual abuse, is responsible for bringing large numbers of suspected child victims into the forensic interview situation. Children are also given forensic interviews in other contexts, such as when it is necessary to determine their knowledge about crimes against other persons. The accuracy of children's reports in legally relevant situations has been of concern for over a century. Initially, courts assumed that children were highly suggestible, dangerous witnesses who were not competent to give court testimony (Davis, 1998; Goodman, 1984). Although very early social science research supported this assumption (Whipple, 1911), modern research reveals that even young children can be accurate witnesses when questioned about meaningful events under optimal reporting conditions (Eisen, Quas, & Goodman, 2002; Goodman & Bottoms, 1993; Saywitz, Goodman, & Lyon, 2002).

In this paper, we outline important considerations for conducting forensic interviews with children who are witnesses or alleged victims. Consistent with our own professional training and backgrounds (as a criminal prosecutor, an experimental psychologist, and a social worker who directs a children's advocacy center, respectively), we provide practical recommendations and we emphasize how those recommendations are based upon empirical research. We begin by discussing the basic principles of the forensic interview and general considerations for any forensic interview, such as how to word questions. Then, we review some of the best structured forensic protocols currently available and provide a detailed, practical blueprint for conducting a structured forensic interview with child witnesses and alleged victims. Then, we discuss special considerations for interviews with children of different age groups and children who have special needs or circumstances, and interviews involving various crime circumstances such as physical abuse, kidnapping, etc. We end with suggestions to assist legal and social service professionals in accessing social science research literature relevant to forensic interviewing.

Note that although our discussion tends to focus on forensic interviews conducted with suspected child abuse victims, our recommendations are also appropriate for child witnesses who might be involved in other types of situations. In addition, the interviewing considerations and techniques we discuss have the same applicability at both the investigative stage of a case and in trial practice. We aim for our recommendations to be useful to a multidisciplinary audience, including social service professionals, law enforcement officers, prosecutors, judges, and others who might conduct forensic interviews with children.

BASIC PURPOSES AND PRINCIPLES OF THE FORENSIC INTERVIEW

Oftentimes, the successful investigation and prosecution of criminal offenses hinges on obtaining reliable information from child victims and/or witnesses. Sometimes, knowledge of what has occurred comes solely from information the child provides during the investigative interview. Primarily three decisions are made based on the results of the investigative interview: child protection decisions, criminal charging decisions, and therapeutic and supportive intervention decisions. The goal of the investigative interview is to obtain information to assist with each of these decisions, without obtaining inaccurate or misleading information. Thus, it is critical that the forensic interview be conducted with skill and integrity. Interviewing children is a task that requires an open, yet analytical and critical perspective. This perspective is necessary to avoid reaching inaccurate conclusions: concluding that an event has occurred when it has not or concluding that an event has not occurred when it has. That is, two goals are paramount: guarding against false accusations of innocent persons, and detecting actual abuse so that children can be protected from future risk. These compatible goals are both safeguarded with forensic interviewing that follows established practices for obtaining accurate information from children.

There is consensus among researchers and practitioners on the underlying principles that should guide interviews with children who might have been a victim or a witness to a crime. For example, the forensic interview should be conducted in a manner that minimizes children's distress. The degree of distress experienced by child victims and/or witnesses can be significant (Goodman et al., 1992; Runyan, 1993). Stress might be ameliorated by minimizing the number of interviews and ensuring that the forensic interview is conducted by a well-trained and sensitive interviewer (Yuille, Hunter, Joffe, & Zaparniuk, 1993).

Minimizing child stress will itself help foster another key principle guiding forensic interviews: the need to protect against improper influences on memory and reports. Specifically, care should be taken to conduct a thorough, open-minded, and sound interview. This is done by maximizing the use of techniques that will elicit reliable information and minimizing the use of highly leading or coercive questions that could change or contaminate the child's memory of past event(s) (e.g., Poole & Lamb, 1998; Yuille et al., 1993). Social science research and practice clearly illustrate that reports about events are most likely to be accurate when they are generated freely by the child. Thus, every effort should be made by interviewers to create a questioning environment that enhances free recall and minimizes interviewer influence (Lieb, Berliner, & Toth, 1997). Of course, improper influences can come from other sources as well, and it is helpful for investigators to know whether children are experiencing pressure to reveal or conceal information.

GENERAL CONSIDERATIONS FOR INTERVIEWING CHILDREN

In this section, we discuss general recommendations for conducting a forensic interview, such as how to word questions and whether and how to use interview aids. In applying these recommendations, however, interviewers will need to recognize and accommodate individual differences among children. That is, no two children are alike, even children of the same chronological age. Therefore, for example, it is impossible to dictate exact techniques to use with children of certain ages. Instead, interviewers should be sensitive to a child's developmental level with regard to language (Carter, Bottoms, & Levine, 1996; Walker, 1994) and cognition. A child's developmental level determines, in part, the necessary manner of questioning and the type of information that can be obtained. For example, compared to older children, young children, especially pre-schoolers, often do not have well-developed memory retrieval strategies and sometimes need focused questions to produce descriptions of events, even though they might recall them well (Kail, 1990). Within general guidelines, adjustments of question content and wording are often necessary with younger children for a successful and competent interview. Children's cognitive and language capacities improve with age, and, as a result, so does their ability to provide information routinely of interest in a criminal investigation.

With age, socio-emotional development also occurs. Compared to younger children, adolescents might present with a more complex emotional landscape that can affect the interviewing process. Adolescents can appear more mature than they actually are. They can be more susceptible than younger children to complex socio-emotional concerns accompanying disclosure of information, especially sexually explicit information (Goodman & Schwartz-Kenney, 1992; Saywitz, Goodman, Nicholas, & Moan, 1991). Also, an interviewer's insensitivity to possible emotional instability and other special adolescent issues can place the adolescent at significant risk for a number of other problems such as suicide, running away, etc.

Interviewers should also be sensitive to individual differences in children's cultural backgrounds. For example, culture can affect the child's and family's attitudes toward the investigation. The interviewer should recognize the degree to which the child and family have assimilated into the dominant culture, the level of English proficiency, cultural or familial norms that might conflict with the interviewer's ability to gain the child's trust, etc. Understanding the cultural dynamics of the family can assist in understanding events in the child's life and the manner in which the child and his or her family react to the child's victimization and/or their contact with the criminal justice system (Fontes, 1995).

We return to the subject of individual differences and their implications for forensic interviewing in later sections, where we provide more detail about considerations for interviewing special child populations, including the pre-school-aged child, the adolescent, the child with disabilities, etc.

Wording Questions

There are many ways to formulate and word questions or comments, some that elicit extensive and accurate responses, and some that elicit simple, incomplete, and even incorrect responses. Interviewers should be sensitive to how they word questions.

Question Suggestiveness. Interviewers need to pay particular attention to the level of suggestiveness in their questions (for a detailed consideration of the literature on children's suggestibility and its implications for forensic interviewing, see Saywitz & Lyon, 2002). There is no exact definition of suggestiveness that would allow for specifically identifying questions as "suggestive" or not. Suggestiveness is best conceptualized as a continuum, and many terms are used to refer to questions along various points of this continuum. The continuum ranges from very open-ended, non-leading questions to highly leading or coercive questions (with questions that might be termed "closed" and "mildly leading" questions in the middle of the continuum). Further, suggestiveness is determined not only by the specific content of a question, but also by the larger situational context. For example, even the least suggestive interviewing techniques can be offset by suggestive events occurring prior to the interview. If someone has persuasively or repeatedly suggested false information to the child before an interview, the child might give inaccurate responses to even the least leading questions, as adult witnesses might in the same situation (for review, see Eisen, Quas, & Goodman, 2002). That is, children's suggestibility should be considered in the context of adult suggestibility. There is sometimes an implicit assumption that child and adolescent witnesses are always more susceptible to suggestive influences than adult witnesses. In fact, adults can also be highly suggestible under certain circumstances, including some of the misleading situational and interview tactics described next (for review, see Wrightsman, Greene, Nietzal, & Fortune, 2002).

The least leading forensic interview questions are usually termed "open-ended" or "free-recall" questions. They contain little information, such as "What happened?" "Tell me everything you can remember about that." Open-ended questions encourage children to give elaborative and narrative responses. It is important to obtain as much information as reasonably possible from children by using open-ended interview techniques, because as elaborated below, research has shown that children's responses to open-ended questions are often (but not always) quite accurate.

Even so, research and experience both illustrate that asking only open-ended questions might increase the possibility of a child omitting portions of their recollection, particularly young children or children who might be reluctant to discuss their abuse. Thus, to obtain complete information from children, after open-ended prompts have been exhausted, it might be necessary to ask questions that are less open-ended, such as "You said you rode in a car. What color was the car? Where did you go?" These questions are variously referred to as closed, focused, directive, or specific questions. Closed questions generally elicit narrowly defined responses. These questions have the advantage of prompting children for specific information and keeping a description focused; however, overuse of this from of questioning can discourage children from freely providing fully detailed accounts of an event. Directed or specific questions are sometimes necessary, however, because children–especially young children–have difficulty reporting experiences because they lack "metamemory" skills such as how to search for knowledge stored in memory and how to report knowledge in a structured manner (Quas, Goodman, Ghetti, & Redlich, 2000). They also can have difficulty remembering the sources for their memories (e.g., distinguishing between details that they experienced versus were told about). In addition, they are sometimes reticent to report embarrassing details of an event even if they remember the details. For example, even children as old as 10 years of age in studies by Goodman, Quas, Batterman-Faunce, Riddlesberger, and Kuhn (1997) and Saywitz et al. (1991) were reluctant to disclose details about genital touch during medical procedures until they were questioned with focused, as compared to free recall, questions. Thus, non-coercive direct questioning can help children recall events accurately.

Leading questions contain information or include assumptions that have not been previously mentioned to the child (e.g., "Was the dress you were wearing blue?" when, in fact, the child has not mentioned a blue dress). The danger of leading questions is that they might be *mis*leading (contain information that is not accurate) and that the child might incorporate the inaccurate information into his or her report. If it is necessary to ask mildly leading questions (which might be appropriate with some reluctant children who are suspected of being in a dangerous situation), it should be done with great care, because, like adults, children give more inaccurate information in response to suggestive questions than open-ended questions. It is important to understand that the danger of obtaining false information in response to leading questions is increased by certain contextual factors. For example, research shows that children, especially preschoolers, are most suggestible when:

- leading questions are asked repeatedly within the same interview or over long periods of time (Ceci & Bruck, 1993);
- leading questions are asked by a biased or high-status interviewer (see Saywitz & Lyon, 2002, for review);
- leading questions are asked by an emotionally intimidating rather than a supportive interviewer (Carter et al., 1996; Davis & Bottoms,

2002a, 2002b; Goodman, Bottoms, Rudy, & Schwartz-Kenney, 1991);

- questioned about peripheral details rather than central issues;
- questioned with developmentally inappropriate language or legalese (Carter et al., 1996);
- false information has been given to the child before the interview, especially if that information is endorsed by other witnesses such as parents (Ceci, Loftus, Leichtman, & Bruck, 1994; Shaw, Garven, & Wood, 1997). Even so, note that children and adults are generally less suggestible about negative and implausible events than about positive and plausible events (Pezdek & Taylor, 2002).

Finally, asking very leading questions ("Bob kissed you on your mouth, didn't he?" when, in fact, the child has previously disclosed no kissing and no involvement of someone named Bob), or asking questions in a coercive context ("If you tell me where it happened, I'll let you play with the toys") greatly increases the risk of obtaining incorrect information from children. These tactics should always be avoided.

In summary, professional and empirical consensus is that the entire interview be structured so that most information is gathered with open types of questions that fall on the less suggestive end of the suggestibility continuum. However, more closed types of questions can be used if necessary to clarify or seek additional information regarding the child's response to open-ended questions.

Negative vs. Positive Questions, Tag Questions. Negative questions are those asked in a negative form; for example, "You don't remember where you were before your dad touched you, do you?" These questions are hard for young children to comprehend. In this example, the question is even worse because of the highly suggestive tag at the end: "Do you?" The tag implies that the interviewer already knows the answer. Negative questions and tag questions should be avoided (Walker, 1994).

Yes/No Questions. Focused questions of a short-answer or multiple-choice format might be more likely to yield correct information than "yes/no" questions, because some children have a bias to respond "yes" to any questions (Peterson & Biggs, 1997). Of course, it would be impracticable to avoid all "yes/no" questions during a forensic interview.

Grammatically Complex or "Double-Barreled" Questions. Grammatically complex questions are difficult to understand. Use of passive voice, multiple nested phrases, vague pronoun references, etc., can all make comprehension of sentences difficult. "Double-barreled" or "compound" questions are those in which two or more questions are contained in one.

Combining even simple questions can make understanding the question difficult, which could lead to less reliable answers (Perry, McAuliff, Tam, & Claycomb, 1995; Walker, 1994). For example, consider this question: "Are you telling me what happened to you because you want to or because your mom told you that you have to?" To which embedded question would a child respond? Rather than asking these complex questions, it is recommended that interviewers ask several simple questions. For example, "Do you want to tell me what happened to you?" Then, "Did your mom want you to tell me anything?"

Note that very young children might have difficulty answering "before" or "after" questions; thus, gathering information regarding the timing of incidents must be done carefully (Walker, 1994).

Jargon, Legalese, and Technical Terminology. Jargon, legalese, and technical terminology are generally understood in a specific way by a certain group or profession and might not be understood in the same way or at all by those outside the group or profession. Studies reveal that using difficult vocabulary can decrease the accuracy of children's reports (Carter et al., 1996; Perry et al., 1995). In addition to the child not understanding technical words, the child might misinterpret these words to mean something other than intended. This could lead to the child's embarrassment or to the interviewer misinterpreting the child's statement. Rather than using jargon, legalese, and technical terminology, everyday language is preferred (Fisher & Geiselman, 1992); for example, "Did you say . . . ?" rather than "Did you allege . . . ?" (Walker, 1994).

Style and Tone of Questioning. Children respond not only to the verbal content of a question, but also to the way in which it is asked. Pace, timing, and tone of voice can affect the quality of a child's response. For example, the speed at which a question is asked can influence the speed at which the answer is given (Fisher, Geiselman, & Raymond, 1987). Asking another question immediately after the child responds limits the amount of time the child has to think about his or her answer and to elaborate. If questions are asked in this manner throughout the interview, the child might offer abbreviated responses throughout the interview (Johnson, 1972). Extended pauses and silences convey to the child that the interviewer is allowing for extended responses and descriptions (Dillon, 1982).

In addition to pacing, the non-verbal behavior of the interviewer has been shown to affect the way in which a child responds. That is, a child's emotional state can interfere with his or her ability to recall and describe events (Saywitz, 1995; Saywitz & Snyder, 1993). An interviewer can have a significant impact on a child's emotions during an interview. Several studies have now shown that children who are interviewed in a warm, supportive environment are less suggestible than children interviewed in an intimidating environment (Carter et al., 1996; Davis & Bottoms, 2002a, 2002b; Goodman et al., 1991). Supportive interviewing in these studies was operationally defined as the interviewer's use of warm vocal tones, supportive eye contact, frequent smiling, rapport building, and sitting with a relaxed body posture. Davis and Bottoms (2002a) found evidence that social support helps children by increasing their perceived ability to resist an interviewer's suggestions, and in turn, decreasing their suggestibility. There is also evidence that an interviewer's facial expressions (e.g., frowning, tensing forehead and brows, looks of disbelief and boredom) can imply to the child that his or her statements are somehow wrong or undesired (Garbarino, 1997). For all these reasons, it is recommended that interviewers monitor their personal style to avoid verbal or non-verbal cues that could cause a child to become anxious, scared, or stressed.

Use of Interview Aids

On a case-by-case basis, the forensic interviewer may decide to use interviewing aids, such as freehand drawings or diagrams, or, in sex crime cases, anatomical drawings or anatomically detailed dolls to assist the child in describing the event(s). The best use of interview aids is to clarify a disclosure that has already been made. It is recommended that they not be used to obtain the initial disclosure before less directive methods of interviewing have been attempted. When used, care should be taken not to present the aids as part of a play activity, which might encourage fantasy use of the aids. Instead, when allowing the child to draw or use an aid during the interview, the interviewer should encourage the child to explain verbally what he or she is drawing or doing. Drawings produced during the interview need to be labeled with the child's name, date, and quotations from the child's description of the drawing, as well as signed by the interviewer.

Interviewers might want to use aids such as dolls with pre-schoolers, whose language abilities have not fully developed. Unfortunately, research suggests that anatomically detailed dolls can be a source of suggestion for preschool-aged children, particularly when combined with leading questions. Children younger than 4 years (and especially younger than 3 years) often do not even have the symbolic skills necessary to even understand that dolls can represent people (deLoache, 1995).

Thus, caution should be used in using dolls with this age group. However, dolls can be helpful for older children in detailing an already established disclosure (see Boat & Everson, 1993; Everson & Boat, 2002; and Koocher, Goodman, White, Friedrich, Sivan, & Reynolds, 1995, for excellent and comprehensive reviews of the research on dolls). The American Professional Society on the Abuse of Children's (APSAC, 2002) guidelines also provides helpful advice for using dolls.

Drawings, dolls, and diagrams can be effective tools for communication or clarification, but it is not recommended that they be used to determine, through the interviewer's interpretation, whether a crime has occurred (Hiltz & Bauer, 2003). The child's use of the aid should be evaluated in light of all of the other evidence compiled in the investigation.

THE INTERVIEW PROCESS

Structured Interview Protocols

Although there are still many unanswered questions about children's eyewitness abilities, a number of good research-based interview protocols are currently available to guide interviews, including the "Step Wise Interview" (Yuille et al., 1993), the "Cognitive Interview" (Fisher & Geiselman, 1992), a "flexible protocol" discussed by Poole and Lamb (1998), and the "NICHD Investigative Interview Protocol" (e.g., Sternberg, Lamb, Esplin, Orbach, & Hershkowitz, 2002). (There are also a number of training programs that teach principles from these and other protocols. For example, see Vieth, this volume, and Holmes & Vieth, 2003, for a discussion of the Finding Words training provided by Corner House and the APRI National Center for Prosecution of Child Abuse. The American Professional Society on the Abuse of Children also provides trainings.)

These and other protocols have similar characteristics and are based upon research and experience. For example, the NICHD Investigative Interview Protocol, developed by researchers at the National Institute of Child Health and Human Development (e.g., Orbach, Hershkowitz, Lamb, Sternberg, Esplin, & Horowitz, 2000; Sternberg, Lamb, Orbach, Esplin, & Mitchell, in press), is similar to and informed by the Step-Wise Interview and Cognitive Interview (Fisher & Geiselman, 1992), but is more highly scripted. It is described in detail in a chapter written by Sternberg and colleagues (2002). The protocol begins with the interviewer introducing him/herself and explaining to the child that he/she will need to describe events in detail, tell the truth, and say "I don't understand," and "I don't know" when appropriate. Rapport building is a key component of the interview, and sets the stage for the rest of the interview by, in effect, training the child to provide detailed information in response to open-ended prompts. Specifically, during rapport building, the child is asked to describe one or more recent neutral events in great detail, in response to nondirective cues (e.g., "Tell me all about that") from the interviewer.

After rapport building, the interviewer moves toward the topic under investigation with as little direction as possible, beginning with "Tell me why you came to talk with me today," and then moving progressively through a series of scripted questions that are more focused, but that do not include specific information about the allegation (see the chapter referenced above for a list of these questions). Most children in studies testing the NICHD protocol disclose after these questions, even though the questions do not include allegation details. If and only if these open-ended questions fail, Sternberg et al. (2002) suggest the use of very minimally leading questions such as "I hear that something might have happened to you at [location or time of incident]." But they recommend only cautious use of such questions, noting that "the use of leading or suggestive questions to initiate the substantive discussion may contaminate the child's response or even foster a false allegation. As a result, we urge interviewers to examine carefully the risks associated with leading questions against the importance of obtaining information from possible victims. . . . Even risky questions are sometimes necessary, but interviewers should also consider terminating the interviews and resuming on another occasion" (Sternberg et al., 2002, p. 426).

Once a child has disclosed the target abuse, other free recall invitations are given, beginning with "Tell me everything that happened from beginning to end as best you can remember." These invitations are supplemented when needed with prompts such as "And then what happened?" After the child mentions people or events, specific information is obtained with contextual cues such as "Did that happen one time or more than one time?" or "Earlier you mentioned X. Tell me everything about that." More directive questions (e.g., "When?" "What color") are used only if this type of questioning fails to uncover pertinent information. Yes/no questions are avoided unless absolutely necessary, and suggestive questions are discouraged.

Laboratory and field studies in multiple countries have revealed that, compared to standard interview techniques, the NICHD protocol prompts more accurate statements from child witnesses. Further, interviewers trained in this structured technique conduct higher quality, less suggestive interviews.

A RECOMMENDED FORMAT
FOR INTERVIEWING CHILD WITNESSES
AND ALLEGED VICTIMS

We encourage forensic interviewers to become familiar with the available protocols referenced above and to follow interview procedures that are consistent with established guidelines. Next, we describe in general terms a suggested process for interviewing that is informed by and consistent with the available protocols mentioned above, especially the Step Wise Interview (Yuille et al., 1993) and research evidence. The process we suggest is meant to serve as a guide and is not intended to prevent the often spontaneous and fluid conversation that occurs between a child and an interviewer. Note that although we recommend following established guidelines, the fact that an interview varies in some way from any recommended approach does not determine whether a report is accurate. Judgments about the accuracy of an account should be made by evaluating all of the available information or evidence, not simply how a particular interview was conducted.

Introducing the Child to the Interview Process

It is recommended that interviewers develop a standard manner in which they introduce themselves to the child and the child to the interview process. For example, "My name is _____ and I am a (state's attorney, police officer, doctor, social worker, etc.). My job is to talk to children about things that might have happened to them or about things that they might have seen." If the interview is being recorded, the videotaping can be explained during this phase.

After this, the interviewer can explain how questions will be asked and how answers should be given. A child should be told that the interview is not a test and that he or she should say "I don't know," or "I don't understand" if they are unsure of the answer to a question or unsure what the question means. The child should also be instructed to correct the interviewer if the child's statement has been misunderstood. The child also needs to know that if he or she wants to break from the interview for a few minutes, he or she just needs to ask.

It is also appropriate early in the interview process to initiate a discussion about the importance of telling the truth. In some jurisdictions, a child's out-of-court statements regarding a physical or sexual act committed against that victim (including statements made during a forensic interview) may be admitted in court as substantive evidence in specific situations. Thus, for both investigative and trial purposes, it is recommended that the child be reminded of the need to tell the truth. It might also be deemed appropriate to assess whether the child understands lies and truth. This should be assessed with developmentally appropriate methods (Bussey, Lee, & Grimbeek, 1993). Research illustrates that asking the child to identify concrete examples of statements of truth and lies is a much better means of assessment than asking the child to define or describe the difference between the two (Lyon, 1996, 2002a). Further, research by Karen Saywitz and Tom Lyon reveals that care should be taken in choosing the actual examples. Specifically, the child might be reluctant to label a statement made by the interviewer or the child him or herself as a lie, because even young children understand that a lie is wrong and that labeling a statement as a lie would be accusatory. Thus, asking a child to identify examples such as "If I said I was your mom, would that be a lie?" or "If you said you were purple, would that be a lie?" can underestimate the child's understanding of lies. Saywitz and Lyon's technique avoids this difficulty by using a neutral third party in examples–fictional figures in a drawing. In the drawing, for example, one figure tells a lie, and one figure tells the truth. The child is then asked to make a choice between the two ("Which person told the lie?"). With this picture method, the child does not have to fear labeling the interviewer or him or herself as a liar; further, memory and language demands are lessened. (A version of this method for determining children's understanding of oaths has been designed for use in forensic interviews and is available directly from Lyon and Saywitz.)

Note that children under the age of 4 years of age might not be able to answer questions accurately about truths and lies, regardless of the way this topic is presented to them. This does not mean that children of this age cannot tell the truth. Moreover, no investigative interview should not stop solely because a child (of any age) is unclear on some concepts or cannot identify truths and lies. Instead, the investigator should attempt to gather as much information as possible and then proceed with the investigation as circumstances dictate.

Finally, regarding in-court testimony, the Federal Rules of Evidence Rule 601 dictate that there is no specified age at which a person becomes competent to testify; instead, every person is presumed to be a competent witness regardless of chronological age. If a party in a case has a question regarding the competency of any witness, the judge can hold a competency hearing to determine whether the witness is capable of expressing him or herself regarding the matter at issue and whether the witness is able to understand the duty to tell the truth. A child does not have to give "perfect" answers to all of the questions in order to be found competent to testify; the child's responses should be judged in their entirety to make that determination. Also, even in court, it is *not* necessary that the child is able to explain the difference between a truth and a lie; the test is whether or not the child understands the consequences of telling a lie.

Rapport Building

Rapport building is an important phase of the interview for several reasons. During rapport building, the child can be asked to give free narrative accounts of neutral events in his or her life. As found by research investigating the NICHD protocol, and as suggested by Yuille et al. (1993), this will increase the likelihood that the child will provide information freely in the later parts of the interview. Topics that could be discussed during this phase include school, family, friends, birthdays, sports, music, etc. The younger child might wish to draw with the interviewer, recite numbers or the alphabet, or talk about family or pets. Spending sufficient time discussing general or non-stressful events also allows the child to relax and allows the interviewer to observe the child's linguistic, cognitive, and social skills (Yuille et al., 1993). Talking about pets might uncover animal abuse, which often accompanies domestic violence and child abuse situations in the home (Boat, 1995). Discussion of animal abuse can be a natural segue for a child to discuss their own abuse.

As suggested by Yuille et al. (1993) and Sternberg et al. (2002), it is a good idea to ask the child to describe in detail some past, neutral event(s) that can be verified (e.g., "How did you get here today?"). This should be done in a natural way, ideally using information the child has spontaneously brought up previously. The description of the event allows the interviewer to assess informally the manner in which the child responds (e.g., does the child provide unsolicited elaboration or does the child respond with short phrases, void of detail?). It also sets the stage for the interview as the interviewer introduces the form of questioning: requesting narrative accounts by asking open-ended questions, followed up if necessary with focused questions. For example:

Interviewer (I):   How did you get here today? "Tell me everything
                   that happened from beginning to end as best you can
                   remember."
Child (C):   My mom brought me.
I: Tell me everything you can remember about your
                   trip.
C: We came in the car. It's in the parking lot!
I: Tell me all about that.
C: Well, my car is kind of big and kind of small.
I: Um hmmm, tell me more about it.
C: It's green.
I: Anything else?
C: It makes a loud noise when you honk the horn!
I: What about your trip here? Tell me all about that.
C: I sat in the back.
I: What else?
C: I ate crackers on the way here.
I: Anything else?
C: I don't know.

During rapport building, the forensic interviewer should try to determine whether a child's immediate emotional or psychological state is an obstacle to communication. For this reason, interviewers should have a basic understanding of the psychological impact of experiencing and witnessing crimes on children of different ages. (See Myers, Berliner, Briere, Hendrix, Jenny, & Reid, 2002, for a discussion of the major forms of child maltreatment and trauma such as neglect and physical, emotional, and sexual abuse, and see Berman, Silverman, & Kurtines, 2002, for a discussion of the effects of witnessing community violence on children.) Traumatized children sometimes function at a psychological level that is less mature than normal (Pynoos & Eth, 1984). If the child appears scared or "distant" during the interview, he or she could be experiencing extreme stress, even post-traumatic stress disorder symptoms. It could be helpful to ask about feelings and encourage the child to talk about what he or she has been experiencing. Although it is inappropriate to attempt to counsel the child in this setting, the child might need to discuss his or her feelings as a way to gain control of them for the moment and complete the interview process.

Broaching the Issue of Alleged Crime Events

The purpose of this phase is to move the interview into a discussion of the allegations in question. Introducing the topic of concern should begin through general, open-ended questions (e.g., "Do you know why you are here today?"). If the child does not respond to this question with an account of the topic to be discussed, it might be necessary to proceed to more focused questions. For example, Yuille and colleagues (1993) suggest questions such as "Has anything happened to you that you would like to tell me about?" If the child is still reluctant, the interviewer can explain that he or she speaks with many children about "all kinds of things," such has family problems, problems with friends, problems with some people hurting animals or other people, etc. The NICHD interview protocol, as discussed above, provides a set of specific and increasingly focused questions that can be asked in a scripted way to avoid the need for suggestive questions. The interviewer should not, for example, suggest the identity of the alleged offender(s) or suggest what might have happened during the events in question.

If the child continues to resist providing a narrative account, the interviewer should solicit direction from others on the investigative team, child welfare professionals, etc., about how to proceed with the interview. The interview could be ended and rescheduled. If the team decides to question the child more specifically about the events in question, the allegations should be stated as vaguely as possible (e.g., "Did you tell your mom something happened to you?" or "Did something happen when you were at the store?"). If the child denies knowledge of the events, the interviewer can proceed to clarify the circumstances of the denial. If the child does not recall the events, a consensus should be reached about how to proceed with the interview (or trial preparation, if that is the purpose of questioning) on a case-by-case basis.

Describing the Event

When the child is able to offer a narrative account, however brief, it is recommended that the interviewer proceed with open-ended questioning in a manner that moves from the general to the specific. The interviewer should be a facilitator, encouraging the child to narrate the story of the allegation. Prompts such as "Then what happened?" or "Tell me about that" will aid in this facilitation. The interviewer should listen carefully to the child and not be impatient. The interviewer should avoid rushing, interrupting, correcting, or challenging the child (Yuille et al.,

1993). After the child appears to have exhausted his or her free recall of events, the interviewer may proceed to ask more specific or closed questions, but only if needed. As new information is gained, the interviewer should return to open-ended question wording, soliciting narrative about the new area of information (see example below). At all times, the interviewer should be sensitive to the highly personal nature of the child's experiences. This can be addressed by questioning the child about the less emotional or intimate aspects of the events first (e.g., preceding events, where the incident occurred, potential witnesses, etc.) and then gradually moving into questioning about the specific allegations and surrounding details. For example, after a child has given a free narrative account of the events, questioning might proceed as follows:

Interviewer (I):	OK, I think I'm beginning to understand what happened. How many times did this happen? (Specific question about frequency)
Child (C):	About three, I think.
I:	Please tell me everything you can remember about one of those times. (Request for narrative account)
C:	I remember the time at my step-mom's the best because my brother almost walked in on us.
I:	Let's talk about that time. (Request for narrative directed at a single incident)

The interviewer might need to remind the child of the interview "rules" (e.g., "If you don't understand the question, just say 'I don't understand'," or, "It's ok to say 'I don't know'"). If the child seems to find it difficult to talk about certain aspects of the event (e.g., the child repeatedly states that he or she doesn't know or doesn't remember), the interviewer might be able to distinguish lack of memory or knowledge from other difficulties by asking whether the child really doesn't know or whether the child just isn't ready to talk about the event(s). The interviewer could ask the child what he or she thinks will happen after the child talks about the occurrence(s). If the child indicates fear, the interviewer can determine the source and attempt to reassure the child in an honest manner. The topic can then be raised at a later point in the interview. Note that this kind of questioning should not be done before the child has freely disclosed the event, nor should it be done in a manner that suggests to the child that the interviewer will not take "I don't know" for an answer.

If the child becomes distressed during the interview, the focus of questioning should shift to more neutral topics. When the child has recovered, questions can again focus on the distressing topic. This switching of topics can happen a few times until the child can talk about stressful events (Yuille et al., 1993).

In situations where a child might be a witness to a crime rather than a victim, the focus of the interview is to determine whether or not the witness has any information regarding the alleged offense. The child witness might have actually witnessed the event, or the child might be a circumstantial witness who has information that can aid in the investigation. Using techniques just described, the interviewer should attempt to elicit all of the details of the child's knowledge-all events before, during, and after the offense. The interviewer could ask the child to describe what happened based on knowledge gained from all of the senses (e.g., How many gunshots did you hear? What did the drink taste like?). It is extremely important to the investigative process that the child's knowledge and ability to perceive the events be fully explored (e.g., Why couldn't the child see exactly what happened? Did the child have on his or her glasses at the time?). An additional consideration is that non-attorney forensic interviewers need to be familiar with the legal elements of any applicable criminal offense (i.e., the actions and motivations that constitute a crime) as well as laws regarding the admissibility of evidence. For example, if the child was a witness to a shooting, the interviewer should ask the child if the victim said anything after he was shot. (This would be important because the victim's statement to the child about the identity of the offender might be admissible in court as a spontaneous declaration, an excited utterance, or dying declaration, as per Federal Rules of Evidence 801.)

Specific Topics for Questioning

The following are suggested areas for exploration during the interview when details of any crime are being gathered.

General Description of Child's Current Living Situation. The interviewer should get a sense of the nature of familial and home relationships as they are perceived by the child. Understanding the child's home and social environment, including visitation arrangements, daycare, school, and for older children, gang affiliation, employment status, pets, and extracurricular activities might be important if they relate to the crime.

Description of the Disclosure Process. The interviewer should encourage the child to describe the specific context of his or her previous disclosure of the crime. To whom, if anyone, did the child previously relate the information? When and why did the child tell? What was the response from those whom the child told? If the child has made a previous statement regarding the incident, the interviewer should review that statement prior to the interview and/or speak to the person to whom the child disclosed. Note, however, that in this case, psychological research calls for the interviewer to be aware of the effect this additional information might have on his or her beliefs about the incident in question, and to take special care to retain an open mind regarding what might have happened. That is, an interviewer should be aware of the hypotheses that he or she is developing about what might have happened, and be vigilant in not allowing those hypotheses to bias the questions he or she asks the child (e.g., Dallas & Baron, 1985; for discussion, see Poole & Lamb, 1998).

Description of the Incident. A detailed description of the incident(s) includes information about the alleged offender, other possible victims or witnesses, where the incident occurred, the context of the incident, and the details of the event itself. If the case history suggests that the child has been victimized and did not immediately report the event, this issue should be probed in a gentle, non-accusatory manner. The interviewer could inquire about why the child reported the event when he or she did (instead of asking why the child did not tell about the allegations sooner, implying that he or she should have).

Repeated Abuse Incidents. Special consideration should be given when children have allegedly experienced repeated instances of abuse rather than one discrete event. Research reveals that repeated experience with events, including stressful events, might help rather than hinder children's memory for central aspects of the events, because children (like adults) form a "script memory" for the common elements of the repeated events (Bearison & Pacifici, 1989; Goodman, Quas, Batterman-Faunce, Riddlesberger, & Kuhn, 1994). However, memory for peripheral details, which might differ across the events, might suffer. Further complicating this issue, it is difficult for adults to determine what children consider to be central or peripheral details. Interviewers need to understand that when script memories are formed for a repeated type of event, memory for individual instances of the repeated event can suffer. Thus, it could be difficult for children to distinguish the individual events, even though they retain script memory for the central aspects of the repeated event (Farrar & Goodman, 1992). Developers of the NICHD protocol suggest inquiring first about the last known event, because it will be the freshest in the child's memory and perhaps easiest to remember. In any case, if there are multiple events, the interviewer should not necessarily expect the child to be able to recall the details of each individual event with specificity. The interviewer may ask the child to put the events in a temporal context by asking the child to associate the events with other memory-triggering events, such as holidays, school vacations, birthdays, etc. The child's own memory cues or triggers might assist the child in recalling more specific information about particular dates and offenses.

Description of Physical Evidence. The child should be encouraged to recall whether items were directly or indirectly used during the crime and where the items were located. Such items might include weapon(s), vehicle(s), property taken, items possessed/touched by the alleged offender(s), and items containing biological samples (e.g., blood, saliva, semen, etc.). In sex offense cases, items might include sexual aids, lotions, birth control devices, pornographic materials, items given to the child by the alleged offender (e.g., gifts, cards, letters), child's diaries or calendars (if abuse is noted or child marked days in a special way), and photographs with or taken by alleged offender (pornographic or non-pornographic).

Pornography Allegations. If it is suspected prior to or discovered during the interview that the alleged offender exposed the child to pornography or involved the child in the creation of pornography, it is important to have the child describe these activities in as much detail as possible (see Shepherd, Dworin, Farley, Russ, & Tressler, 1992, for more information). The pornography involved in the sexual abuse could include photos, magazines, videos, movies, or computer-generated images. The child should be questioned about the availability of these materials: Was it shown intentionally to the child or did the child come upon these materials by accident or through curiosity? The child should be asked to describe the equipment used to film or display pornography and where the alleged offender stores it. The child should also be asked if he or she can identify other children who are depicted in the pornography. Such information could be used to show probable cause for obtaining a search warrant and could aid law enforcement during a subsequent search.

History of Prior Abuse. Depending on the child's age and ability to communicate, the interviewer should attempt to determine if the child was a victim of prior abuse. This is important for several reasons; for example, to determine if prior abuse might explain age-inappropriate knowledge of sexual behaviors, or whether there are alternative explanations of the current allegations, etc. If the child states that he or she has previously been abused and the abuse was investigated, the interviewer should make note of this but not question the child further. If the child states that he or she has previously been abused and the abuse was *not* investigated to the child's knowledge, the interviewer should obtain enough information to call the child abuse hotline or file a police report.

Other Crimes. During the course of the interview, it is possible the child witness will make statements about other crimes (e.g., physical or sexual abuse to that child, witnessing another crime, etc.). That information should be noted; however, it is recommended that the interviewer not interview the child regarding those allegations during this interview, unless they have a direct bearing on the allegation currently under investigation. For example, a child's discussion of animal abuse and domestic violence might trigger his or her own allegations of abuse. In these cases, the interviewer can follow up on the newly disclosed information by opening a new investigation, relating the information to the investigators working on that case, etc.

Inconsistencies. During a child's interview, there can be inconsistencies among the child's current statements and other sources of information such as the child's prior statements, physical evidence, eyewitness accounts, etc. Inconsistencies are not necessarily indicators of inaccuracy and are often noted in young children's reports of past events (particularly preschoolers' reports; Fivush, 1993).

Inconsistencies can be due to a number of factors: language skills, developmental stage, fatigue, the tendency mentioned above to remember central details but not peripheral details of repeated events, etc. For example, young children have a limited concept of time and temporal order. This could result in a child alternately reporting that an event occurred in October and in December. An interviewer could explore such an inconsistency by asking the child questions regarding the weather (Was it hot? cold?), preparations for the holidays, etc. Also, note that what might seem like inconsistency might be the child describing multiple events. Generally, the interviewer should pursue inconsistencies through sensitive probing (e.g., the interviewer could display genuine confusion to the child). Sometimes it will not be possible to resolve inconsistencies during the interview or by consulting other sources such as witnesses or corroborative circumstances. In those cases, it is in the interest of justice to note the inconsistencies along with the rest of the child's statement.

Recantation. It is not unusual for a child to recant allegations before, during, or after an investigative interview (see Lyon, 2002b, and Pipe, Lamb, Orbach, & Cedarborg, in press, for discussion). Some recantations are false, made for many reasons, including familial, parental or peer pressure, fear, embarrassment, threats, etc. Other recantations are truthful, and the interviewer should be open to that important possibility. Recantations should be treated as any other relevant information and investigated impartially. For example, the interviewer might examine the timing and context of the recantation. Was the recantation spontaneous? Who was present? What was the family's/community's response to the crime? Was the recantation made face-to-face or in writing? In some cases of recantation, the interviewer might find it helpful to question the child's caretakers, friends, etc., to determine the circumstances of the recantation. The interviewer should question the child about the recantation in a non-threatening manner.

If, upon questioning, the child maintains the recantation, the interviewer should further investigate both the original and current statements. If there is evidence to show that the recantation was improperly produced or encouraged by another person or was intended by the child to discourage the investigation or the prosecution, the child can be presented with that information and questioned further. If there is no evidence to show that the recantation was improperly motivated, the recantation might, in fact, be true, and so the child should be questioned regarding the motivation and circumstances behind both statements.

If circumstances warrant, a second related investigation could be opened against any person who deliberately attempted to thwart the investigation or prosecution and therefore impede justice. This is known as suborning perjury or improper communication with a witness, and would include coercing a child to make a false statement or recant a true report.

Ending the Interview

When the interviewer believes the interview is completed, he or she might wish to consult with others (e.g., investigative team members, trial partners) to determine if there is a need for further questions. Even if more questions are called for, if the child appears too tired or stressed to continue with the interview, a follow-up interview (although often not desirable) might be required. Ideally, the same interviewer will conduct that second interview. At the end of an interview, the child might be asked if there is anything else he or she thinks should have been asked, but was not. Once it is determined that there are no further questions, the interviewer might find it helpful to review the details of the report (i.e., the details that the child gave during the interview only) with the child and ask the child if that report is accurate or whether additional information should be added.

To end the interview, the interviewer should bring the conversation back to more neutral topics, allowing the child to regain his or her composure. If the child is finished, he or she should be thanked for his or her participation, regardless of the outcome of the interview. The interviewer (e.g., investigative team member, co-counsel, victim-witness personnel) should explain to the child what will probably happen next in the investigative or prosecutorial process. Care should be taken to avoid promises about future events (e.g., "We will make sure that you won't miss school because of this."). Finally, the child's questions should be solicited and answered, and the child can be told how to contact the interviewer should he or she have any other questions or recall any other information. In that case, another interview can be arranged.

INDIVIDUAL DIFFERENCES AMONG CHILDREN: SPECIAL VICTIM POPULATIONS

Across all studies of children's memory and suggestibility and eyewitness testimony abilities, there is variability in children's performance even among children of the same chronological age. Much of this variability is probably accounted for by individual differences in children's abilities. The more that future research addresses this issue, the more information forensic interviewers will have to help them accommodate the individual abilities and needs of particular children. In terms of individual difference factors, age is still the single best predictor of children's abilities. At this time, conclusions about the effects of other individual differences on memory and suggestibility are somewhat speculative, but becoming more definitive as the research base grows (Quas et al., 2000). For example, there is some preliminary evidence that children with poorer attention skills are sometimes less accurate than other children, but that this can be overcome with warm, supportive interview techniques (Bottoms, Davis, Nysse-Carris, Haegerich, & Conway, 2000). Research reveals that better memory for stressful medical procedures is found in children who have temperaments that are the most adaptable and open to new experiences (Merritt, Ornstein, & Spicker, 1994) and in children who are most securely attached to their parents and who, therefore, have better communication with and support from their parents (Goodman et al., 1994, 1997). Also, preschoolers, who have poor source-monitoring skills (i.e., they have difficulty distinguishing among various sources for their beliefs or memory), are sometimes more suggestible than other children (Leichtman & Morse, 1997). Future research needs to replicate these findings and explore other factors that can identify children who might be particularly vulnerable to inaccuracy during forensic interviews.

Next, we focus on other individual difference factors that are known to affect children's abilities, and how those factors can be accommodated practically in the forensic interview. Specifically, we discuss age factors (special considerations for very young and for teenaged children) and disability issues. Finally, we also discuss special considerations for the child who is a suspected victim of physical abuse rather than sexual abuse.

The Pre-School Aged Child (3 to 5 Years of Age)

For developmental reasons, it is generally recommended that children under 2 years old not be interviewed. Children between 2 and 3 years old could be assessed for child protection concerns but should be evaluated on a case-by-case basis to determine whether their cognitive and linguistic skills are developed to the extent necessary to participate in a forensic interview (Hewitt, 1997). Forensic interviews with such young children should be approached very cautiously. Below, we provide recommendations for interviewing children aged 3 years and older.

Scheduling. The young child needs to be seen as soon as possible and therefore should receive priority in scheduling if possible (Hewitt, 1997). Sensitivity to a child's daily schedule and routine should result in minimal disruption for the child.

Snacking. Caretakers should be reminded to make sure that their child is well fed prior to arriving at the interview. If a child complains of hunger, healthy snacks should be offered by someone other than the designated interviewer.

Questions. As discussed above, research reveals that, compared to older children, young children lack linguistic skills, the skills needed to perform a thorough memory search, and the understanding of what information might be pertinent to an investigation. Therefore, they might not provide a great deal of information in response to free recall questions (Carter et al., 1996; Goodman et al., 1991), and it might be necessary to narrow the focus for young children by using specific questions; however, these questions should still allow children to answer in an

open-ended fashion. Interviewers might need to take more time orient-
ing young children to the interview itself (e.g., "I'm interested in getting
to know more about you today. I'm going to ask you some questions. I
might write down some notes so that I can remember what you say".) It
is recommended that questions be direct (e.g., "Your mom or dad didn't
tell me about your family. Tell me everything you can about all the people in your family"). As much as possible, suggestive questions should
be minimized. Also, as discussed elsewhere, although it is tempting because of their lack of language skills, it is not appropriate to use interview aids such as dolls to prompt disclosures from children. This is
especially true for children younger than age 4, many of whom do not
yet possess the symbolic skills necessary for representing themselves
and other people with dolls (deLoache, 1995).

An interviewer should take care to use words and terms that are developmentally, socially, and culturally appropriate. Note whether a child uses id-
iosyncratic words or different words or phrases to describe the same object
or concept (e.g., "basement" = "Johnny's room"). Although children comprehend many adult-like language features by about first grade, language
skills develop across the lifespan (Whitehurst, 1982). Young children are
particularly vulnerable to linguistically complex questions (Carter et al.,
1996; Perry et al., 1995; Walker, 1994). Complex questions are those that
(a) are simply too long; (b) use pronouns ambiguously; and (c) contain
age-inappropriate words, expressions, and sentence structures such as embedded clauses and nested questions (e.g., "Did you say you asked her to
go to the store?"), multiple prepositional phrases (e.g., "Did you say that
Sam put the video in the red box in the VCR under the TV?"), negatives
("Didn't you say it was Sam who went to the store?"), and/or passive voice
("Was the ball thrown by Sam?"). A particular danger is that even though
the child might not understand complex questions, he or she might try to
answer them anyway, often incorrectly. This is exacerbated by the fact that
young children sometimes are not even aware that they do not understand
complex questions (Markman, 1979). Thus, it is best for interviewers to
make a conscious effort to avoid complex sentence structures.

Length of Interview. Because young children have an especially limited attention span, interviewers and observers should be sensitive to
children's verbal and non-verbal cues in determining the length of the
interview. The interviewer should not bribe, entice, or lure a child into
the interviewing room or, once there, into staying. The child should be
encouraged to use the bathroom prior to the interview and should be
given breaks as needed. The young child should be reassured that his or
her caretaker is waiting. If the child is escorted to the caretaker for a

brief period of time, it is recommended that he or she not be left alone with the caretaker. If the child refuses to go back to the interview, a decision should be made concerning whether to conclude the interview.

Limit-Setting. Recognizing that young children are the most forthright when comfortable, they should be allowed to move about in the interviewing room (which should be relatively free from distractions). Note, however, that some young or particularly inattentive children might be more comfortable with limits set on their mobility. In either case, the interviewer must discourage any activity that will place a child at risk of harm.

Others Present During Interview. Occasionally, the young child will be unable to talk to interviewers outside the presence of a familiar caretaker or relative. In these circumstances, a non-offending caretaker or support person (who is not a witness in the investigation or prosecution) may be present during the interview. The caretaker should be instructed not to initiate conversation with, question, or answer for the child. The person should also be instructed to sit behind the child (to avoid eye contact or behavioral signals).

The Pre-Adolescent and Adolescent Child (11 to 18 Years of Age)

Pre-adolescent and adolescent children sometimes appear to be more mature than they really are. Although older children have better memory skills and are less suggestible than younger children, pre-adolescent and adolescent children often have complex social and emotional issues that require special sensitivity in the interview process. For example, these children might have overt emotional or behavioral problems in response to victimization. These children sometimes disclose their involvement only after other problems emerge, such as academic failure, suspension, or truancy; legal trouble; drug or alcohol use; depression; suicidal or homicidal tendencies; running away; etc. Next, we provide some specific recommendations for interviewing children of this age group.

Repeated Interviews. Pre-adolescents and adolescents, like younger children, should not be subjected to repetitive interviews. Being asked to repeat their statements to interviewers might cause them to re-experience trauma-related emotional difficulties, such as shame and embarrassment. If repeated interviews are unavoidable, at the second and subsequent interview, prior interviews should be discussed and the purpose for the current interview (e.g., additional investigation, trial preparation) should be explained. The child should be allowed to express his or her feelings about being asked to repeat information.

Interviewer Gender. Pre-adolescents and adolescents should be given a choice of interviewer gender, if possible. The interviewer should not assume that children will prefer an interviewer of their same gender, given possible complexities in their cases. For example, a girl who was victimized by her father might feel more immediate anger towards her mother, perhaps viewing her as powerless. She might wish to speak to a man.

Delayed or Reluctant Disclosures. It is not unusual for children (of any age) to delay disclosing their victimization or knowledge of criminal activity (see Lyon, 2002b, and Pipe et al., in press, for discussion). Interviewers should be aware of the circumstances surrounding the child's disclosure in all cases, but especially in cases involving pre-adolescents and adolescents, where the issue of blame and fault are of primary concern. For example, in situations where a relative is the offender, the child might have disclosed to a caretaker who sided with the offender prior to a full investigation. The caretaker might even feel threatened by the disclosure (which could lead to loss of children, partner, and/or income) and might be angry at the child for his or her disclosure. Caretakers accusing a child of seduction or lying, or who otherwise place blame on a child, could discourage the child from speaking at all. Other reasons for delayed disclosure include shame and embarrassment, fear of not being believed, fear of drawing attention to themselves, fear of police involvement, and/or previous involvement with law enforcement. The interviewer should, if possible, have knowledge of any negative reactions that the child experienced since disclosure. To determine at the outset of an interview whether the child is motivated to avoid disclosure for any of these or other reasons, the interviewer could ask questions such as "Whose idea was it to talk to the investigators?" or "How do you feel about being here today?" and "Do you understand what's happening?" In cases where negative reactions have occurred, the interviewer could address these matters with the child prior to the interview and seek the child's cooperation.

Issues Involving Consent. Before children have reached the statutory age of consent, which varies from state to state, the law does not recognize their ability to consent to have sexual relations. In many cases, it will be important to determine whether the offender was informed about the child's age. In cases involving pre-adolescents and adolescents, however, the issue of consent can be more complex than merely determining the biological ages of the child and alleged offender or even whether the child's actual age was understood.

For example, a child might be involved in an "under age relationship," a relationship that the child (and perhaps even the offender) consider to be a normal romantic relationship, but which is in reality statutory rape. Such cases can be challenging because children in these relationships often develop a bond with the alleged offender and will not admit to the sexual relationship in order to protect the offender. Although such a child might not acknowledge his or her victimization, the child might admit to circumstances surrounding his or her relationship with the offender, and those admissions could lead to evidence sufficient to sustain a conviction (DNA, circumstantial witnesses, physical evidence, etc.). To increase the chances of uncovering such information, investigators can explore the exploitative aspects of the relationship. Was the child keeping the relationship secret from friends, family, teachers, and others? How would the child and the alleged offender make contact (i.e., through secret code, e-mails, a person acting as a go-between)? If the child and offender had clandestine meetings, when and where did they occur? Another avenue for investigation is to determine whether the child received a medical examination or treatment during the period he or she was involved with the offender. This might lead to evidence that the child was prescribed birth control, treated for a sexually transmitted disease, pregnant, etc. Although the collateral information collected through such inquiries might not provide probable cause to arrest the suspected offender, it might provide sufficient grounds for implementing a protection plan.

A related consideration is the issue of the child's own understanding (or misunderstanding) about the concept of consent. For example, in an acquaintance rape situation, wherein a child might know and trust the abuser, the child might mistake his or her own passivity (due to fear or other factors) for consent. If the child believes that giving consent means not aggressively fighting back, he or she might feel guilty and be reluctant to cooperate with the investigation or prosecution. In these cases, after a child has disclosed abuse, it might be advisable to remind the child that no matter what he or she says, and no matter what happened, the interviewer understands that he or she is not at fault for the abuse.

Risk of Recantation. Children of all ages could recant their abuse, although there is not yet a clear understanding of how often this occurs (for discussion, see Lyon, 2002b; Pipe et al., in press). Pre-adolescents and adolescents might be at particular risk because they are better able to understand the ramifications of their disclosure and the possible effects of their cooperation with the criminal justice system (e.g., publicity, schedule disruption, negative peer or familial response, etc). The interviewer might need to speak at length with these children about how their life has been since their disclosure, rather than confronting them, however gently, about the disclosure itself. The information about their life after disclosure could provide insights about the recantation that can guide further questions.

Confidentiality in the Interview. Pre-adolescents and adolescents might be very sensitive to the issue of confidentiality. The interviewer should discuss with the child the extent of information he or she would like his or her parents to know. The interviewer could plan with the child how to talk to his or her parents about the incident at both the post-interview meeting and in future conversations with the parents. (The interviewer should also explain videotaping, if applicable.) The interviewer should not make promises that are unenforceable (e.g., "You will never have to testify in court." "This will be easy." "We won't tell your parents what happened.")

If the child will testify in court, the non-confidential nature of the child's testimony should be discussed with the child prior to any hearing. It should be explained that the law requires the defendant's presence at any hearing, and that therefore the defendant will be physically present in the courtroom with the child. (In some jurisdictions, the judge determines at a pre-trial hearing whether or not the child can testify in camera via closed circuit television.) It should also be explained to the child that the courtroom is a public forum and that members of the public such as the press will be present in the courtroom.

Other Concerns. Adolescents' situations might be so complicated that social service intervention is necessary. Investigators should facilitate such intervention if the interview uncovers concerns such as the need for relocation due to harassment or threats, pregnancy or risk of pregnancy, risk of contracting STDs and/or HIV, risk of running away, need for case management and advocacy (particularly if child is placed in a shelter), the need for crisis intervention and/or counseling, the need for suicide assessment, etc.

Children Who Have Disabilities

Children and adults with disabilities are far more likely than their nondisabled peers to be maltreated (Verdugo, Bermejo, & Fuertes, 1995). Yet their claims are unlikely to be reported to authorities, acted on by authorities if reported, or prosecuted in court (Kebbell & Hatton, 1999; but see *Illinois v. Spencer*, 1983 and *People v. Karelse*, 1985, for exceptions). This could contribute to their vulnerability. That is, it might be assumed that children with disabilities cannot give accurate reports of abuse or that their accusations will not be believed by investigators or by jurors should cases go to trial. In fact, Seidman (2000) found that some adults with mild intellectual disabilities are not necessarily unreliable in recalling past events of a sexual nature, and Dent (1986) suggests that with non-leading questioning, children with mild mental retardation might not necessarily be poorer witnesses than other children. Further, one jury simulation study shows that adolescents with mild intellectual disabilities are sometimes perceived by jurors to be even more credible than nondisabled victims (Bottoms, Nysse-Carris, Harris, & Tyda, 2003).

Thus, it is important not to dismiss the potential for victims with disabilities (even those who have intellectual disabilities) to participate in forensic interviews or even give courtroom testimony. There are a number of unique issues to consider when interviewing children who have disabilities (Poole & Lamb, 1998), as we discuss next.

Prior to the Interview. If it is learned prior to the interview that the child has a disability, it is important to gather information about the disability and its implications for interactions with the child. It is recommended that caretakers (or the person who knows the disabled child best) be questioned regarding general communication and behavioral concerns (Davies, 1997). Several types of information regarding the child's general abilities might be gathered:

- What is the nature of the child's disability? What is the type and extent of the impairment? Does it present the child with physical, emotional, or intellectual challenges? For example, if the child is reported to have learning disabilities, it is important to understand the extent of the learning disability, if possible. A child might have a specific or focal deficit in one area of learning, for instance. If this is the case, questioning can be adjusted to accommodate this disability.
- How does the child adapt to new environments and new people? If accommodations are needed, arrangements should be made prior to the interview. Because many children with disabilities have difficulty adjusting to unfamiliar environments, special consideration can be made regarding where the interview will occur. If the child is interviewed at a non-child advocacy center or non-law-enforcement facility, the interviewing space should be as neutral as possi-

ble (e.g., not the child's bedroom). In some cases, more than one interviewing session might be necessary for a full disclosure.

- How does the child manage anxiety? For example, certain disabilities will be characterized by repetitive behaviors (stereotypy), such as rocking, hand flapping, head hitting, etc. In the case of excessive displays of these behaviors, which could indicate stress, the child should be reminded that he or she can ask for a break or stop the interview at any time.
- What are the child's "anger triggers" (e.g., What happens if he or she is asked to repeat his or her answers)?
- Has the child been exposed to violence (actual or simulated as in video games, movies)? Resided in a home where violence or sexual abuse is known or suspected? Been in the care of a registered or known sexual offender? Had a history of injuries? Displayed difficulty in walking or sitting? Had torn, stained, or bloody clothing? Been exposed to pornography? Been pregnant or had an STD? Experienced genital pain, itching, or bleeding?

Answers to these questions will help determine if the child needs to be prepared for the interview in any way. In addition, it is important to determine if the child is currently taking any medication and how this could influence his or her behavior, ability to communicate, and memory. Caretakers should be asked about the best time to interview the child, considering the child's routine and the effects of the medication. It is important to remind the caretaker to be sure the child receives his or her medication on the day of the interview or testimony. It is recommended that interviews or testimony be scheduled during the period when the medicine is most effective. If there are any questions, the interviewer should note the type of medication the child is taking and consult with a physician prior to the interview or testimony.

Also, if the child uses adaptive equipment, such as hearing aids, a wheelchair, or a helmet, it is important to recognize that this equipment might be considered by the child to be an extension of the body and should be treated as such. Note that wearing a helmet could impair hearing.

Finally, the Americans With Disabilities Act requires that, if a person with a disability requests an interpreter, one must be provided. For purposes of forensic interviewing, it is recommended that a certified and neutral interpreter agreed upon by the team conduct interpretation. It is essential that an interpreter understand his or her role in the interview so that he or she will not, for example, answer for the child when the child is slow to respond or unintelligible. The interpreter should be seated in the interview room in such a manner that his or her face can be seen at the same time as the child's. Note that interpreters using "facilitated communication" should be completely avoided. This is a highly controversial and questionable technique by which communication (typing on a keyboard) is "facilitated" through the assistance of a "facilitator" who uses a hand-over-hand technique to guide a child's hand across a keyboard. There is no empirical evidence that supports the use of this technique in a forensic interview setting (for reviews, see Jacobson, Mulick, & Schwartz, 1995; Heckler, 1994).

Questioning. When questioning the developmentally delayed or mentally retarded child, the severity of retardation or delay must be determined to the extent possible, and questions should be adjusted to reflect the child's mental age rather than chronological age. Despite knowledge of a child's mental age or the level of demonstrated social skills, the interviewer should not overestimate the child's comprehension and communication skills. The interviewer should assess the child's use of words during rapport building and capitalize on the words the interviewer is confident the child understands. In addition, the interviewer should be particularly sensitive to potential suggestibility, as with young children. Because of the highly structured and dependent environments in which many disabled individuals live, they might have more acquiescing communication styles (Davies, 1997). It is important, therefore, that the child with disabilities be frequently reminded that he or she can disagree if anything said is either wrong or misunderstood.

It is also important to note that mental age does not necessarily predict the type of interviewing aids that could be necessary. For example, an 18-year-old with a mental age of 5 might not want to use anatomically detailed dolls to describe incidents. In other words, mental age does not automatically define social age. Issues of consent to sexual acts sometimes arise in investigations with adolescents who are intellectually disabled. The child must be questioned with great sensitivity surrounding the context in which he or she claims to have consented to sexual relations (for discussion of consent among the disabled, see Tharinger, Horton, & Millea, 1990).

Emotional Disabilities. Some individuals with disabilities lack the coping mechanisms of non-disabled individuals and could demonstrate more acute post-traumatic stress symptoms during an interview. If the interviewer suspects this, the interview can be paced accordingly or stopped to prevent overwhelming the child. If the child has an emotional disability, attempts to make the interviewing environment as comfortable as possible could be useful. For example, the child can bring a favorite toy or stuffed animal or pet (if the facility allows) into the interview room. Although the child often has a right to have a caretaker or advocate present during the interview, it is recommended that others not be allowed in the interview room during the interview if possible. If, however, the child is distraught and/or the interview could not otherwise proceed, a support person should be allowed, provided that the person has agreed to remain silent and not to guide the child's responses in any way.

Victims or Witnesses Who Are Suspected Juvenile Offenders

Occasionally, child victims or witnesses who are being interviewed are also alleged to be, known to be, or disclose that they are perpetrators. If a child has a documented history of committing criminal acts, the interviewer could tell the child in the beginning of the interview that the purpose of his or her interview is to talk about what the child experienced, not about acts allegedly perpetrated on others. If, during the interview, the child spontaneously discloses information about offenses that he or she perpetrated on others, that information should be noted, but no specific questions regarding that disclosure should be asked at that time. Questioning about possible offenses is beyond the scope of a forensic interview. The focus of the interview should remain on the facts currently under investigation.

Soon afterward, a break in the interview can be taken so a decision can be made about how to proceed. To protect the child's rights, questioning regarding juvenile offenses should be conducted by law enforcement in accordance with state and federal laws (e.g., state juvenile codes, *Miranda v. Arizona*, 1966). If it is decided to address the possible perpetration in a subsequent interview, the child can be informed that someone else (e.g., the police or a child protective services investigator) will talk with him or her about the potential offenses.

Child Physical Abuse Victims

Many of the same techniques suggested for interviewing children regarding sexual abuse and other crimes are appropriate when physical abuse is suspected. The following suggestions, however, are tailored to the forensic interview of alleged physical abuse victims. (For more information on recognizing intentional physical maltreatment, see Johnson, 1996, and for a discussion of physical abuse generally, see Myers et al., 2002.)

A careful physical evaluation by a physician who has training and experience in recognizing abuse-related injuries should be conducted at the earliest possible time to determine if there are bruises, scars, burns, or other physical evidence of abuse. If the interviewer notices or the child mentions visible marks, photos should be taken of the marks (or lack thereof) by an evidence technician from the police department or other designated person, regardless of the age of the injury (see the American Professional Society on the Abuse of Children's "Recommendations on Photographing Abuse Injuries"). The need for photos should be explained to the child, and emotional support should be provided to the child during the photographing procedure. In the case of recent injury, the child's caretaker should be informed that follow-up photos will be necessary to document the severity of the injury and the process of healing. As with all abuse cases, the child and his or her caretaker should be interviewed about the allegations and circumstances separately, if possible. In addition to photographs of the injuries, other documented information collected from the caretaker and the child should include information such as the following:

History of the Injury. The interviewer should document the name of the informant (if any); the date, time, and place of the injury; how the injury occurred; who witnessed the injury; when the injury occurred; and the history from the child.

Discipline. The interviewer might question the child about discipline (who does it, and how and why it is done), and about current and past marks left on his or her body as a result of discipline or other physical assaults. The interviewer could ask specifically how each adult who cares for the child handles discipline (what, in detail, is the nature and frequency of the abuse or discipline?). Particular attention should be paid to any unusual method of discipline (e.g., manacles, locking in closet, tying to bed, etc.). Inquiries can be made about objects that might have been used to hit the child (e.g., What is the item? What is its size, color, etc.? Where it is usually kept?). If the child was burned, with what were they burned? Did anyone attempt to treat the burn?

Preceding Events. The forensic interviewer should ask the child about events that preceded the abuse (e.g., arguing, fighting, bathing, dressing, use of drugs or alcohol by the alleged offender, etc.).

Witnesses. The interviewer should inquire about other possible witnesses such as other children, neighbors, friends, or relatives. The interviewer should ask the child if anyone else was present during the abusive act(s), if the child told anyone (and what resulted from this disclosure), and what type of discipline (or abuse) the child has observed the alleged offender inflict on other children. If the child alleges that a caretaker in his or her home is the abuser, the interviewer might ask the child about the relationship among the adults in the home (e.g., domestic abuse, alcohol or drug use, etc.). If there were no other eyewitnesses, did the child scream or cry and could anyone have heard the child's cries?

Child's Medical History. The interviewer might question the caretaker and child about past medical care they received or needed, previous traumas, hospitalizations, behavior problems, developmental delays, etc. A suspiciously large number of past hospitalizations or other medical treatments could indicate Munchausen Syndrome by Proxy, a condition in which a caretaker fabricates medical problems that the child does not actually have, to gain sympathy and attention for the caretaker him or herself (Johnson, 1996; Rosenberg, 1987).

Sibling History. The interviewer might find it useful to query the child and/or the child's caretaker regarding abuse, trauma, and even deaths of siblings (number of deaths and age at time of death, gender of siblings, etc.).

Parental History. History taken from both offending and non-offending parents can include inquiries into the following areas: domestic violence in the home, past or current drug or alcohol abuse, history of sexual abuse, parental psychiatric history, parental support systems, pregnancies, and previous child protective involvement.

ADDITIONAL CONSIDERATIONS

Multi-Victim Investigations

In some investigations, several children might need to be interviewed as potential victims. If more than one child is present to be interviewed, children should be kept separate before and during all of the interviews. Children should not be allowed to confer and communicate with each other during the interviewing process. Further, under some circumstances, children and caretakers should be instructed to not talk with each other about their statements.

Investigative agencies should formulate a protocol for dealing with potentially problematic situations involving large numbers of suspected victims (see Lanning, 1989, and Pence & Wilson, 1994, for detailed multi-victim investigation protocols). When these cases arise, interviewers should quickly determine the number of children who need to be interviewed and devise the best strategy for handling the interviews thoughtfully. If a large number of children need to be interviewed, it is advisable for several teams to be formed to interview the children, enabling the investigators to interview several children concurrently.

In such investigations, it might not be feasible to interview all children at an advocacy center or law enforcement agency. When arranging interviews outside of an advocacy center or law enforcement agency, a location should be found that is neutral and distraction free. Unless there is no reasonable alternative, it is best not to interview the children at home or at the site of the alleged abuse.

If there are a large number of potential victims and witnesses, a coordinator should be designated to arrange activities: scheduling, transportation arrangements, communications among interviewers and child's caretakers, etc. The coordinator should also ensure that potential witnesses and their caretakers do not wait in the same location with other witnesses, and that they are cautioned against discussing the case with others. The coordinator might also be responsible for gathering medical reports and other documentation and for determining what information should be shared among team members (Lanning, 1989).

When interviewing each child, the team should assess the child not only as a potential victim but also as a potential witness to other crimes. The child should be asked in a non-leading manner to describe everything the child has seen or knows that is related to this investigation. The interviewer should inquire as to the basis of the knowledge (if it is not first hand).

Child Kidnappings

Cases involving abducted children should be considered high priority, emergency investigations. As soon as possible after the child is returned to safety, it is recommended that the child be physically examined and, if emotionally able, interviewed. Circumstances of the investigation should dictate which (the physical exam or the interview) should be conducted first. Because these cases often involve a great deal of publicity, it is imperative that the child be shielded from reporters and any non-familial and non-investigative personnel. Families of abducted children are in distress, and they should be provided time to reunite privately so that the family is reassured about the safety of the child.

The same interviewing recommendations given above for other child witnesses should be followed for kidnapping victims, with the addition of the following areas of specific questioning.

Preceding Events. What was the child doing prior to the abduction? Were there prior contacts with the alleged perpetrator? Was the child aware of any plans to abduct him or her?

Transportation. How was the child transported? Can the child describe the vehicle, including objects inside the vehicle?

Destination(s). Where was the child taken during the abduction? Each scene should be described in detail, if possible. Was the child told where he or she was going?

Involved Persons. Whom did the child encounter during the abduction and what was the detailed nature of each encounter? Is the child aware of other individuals with information? Can the child describe the person(s) involved, if strangers?

Conversations. What did the abductor or others say to the child during the abduction? Did anything happen or was anything said that did not make sense to the child? Was the child instructed what to say when talking to others?

Timing. It is important to understand in detail what happened and when. Creation of a timeline can be useful in helping the child organize the order in which events occurred.

Commission of Other Crimes. Were other crimes committed during the abduction, such as sexual abuse, physical abuse, substance abuse, theft, exposure to or manufacturing of child pornography, etc.?

Bizarre or "Ritualistic" Abuse Allegations

During the course of an investigation, children might make extremely unusual allegations of abuse or circumstances surrounding the abuse. For example, they could allege abuse involving religious or quasi-religious ceremonies and symbols, multiple perpetrators and victims, animal or human sacrifice, or cannibalism. Such allegations, which emerged in the mid-1980s but are less common today, are generally known as "ritual abuse" or "satanic ritual abuse." Research reveals that ritual abuse claims are rarely substantiated with conclusive evidence, particularly those cases involving allegations of organized satanic cult activity (Bottoms, Shaver, & Goodman, 1996; Lanning, 1992, 1991). However, there is good evidence for abuse related to other religious beliefs; for example, abuse perpetrated by religious authorities, beatings motivated by biblical writings and beliefs, and religiously motivated medical neglect (for which parents

are protected from prosecution in some states, though this is being chal-
lenged and changed increasingly; Bottoms, Nielsen, Murray, & Filipas,
2004; Bottoms, Shaver, Goodman, & Qin, 1995; Goodman, Bottoms,
Redlich, Shaver, & Diviak, 1998).

If a child makes ritualistic allegations, or any other type of equally
implausible allegations, the history of the case should be examined
carefully. It might be helpful to interview all of the people to whom the
child disclosed. The goal at this stage of the investigation is to verify exactly what the child said to whom and in what time sequence. This process can give the investigators a more detailed history regarding the
allegations and the process of disclosure; it might also give the investigators an opportunity to evaluate the child (and the people who might
have influenced the child) for motive and bias. It should also allow investigators to explore potential sources for the bizarre, age-inappropriate information included in the child's allegations (e.g., films, television
shows, heavy metal band music, other victims, previous therapists;
Goodman, Quas, Bottoms et al., 1997).

When investigating such cases, investigators should remain open to
the possibility that some form of maltreatment might have actually occurred, but the child could have embellished those true allegations with
inflated, bizarre details that are false. There are a number of potential
explanations for this embellishment, each of which should be considered by the investigating team (Dalenberg, 1996; Dalenberg, Hyland, &
Cuevas, 2002; Everson, 1997; Lanning, 1989):

- The bizarre details might have been suggested to the child through
  various misleading sources such as the media, parents, previous interviewers, or therapists (Loftus, 1992; Weir & Wheatcroft, 1995).
- The trauma of the actual abuse (present or past) might psychologically affect a child in a way that leaves him or her more open to
  suggestions and to reporting distortions in an otherwise true story
  (Ganaway, 1989).
- The perpetrators of the crime might have staged bizarre events to
  ensure that the child would report implausible details and not be
  believed (Lanning, 1989, 1992).
- The child might have exaggerated the claim to gain sympathy or
  approval from listeners or might have misunderstood the actual
  events (Everson, 1997).

Thus, children's allegations should not be automatically discounted
because of exaggerated details; however, as the number of fantastic de-

tails in a disclosure increases without corroboration, increased skepticism might be warranted.

UNDERSTANDING AND USING THE RESULTS
OF SOCIAL SCIENCE RESEARCH

We return now to a theme we introduced early in this paper: The best forensic interviewing practices are informed by knowledge obtained from social science research studies. Throughout this paper, we have provided references to studies that support our recommendations. To the greatest extent possible, investigators should remain aware of the current knowledge base, by reading articles and books written by researchers and attending training sessions where research results are discussed.

Accessing the Research. Many studies of children's testimony are published in psychology journals (e.g., *Child Development, Journal of Applied Social Psychology, Psychological Bulletin, Applied Developmental Science*) or interdisciplinary journals (e.g., *Law and Human Behavior, Child Abuse and Neglect, Child Maltreatment*). The contents of such journals can be searched by keywords and/or author names using various search engines (e.g., Current Contents, PsychInfo) available at university libraries and some public libraries.

Because forensic investigators have different professional training than social scientists, it can sometimes be difficult to access or interpret some research. Because of the reward structure at universities (for promotion, tenure, and raises), researchers who are professors usually write articles using technical language and styles appropriate for audiences of other researchers rather than for audiences of legal or social service professionals. Even so, researchers are quite motivated to help front-line professionals access their research. In fact, when psychological knowledge reaches a stage where it indicates specific directives for law or policy, social scientists have a moral duty to disseminate it to the professionals who can affect change (Reppucci, 1985). Thus, investigators should not hesitate to ask researchers directly about obtaining or interpreting their (or others') research. Most researchers are affiliated with universities or research institutes, and they can be reached easily by electronic mail. (Their addresses can usually be found quickly through an Internet search.) Increased contact between researchers and investigators will be advantageous to both parties; forensic investigators are a key source of ideas for future studies that will be of benefit to the field.

We also suggest that investigators take advantage of books that researchers write specifically for more general audiences. For example, in addition to other books we have referenced throughout this paper, the following volumes provide excellent, reader-friendly summaries of research findings and direct recommendations for forensic interviewing: *Memory and Suggestibility in the Forensic Interview* (Eisen et al., 2002); *Investigative Interviews of Children: A Guide for Helping Professionals* (Poole & Lamb, 1998); and *Children's Testimony: A Handbook of Psychological Research and Forensic Practice* (Westcott, Davies, & Bull, 2002). In addition, the *APSAC Handbook on Child Maltreatment* (Myers et al., 2002) also provides an excellent summary of research on interviewing children in and out of court, written by Saywitz et al. (2002). That handbook also includes chapters about most forms of child maltreatment. Finally, *Children, Social Science, and the Law* (Bottoms, Kovera, & McAuliff, 2002) provides reviews of social science evidence related to children's eyewitness testimony and other topics such as expert testimony on children's suggestibility, courtroom innovations for child witnesses, youth violence and juvenile justice, children's legal rights, children's legal representation, divorce and custody, adoption, etc. We have cited other good resources throughout this paper, and we have listed even more in our Appendix.

Interpreting and Using the Research. There are several issues to keep in mind when interpreting and evaluating research on children's eyewitness testimony. For example, as recognized by the US Supreme Court (*Daubert v. Merrell Dow Pharmaceuticals*, 1993), the most trustworthy research will be published (or eventually publishable) in well-known peer-reviewed journals and conducted by researchers affiliated with respected institutions of higher education or research institutes. Sometimes, but not always, the research will have been funded by federal research grants. These facts will usually, but not always, ensure that the research is solid in terms of basic scientific issues such as random assignment of subjects to experimental conditions, adequate number of subjects, presence of a control group or comparison group to which the treatment group(s) can be compared, etc.

It is also important to consider how generalizable laboratory findings are to the real world of child abuse investigations. Quas et al. (2000, pp. 243-244) offer the following advice to investigators seeking to interpret child witness research and generalize it to forensic practice:

- Note the age of children in a study and understand that results might not generalize to children of different ages.
- Understand that the type of event children witness in a study (emotional, negative, positive) can influence the generalizability of results.

- Examine the type of questioning techniques used in the study and consider whether they are like those used in investigatory practice. If multiple suggestive techniques are used simultaneously in a study, one cannot know which one caused associated changes in children's accuracy, or even whether one of the techniques alone could have a similar effect.
- Understand that statistically significant results are often, but not always, meaningful in a practical sense. For example, a difference in the performance of two groups of children who receive different interview protocols might be statistically significant, but the absolute difference might be too small to justify a change in forensic practice. Consistent replication of the result in other studies, however, would lend credibility to the finding.
- Realize that researchers examine differences between groups of children, or trends in results across multiple children. In contrast, forensic investigators and the courts are concerned about the accuracy of individual children in specific cases. Thus, findings from studies are not necessarily generalizable to every child. Research on individual differences in children's abilities is just beginning. Eventually, it will help provide information that can be targeted at specific types of children, but that goal is still a few years away, and it is highly doubtful that we will ever have a "litmus test" of the accuracy of individual child witnesses.

CONCLUSION

Children's reports are critical evidence in many cases. It is thus of utmost importance to ensure that the best methods are used to obtain their reports. We have provided the scaffolding on which investigators can build solid forensic interview techniques that will facilitate children's reports, and, in turn, ensure the protection of children who might be involved in abusive situations while also guarding against false allegations that could threaten the rights of innocent persons.

REFERENCES

American Professional Society on the Abuse of Children. (1995). *Photographic documentation of child abuse.* Chicago, IL: Author.
American Professional Society on the Abuse of Children. (1996). *Use of anatomical dolls in child sexual abuse assessments.* Chicago, IL: Author.

American Professional Society on the Abuse of Children. (2002). *Guidelines for psychosocial evaluation of suspected sexual abuse in young children* (Revised). Chicago, IL: Author.

Americans With Disabilities Act of 1990, 42 U.S.C. 12101 et seq.

Bearison, D. J., & Pacifici, C. (1989). Children's event knowledge of cancer treatment. *Journal of Applied Developmental Psychology, 10*, 469-486.

Berman, S., Silverman, W., & Kurtines, W. (2002). The effects of community violence on children and adolescents: Interventions and social policy. In B. L. Bottoms, M. B. Kovera, & B. M. McAuliff (Eds.), *Children, social science, and law* (pp. 301-321). New York: Cambridge.

Boat, B. (1995). The relationship between violence to children and violence to animals: An ignored link? *Journal of Interpersonal Violence, 10*, 228-35.

Boat, B. W., & Everson, M. D. (1993). The use of anatomical dolls in sexual abuse evaluations: Current research and practice. In G. S. Goodman & B. L. Bottoms (Eds.), *Child victims, child witnesses: Understanding and improving children's testimony* (pp. 47-70). New York: Guilford.

Bottoms, B. L., Kovera, M. B., & McAuliff, B. M. (2002). *Children, social science, and law*. New York: Cambridge.

Bottoms, B. L., Davis, S., Nysse-Carris, K. L., Haegerich, T. M., & Conway, A. (2000, March). Effects of social support and working memory capacity on children's eyewitness memory. In B. L. Bottoms & M. B. Kovera (Chairs), *Individual and contextual influences on adults' perceptions of children's reports*. Symposium conducted at the biennial meeting of the American Psychology/Law Society, New Orleans, LA.

Bottoms, B. L., Nielsen, M., Murray, R., & Filipas, H. (2004). Religion-related child physical abuse: Characteristics and psychological outcomes. *Journal of Aggression, Maltreatment and Trauma, 8*(1/2), 87-114.

Bottoms, B. L., Nysse-Carris, K. L., Harris, T., & Tyda, K. (2003). Jurors' perceptions of adolescent sexual assault victims who have intellectual disabilities. *Law and Human Behavior, 27*, 205-227.

Bottoms, B. L., Shaver, P. R., & Goodman, G. S. (1996). An analysis of ritualistic child abuse allegations. *Law and Human Behavior, 20*, 1-34.

Bottoms, B. L., Shaver, P. R., Goodman, G. S., & Qin, J. (1995). In the name of God: A profile of religion-related child abuse. *Journal of Social Issues, 51*, 85-111.

Bussey, K., Lee, K., & Grimbeek, E. J. (1993). Lies and secrets: Implications for children's reporting of sexual abuse. In G. S. Goodman & B.L. Bottoms (Eds.), *Child victims, child witnesses: Understanding and improving children's testimony* (pp. 147-168). New York: Guilford.

Carter, C. A., Bottoms, B. L., & Levine, M. (1996). Linguistic and socio-emotional influences on children's reports. *Law and Human Behavior, 20*, 1-34, 335-358.

Ceci, S. J., & Bruck, M. (1993). The suggestibility of the child witness: A historical review and synthesis. *Psychological Bulletin, 113*, 403-439.

Ceci, S. J., Loftus, E. F., Leichtman, M. D., & Bruck, M. (1994). The possible role of source misattributions in the creation of false beliefs among preschoolers. *The International Journal of Clinical and Experimental Hypnosis, XLII*, 304-320.

Dalenberg, C. J. (1996, Summer). Fantastic elements in child disclosure of abuse. *APSAC Advisor, 9*(1), 5-10.

Dalenberg, C. J., Hyland, K. Z., & Cuevas, C. A. (2002). Sources of fantastic elements in allegations of abuse by adults and children. In M. Eisen, J. A. Quas, & G. S. Goodman (Eds.), *Memory and suggestibility in the forensic interview* (pp. 185-204). Mahwah, NJ: Erlbaum.

Dallas, M. E. W., & Baron, R. S. (1985). Do psychotherapists use a confirmatory strategy during interviewing? *Journal of Social and Clinical Psychology, 3*, 106-122.

Daubert v. Merrell Dow Pharmaceuticals, Inc. 113 S.Ct. 2786 (1993).

Davies, D. (1997, January). *Interviewing adolescent victims about sexual abuse*. Presentation at the San Diego Conference on Responding to Child Maltreatment, San Diego, CA.

Davis, S. L. (1998). Social and scientific influences on the study of children's suggestibility: A historical perspective. *Child Maltreatment, 3*, 186-194.

Davis, S. L., & Bottoms, B. L. (2002a). Effects of social support on children's eyewitness reports: A test of the underlying mechanism. *Law and Human Behavior, 26*, 185-215.

Davis, S. L., & Bottoms, B. L. (2002b). The effects of social support on the accuracy of children's reports: Implications for the forensic interview. In M. Eisen, J. A. Quas, & G. S. Goodman (Eds.), *Memory and suggestibility in the forensic interview* (pp. 437-458). Mahwah, NJ: Erlbaum.

DeLoache, J. (1995). The use of dolls in interviewing young children. In M. S. Zaragoza, J. R. Graham, G. C. N. Hall, R. Hirschman & Y. S. Ben-Porath (Eds.), *Memory and testimony in child witness* (pp. 160-178). Thousand Oaks, CA: Sage.

Dent, H. R. (1986). An experimental study of the effectiveness of different techniques of questioning mentally handicapped child witnesses. *British Journal of Clinical Psychology, 25*, 13-17.

Dillon, J. T. (1982). The effect of questions in education and other enterprises. *Journal of Curriculum Studies, 14*, 127-152.

Eisen, M., Quas, J. A., & Goodman, G. S. (2002). *Memory and suggestibility in the forensic interview*. Mahwah, NJ: Erlbaum.

Everson, M. (1997). Understanding bizarre, improbable, and fantastic elements in children's accounts of abuse. *Child Maltreatment, 2*, 134-149.

Everson, M., & Boat, B. (2002). The utility of anatomical dolls and drawings in child forensic interviews. In M. Eisen, J. A. Quas, & G. S. Goodman (Eds.), *Memory and suggestibility in the forensic interview* (pp. 383-408). Mahwah, NJ: Erlbaum.

Farrar, M. J., & Goodman, G. S. (1992). Developmental changes in event memory. *Child Development, 63*, 173-187.

Federal Rules of Evidence. (2000). Rules 601 and 801.

Fisher, R. P., & Geiselman, R. E. (1992). *Memory enhancing techniques for investigative interviewing: The cognitive interview*. Springfield, IL: Charles C. Thomas.

Fisher, R. P., Geiselman, R. E., & Raymond, D. S. (1987). Critical analysis for police interviewing techniques. *Journal of Police Science and Administration, 15*, 177-185.

Fivush, R. (1993). Developmental perspectives on autobiographical recall. In G. S. Goodman & B.L. Bottoms (Eds.), *Child victims, child witnesses: Understanding and improving children's testimony* (pp. 1-24). New York: Guilford.

Fontes, L. A. (Ed.) (1995). *Sexual abuse in nine North American cultures.* Thousand Oaks, CA: Sage.

Ganaway, G. (1989). Historical versus narrative truth: Clarifying the role of exogenous trauma in the etiology of MPD and its variants. *Dissociation, 2,* 205-220.

Garbarino, J. (1997, January). *Eliciting information from young children.* Presentation at the San Diego Conference on Responding to Child Maltreatment, San Diego, CA.

Goodman, G. S. (Ed.). (1984). The child witness [Special issue]. *Journal of Social Issues, 40*(2).

Goodman, G. S., & Bottoms, B. L. (Eds.) (1993). *Child victims, child witnesses: Understanding and improving testimony.* New York: Guilford.

Goodman, G. S., Bottoms, B. L., Redlich, A., Shaver, P. R., & Diviak, K. (1998). Correlates of multiple forms of victimization in religion-related child abuse cases. *Journal of Aggression, Maltreatment & Trauma, 2,* 273-295. Reprinted in B. B. R. Rossman & M. S. Rosenberg (Eds.) (1998). *Multiple victimization of children: Conceptual, developmental, research, and treatment issues* (pp. 273-295). Binghamton, NY: The Haworth Press, Inc.

Goodman, G. S., Bottoms, B. L., Rudy, L., & Schwartz-Kenney, B. M. (1991). Children's testimony about a stressful event: Improving children's reports. *Journal of Narrative and Life History, 1,* 69-99.

Goodman, G. S., Quas, J. A., Batterman-Faunce, J. M., Riddlesberger, M. M., & Kuhn, G. (1994). Predictors of accurate and inaccurate memories of traumatic events experienced in childhood. *Consciousness and Cognition, 3,* 269-294.

Goodman, G. S., Quas, J. A., Batterman-Faunce, J. M., Riddlesberger, M. M., & Kuhn, G. (1997). Children's reactions to and memory for a stressful event: Influences of age, anatomical dolls, knowledge, and parental attachment. *Applied Developmental Science, 1,* 54-75.

Goodman, G. S., Quas, J. A., Bottoms, B. L., Qin, J. J., Shaver, P. R., Orcutt, H., et al. (1997). Children's religious knowledge: Implications for understanding allegations of satanic ritual abuse. *Child Abuse and Neglect, 16,* 1111-1130.

Goodman, G. S., & Schwartz-Kenney, B. M. (1992). Why knowing a child's age is not enough: Effects of cognitive, social, and emotional factors on children's testimony. In R. Flin & H. Dent (Eds.), *Children as witnesses* (pp. 15-32). London: Wiley.

Goodman, G. S., Taub, E. P., Jones, D. P., England, P., Port, L. K., Rudy, L., et al. (1992). Testifying in criminal court. *Monographs of the Society for Research in Child Development, 57*(5, Serial No. 229).

Heckler, S. (Ed.). (1994). Facilitated communication [Special issue]. *Child Abuse and Neglect, 18*(6), 495-540.

Hewitt, S. (1997, January). *Developmentally specific strategies for assessing child abuse allegations involving very young children: 18-36 months (I & II).* Presentation at the San Diego Conference on Responding to Child Maltreatment, San Diego, CA.

Hiltz, B., & Bauer, G. (2003). Drawings in forensic interviews of children. *APRI Update, 16*(3), pp. 1-2.

Holmes, L., & Vieth, V. (2003). Finding words/Half a nation: The forensic training program of CornerHouse and the APRI's National Center for Prosecution of Child Abuse. *APSAC Advisor 15*(1), 4-8.

Illinois v. Spencer, 457 N.E. 2d 473 (Ill. App. Ct. 1983).

Jacobson, J. W., Mulick, J. A., & Schwartz, A. A. (1995). A history of facilitated communication. *American Psychologist, 50*, 750-765.

Johnson, C. F. (1996). Physical abuse: Accidental versus international trauma in children. In J. Briere, L. Berliner, J. A. Bulkley, C. Jenny, & T. Reid (Eds.), *The APSAC handbook on child maltreatment* (pp. 206-226). Thousand Oaks, CA: Sage.

Johnson, N. F. (1972). Organization and the concept of a memory code. In A. Melton & E. Martin (Eds.), *Coding processes in human memory* (pp. 125-159). Washington, DC: Winston.

Kail, R. (1990). *The development of memory in children.* New York: Freeman.

Kebbell, M. R., & Hatton, C. (1999). People with mental retardation as witnesses in court: A review. *Mental Retardation, 37*, 179-187.

Koocher, G. P., Goodman, G. S., White, C. S., Friedrich, W. N., Sivan, A. B., & Reynolds, C. R. (1995). Psychological science and the use of anatomically detailed dolls in child sexual-abuse assessments. *Psychological Bulletin, 118*, 199-222.

Lanning, K. V. (1989). *Child sex rings: A behavioral analysis.* Arlington, VA: National Center for Missing and Exploited Children.

Lanning, K. V. (1991). Ritual abuse: A law enforcement view or perspective. *Child Abuse and Neglect, 15*, 171-173.

Lanning, K. V. (1992). *Investigator's guide to allegations of ritual child abuse.* Quantico, VA: National Center for the Analysis of Violent Crime, FBI Academy.

Leichtman, M. D., & Morse, M. B. (1997, April). Individual differences in preschoolers' suggestibility: Identifying the source. In J. A. Quas & G. S. Goodman (Chairs), *Individual differences in children's memory and suggestibility: New research findings and directions.* Symposium conducted at the biennial meeting of the Society for Research in Child Development, Washington, DC.

Lieb, R., Berliner, L., & Toth, P. (1997). *Protocols and training standards: Investigating allegations of child sexual abuse.* Olympia, WA: Washington State Institute of Public Policy, The Evergreen State College.

Loftus, E. F. (1992). The reality of repressed memories. *American Psychologist, 48*, 518-537.

Lyon, T. D. (1996, Spring). Assessing children's competence to take the oath: Research and recommendations. *APSAC Advisor, 9*(1), 1-7.

Lyon, T. D. (2002a). Child witnesses and the oath. In H. L. Westcott, G. Davies, & R. H. C. Bull (Eds.), *Children's testimony: A handbook of psychological research and forensic practice* (pp. 245–260). West Sussex, England: Wiley.

Lyon, T. D. (2002b). Scientific support for expert testimony on child sexual abuse accommodation. In J. R. Conte (Ed.), *Critical issues in child sexual abuse* (pp. 107-138). Newbury Park, CA: Sage.

Markman, E. M. (1979). Realizing that you don't understand: Elementary school children's awareness of inconsistencies. *Child Development, 50*, 643-655.

Merritt, K. A., Ornstein, P. A., & Spicker, B. (1994). Children's memory for a salient medical procedure: Implications for testimony. *Pediatrics, 94*, 17-23.

Miranda v. Arizona, 384 U.S. 436, 86S. Ct. 1602, 16L. Ed. 2nd 694 (1966).

Myers, J. E. B., Saywitz, K. J., & Goodman, G. S. (1996). Psychological research on children as witnesses: Practical implications for forensic interviews and courtroom testimony. *Pacific Law Journal, 28*, 3-91.

Myers, J. E. B., Berliner, L., Briere, J., Hendrix, C., Terry Jenny, C., & Reid T. A. (Eds.) (2002). *APSAC handbook on child maltreatment* (2nd ed.). Thousand Oaks, CA: Sage.

Orbach, Y., Hershkowitz, I., Lamb, M. E., Sternberg, K. J., Esplin, P. W., & Horowitz, D. (2000). Assessing the value of structured protocols for forensic interviews of alleged child abuse victims. *Child Abuse and Neglect, 24*, 733-752.

Pence, D., & Wilson, C. (1994). *Team investigation of child sexual abuse: The uneasy alliance*. Newbury Park, CA: Sage.

People v. Karelse, 143 Mich. App. 712 (1985).

Perry, N. W., McAuliff, B. D., Tam, P., & Claycomb, L. (1995). When lawyers question children: Is justice served? *Law and Human Behavior, 19*, 609-629.

Peterson, C., & Biggs, M. (1997). Interviewing children about trauma: Problems with "specific" questions. *Journal of Traumatic Stress, 10*, 279-290.

Pezdek, K., & Taylor, J. (2002). Memory for traumatic events in children and adults. In M. Eisen, J. A. Quas, & G. S. Goodman (Eds.), *Memory and suggestibility in the forensic interview* (pp. 165-184). Mahwah, NJ: Erlbaum.

Pipe, M. E., Lamb, M., Orbach, Y., & Cedarborg, A. C. (Eds.) (in press). *Child sexual abuse: Disclosure, delay and denial*. Mahwah, NJ: Erlbaum.

Poole, D. A., & Lamb, M. E. (1998). *Investigative interviews of children: A guide for helping professions*. Washington, DC: American Psychological Association.

Pynoos, R., & Eth, S. (1984). The child as witness to homicide. *Journal of Social Issues, 40*, 87-108.

Quas, J. A., Goodman, G. S., Ghetti, S., & Redlich, A. D. (2000). Questioning the child witness: What can we conclude from the research thus far? *Trauma, Violence, & Abuse, 1*, 223-249.

Reppucci, N. D. (1985). Psychology in the public interest. In A. M. Rogers & C. J. Scheirer (Eds.), *The G. Stanley Hall lecture series* (vol. 5, pp. 121-156). Washington, DC: American Psychological Association.

Rosenberg, D. (1987). Web of deceit: A literature review of Munchausen Syndrome by Proxy. *Child Abuse and Neglect, 11*, 547-563.

Runyan, D. K. (1993). The emotional impact of societal intervention into child abuse. In G. S. Goodman & B. L. Bottoms (Eds.), *Child victims, child witnesses: Understanding and improving children's testimony* (pp. 263-277). New York: Guilford.

Saywitz K. J. (1995). Improving children's testimony: The question, the answer, and the environment. In M. S. Zaragoza, J. R. Graham, G. C. N. Hall, R. Hirschman, & Y. S. Ben-Porath (Eds.), *Memory and testimony in the child witness* (pp. 113-140). Thousand Oaks, CA: Sage.

Saywitz, K., Goodman, G. S., & Lyon, T. (2002). Interviewing children in and out of court: Current research and practice implications. In J. E. B. Myers, L. Berliner, J. Briere, C. T. Hendrix, C. Jenny & T. A. Reid (Eds.), *APSAC handbook on child maltreatment* (2nd ed., pp. 349-378). Thousand Oaks, CA: Sage.

Saywitz, K., Goodman, G. S., Nicholas, E., & Moan, S. (1991). Children's memories of physical examinations involving genital touch: Implications for reports of child sexual abuse. *Journal of Consulting and Clinical Psychology, 59,* 682-691.

Saywitz, K. J., & Lyon, T. (2002). Coming to grips with children's suggestibility. In M. Eisen, J. A. Quas & G. S. Goodman (Eds.), *Memory and suggestibility in the forensic interview* (pp. 85–114). Mahwah, NJ: Erlbaum.

Saywitz, K. J., & Snyder, L. (1993). Improving children's testimony with preparation. In G. S. Goodman & B. L. Bottoms (Eds.), *Child victims, child witnesses: Understanding and improving children's testimony* (pp. 147-168). New York: Guilford.

Seidman, R. R. (2000). *The memory of female witnesses with mild mental retardation: Implications for reports of sexual abuse.* Unpublished doctoral dissertation, University of Illinois at Chicago.

Shaw, J., Garven, S., & Wood, J. M. (1997). Co-witness information can have immediate effects on eyewitness memory reports. *Law and Human Behavior, 21,* 503-523.

Shepherd, J. R., Dworin, B., Farley, R. H., Russ, B. J., & Tressler, P. W. (1992). *Child abuse and exploitation: Investigative techniques* (2nd ed.). Glynco, GA: Department of the Treasury, Federal Law Enforcement Training Center.

Sternberg, K. J., Lamb, M.E., Esplin, P. W., Orbach, Y., & Hershkowitz, I. (2002). Using a structured interview protocol to improve the quality of investigative interviews. In M. Eisen, J. A. Quas & G. S. Goodman (Eds.), *Memory and suggestibility in the forensic interview* (pp. 409-436). Mahwah, NJ: Erlbaum.

Sternberg, K. J., Lamb, M.E., Orbach, Y., Esplin, P.W., & Mitchell, S. (2001). Use of a structured investigative protocol enhances young children's responses to free recall prompts in the course of forensic interviews. *Journal of Applied Psychology, 86(5),* 997-1005.

Tharinger, D., Horton, C. B., & Millea, S. (1990). Sexual abuse and exploitation of children and adults with mental retardation and other handicaps. *Child Abuse and Neglect, 14,* 301-312.

Verdugo, M. A., Bermejo, B. G., & Fuertes, J. (1995). The maltreatment of intellectually handicapped children and adolescents. *Child Abuse and Neglect, 19,* 205-215.

Vieth, V. (2006). Unto the third generation: A call to end child abuse in the United States within 120 years. *Journal of Aggression, Maltreatment & Trauma, 12(3/4).*

Walker, A. G. (1994). *Handbook on questioning children: A linguistic perspective.* Washington, DC: American Bar Association Center on Children and the Law.

Weir, I. K., & Wheatcroft, M. S. (1995). Allegations of children's involvement in ritual sexual abuse: Clinical experience of 20 cases. *Child Abuse and Neglect, 19,* 491-505.

Westcott, H. L., Davies, G. M., & Bull, R. H. C. (2002). *Children's testimony: A handbook of psychological research and forensic practice.* West Sussex, England: Wiley.

Whipple, G. M. (1911). The psychology of testimony. *Psychological Bulletin, 8,* 307-309.

Whitehurst, G. J. (1982). Language development. In B. B. Wolman & G. Stricker (Eds.), *Handbook of developmental psychology* (pp. 367-386). Englewood Cliffs, NJ: Prentice-Hall.

Wrightsman, L. S., Greene, E., Nietzal, M. T., & Fortune, W. H. (2002). *Psychology and the legal system* (5th ed.). Pacific Grove, CA: Brooks/Cole.
Yuille, J., Hunter, R., Joffe, R., & Zaparniuk, J. (1993). Interviewing children in sexual abuse cases. In G. S. Goodman & B. L. Bottoms (Eds.), *Child victims, child witnesses: Understanding and improving children's testimony* (pp. 95-116). New York: Guilford.

APPENDIX

Other Useful References Not Cited Above

American Psychological Association. (1996). *Guidelines for child protection evaluations*. Washington, DC: Author.
Bottoms, B. L., & Goodman, G. S. (Eds.) (1996). *International perspectives on child abuse and children's testimony: Psychological research and the law*. Newbury Park, CA: Sage.
Dent, H., & Flin, R. (Eds.) (1992). *Children as witnesses*. Chichester, England: John Wiley.
Faller, K. C. (1996). *Evaluating children suspected of having been sexually abused*. Thousand Oaks, CA: Sage.
Fisher, R. P., & Geiselman, R. E. (1992). *Memory-enhancing techniques for investigative interviewing: The cognitive interview*. Springfield, IL: Charles E. Thomas.
Fivush, R., & Hudson, J. (Eds.) (1990). *Knowing and remembering in young children*. New York: Cambridge University Press.
Goodman, G. S., & Bottoms, B. L. (1993). *Child victims/child witnesses: Understanding and improving testimony*. New York: Guilford.
Gray, E. (1993). *Unequal justice: The prosecution of child sexual abuse*. New York: The Free Press.
Lanning, K. V. (1992). *Investigator's guide to allegations of ritual child abuse*. Quantico, VA: National Center for the Analysis of Violent Crime, FBI Academy.
McGough, L. S. (1994). *Child witnesses: Frail voices in the American legal system*. New Haven, CT: Yale University Press.
Melton, G. B. (1987). *Reforming the law: Impact of child development research*. New York: Guilford.
Morgan, M. (1995). *How to interview sexual abuse victims*. Newbury Park, CA: Sage.
Myers, J. E. B. (1992). *Legal issues in child abuse and neglect*. Newbury Park, CA: Sage.
Myers, J. E. B. (1992/1994). *Evidence in child abuse and neglect* (Vols I & II). New York: Wiley.

Myers, J. E. B. (1994). *The backlash: Child protection under fire*. Thousand Oaks, CA: Sage.

National Center for the Prosecution of Child Abuse. (1993). *Investigation and prosecution of child abuse* (2nd ed.). Arlington, VA: American Prosecutors Research Institute.

Perry, N. W., & Wrightsman, L. (1991). *The child witness: Legal issues and dilemmas*. Newbury Park, CA: Sage.

Spencer, J. R., & Flin (1990). *The evidence of children: The law and the psychology*. London: Blackstone.

Whitcomb, D. (1992). *When the child is a victim* (2nd ed.). Washington DC: U.S. Government Printing Office.

Wilson, C., & Pence, D. (1994). *Team investigation of child abuse: An uneasy alliance*. Thousand Oaks, CA: Sage.

Zaragoza, M., Graham, J., Hall, G., Hirschman, R., & Ben-Porath, Y. S. (Eds.) (1995). *Memory and testimony in the child witness*. Newbury Park, CA: Sage.

Children First:
National Model for the Vertical Prosecution
of Cases Involving Murdered and Physically
Abused Children

David M. Williams

SUMMARY. Investigations and prosecutions involving murdered and physically abused children are among the most serious and most complex faced by law enforcement professionals. These cases are complicated on legal, factual, medical, and scientific levels. Oftentimes, the evidence against the suspected perpetrator is solely circumstantial. Many of the problems inherent in these investigations can be overcome by prioritizing these cases. The local prosecutor's office can take the

Address correspondence to: David M. Williams, JD, 1001 North Paulina, Chicago, IL 60622.

The author would like to thank the following professionals in the area of child abuse investigation, treatment, and prosecution, whose conversation and discussion has been invaluable as he wrote this paper: Dr. Nancy Jones, Cook County Medical Examiner's Office; Dr. Jill Glick, University of Chicago; Dr. Demetra Sotor, Cook County Children's Hospital; Tem Williams and Mark Williams; Brian Killacky, former Chicago Police Detective, current investigator with the Cook County State's Attorney's Office; and Cook County Assistant State's Attorneys Robert Robertson, Alison Perona, and Scott Cassidy.

[Haworth co-indexing entry note]: "Children First: National Model for the Vertical Prosecution of Cases Involving Murdered and Physically Abused Children." Williams, David M. Co-published simultaneously in *Journal of Aggression, Maltreatment & Trauma* (The Haworth Maltreatment & Trauma Press, an imprint of The Haworth Press, Inc.) Vol. 12, No. 3/4, 2006; and: *Ending Child Abuse: New Efforts in Prevention, Investigation, and Training* (ed: Victor I. Vieth, Bette L. Bottoms, and Alison R. Perona) The Haworth Maltreatment & Trauma Press, an imprint of The Haworth Press, Inc., 2006. Single or multiple copies of this article are available for a fee from The Haworth Document Delivery Service [1-800-HAWORTH, 9:00 a.m. - 5:00 p.m. (EST). E-mail address: docdelivery@haworthpress.com].

Available online at http://www.haworthpress.com/web/JAMT
doi:10.1300/J146v12n03_05

lead in ensuring justice by direct participation in the investigative phase and by ensuring continuity in the prosecution. In this article, I outline a model to ensure that this happens. *[Article copies available for a fee from The Haworth Document Delivery Service: 1-800-HAWORTH. E-mail address: <docdelivery@haworthpress.com> Website: <http://www.HaworthPress.com> © 2006 by The Haworth Press, Inc. All rights reserved.]*

KEYWORDS. Prosecutor, child murder, child physical abuse, team

Too often, there is no one to speak for abused children who, because of their physical or developmental age, cannot advocate for themselves. Child maltreatment statistics are staggering. Each year an estimated one million violent crimes involving child victims are reported to the police; another 1.1 million cases of child abuse are substantiated by child protection agencies (Kilpatrick & Saunders, 1997). Of the 22.3 million adolescents aged 12 to 17, approximately 3.9 million reported having been victims of a serious physical assault. Society often has difficulty believing that those responsible for the health and safety of children, especially parents, are capable of such brutality (North Carolina Child Advocacy Institute, 2000). Statistics prove otherwise. Every year, nearly 1,200 children and youth are murdered by caretakers–most of the victims are 5 years old or younger (U.S. Department of Justice, 1994). In fact, it is more likely that a female will be murdered before the age of one than at any other time in her life (Scarnberg, 2002). Very few criminal acts are more horrible than the murder of infants. Very few criminal acts are also more difficult to prove.

Justice for murdered and abused children can be scarce. Resources are scant. Budgets have been slashed; programs have been combined; emphasis has shifted to contemporary "hot button" topics (e.g., homeland security and financial identity theft). Witnesses are few. Often, the murderer is the sole witness to the crime. These cases are further complicated on legal, factual, and interpersonal levels because the victim and the offender often share a familial relationship (Finkelhor & Ormrod, 1999). Family members, who may be witnesses to prior incidents or are knowledgeable regarding the family's social history, are usually reluctant to get involved with law enforcement or unwilling to "betray" the family. Corroborating physical evidence is often lacking. Frequently, the crime scene is not quickly identified or adequately preserved, resulting in the loss (or potential contamination) of physical evidence. The expert opinion as to manner or cause of death is often subjective, relying on extrinsic evidence and rarely establishing the identity (or intent) of the perpetrator(s). As a result, investigations languish and prosecutions are hampered. And if cases make it in front of a jury, prosecutors face the daunting task of persuading judges and jurors that loving and otherwise law-abiding caregivers beat, shake, and starve their children to death (North Carolina Children's Advocacy Institute, 2000).

All too often, the justice system is also bogged down in political and bureaucratic quagmires. Turf battles (e.g., responsibilities, control) between law enforcement agencies often interfere with the efficient and successful investigation of these cases (Vieth, 1998). Overcoming all these obstacles and conflicts is paramount in finding a more efficient and effective path to the truth. Lines of communication between the evidence gatherers and the evidence interpreters must be opened and maintained. It is equally important to build trust and respect among prosecutors, investigators, doctors, and social workers, recognizing the importance of each other's contributions. Because prosecution is the culmination of a successful investigation, it is incumbent upon the prosecutor to provide this forum and develop this coordination. Yet many prosecutorial models lack a unified approach to prosecution. Most prosecuting offices employ a traditional approach that can be described as assembly-line justice: one prosecutor handles a case at the charging stage; a second prosecutor procures the indictment; and a third prosecutor is assigned as the trial attorney. This revolving door of prosecutors, although effective for most of the caseload, is ineffective in handling these complicated cases. Complex cases demand continuity, prioritization, and specialization. Vertical prosecution can meet these demands.

"Vertical prosecution" means a unified approach to a case–both in philosophy and in personnel. Oftentimes, the same prosecutor handles the case throughout the legal process (San Diego Regional Child Victim-Witness Task Force, 1991). Vertical prosecution is not a new concept. This procedure is already in use across the country to handle a variety of complex criminal cases that include murders, sexual assaults, and gang crimes. In contrast to roles in traditional prosecution models (where the prosecutor becomes involved at or after the charging decision), vertical prosecutors become active in a case at its inception. A vertical prosecutor who is trained and experienced in the specific subject matter can identify problems, coordinate efforts, and facilitate interaction between various agencies throughout the pendancy of the case.

Prosecutors, doctors, investigators, social workers, educators, and the community must give greater priority to child abuse cases. A national survey of prosecutors found that of all cases, child abuse and adult sexual assault required the most time and resources (U.S. Department of Justice, 1999). In many prosecuting offices, adult sexual assault cases have received priority because dedicated units have been created for vertical prosecution, but the murders of children have not been specifically addressed in this fashion. This can be accomplished by creating a specialized unit of prosecutors: the Child Victim Unit (CVU).

In the remainder of this article, I outline the goals and mission of the CVU. Clearly defining the CVU's responsibilities and case acceptance policy will ensure the integrity of the CVU's focus and specialization. In addition to traditional prosecutorial functions, the prosecutors assigned to the CVU are charged with the duty of building relationships among the victims, witnesses, and others (e.g., investigators, doctors, nurses, teachers, clergy, social workers, psychologists) involved in the protection of our children. The prosecutors in the CVU are managers of a system that coordinates the disciplines and facilitates communication in a combined effort to protect our children, educate the community, and reduce the incidents of physical abuse against our youth (Vieth, this volume).

CHANGING THE ROLE OF THE PROSECUTOR

The Requirements of the Prosecutor and the Prosecutorial Team

To increase the likelihood of success in these difficult cases, prosecuting agencies must develop specially trained prosecutors specifically for these cases (Delany-Shabazz & Vieth, 2001). They should be well versed in the technical legal issues and trained to understand complicated psychological and medical issues. They must develop specialized interpersonal skills to handle the intricate familial relationships involved in these cases, as well as be able to work with child witnesses.

The prosecutor's training in the handling of child victim cases should include developing a specialized body of legal knowledge. Child victim cases require more extensive knowledge of certain areas of the law to ensure effective prosecution. First, child victim cases often require expert testimony and knowledge of the corresponding law. Second, these cases utilize specialized evidentiary law such as the hearsay exceptions for the outcries of child victims, the limited use of prior consistent statements, and the introduction into evidence of statements made to medical personnel in the course of treatment. Third, these cases often deal with the difficult interplay between the charge of murder and lesser-included offenses, such as involuntary manslaughter–issues that take considerable resources to defeat.

In the course of the investigation, once the cause of death is ascertained and the identity of the alleged perpetrator is established, the intent of the offender must be determined to decide whether or not criminal charges are warranted. Determining the appropriate charge(s) within existing statutes can be difficult. The key issue is whether the requisite mental state that is required to establish criminal culpability can be proven beyond a reasonable doubt. A defendant's mental state at the time a criminal act was committed is often difficult to prove, especially in child maltreatment or fatality cases (Vieth, this volume). Common defenses that eliminate or reduce criminal intent include accident, natural causes, emotional or mental illness, lack of knowledge that the behavior in question would be harmful or dangerous, or that someone else was responsible. The prosecutor must analyze the totality of the circumstances and facts surrounding a particular case. This includes determining the credibility of witnesses and offender, the evaluation of any corroborating physical or circumstantial evidence, and the consideration of expert opinion. Child victim cases also require a specialized body of medical and psychological knowledge. Violent child abuse cases require an understanding of the physical and the psychological development of children. The medical testimony in these cases is crucial to the success of the prosecution. Medical testimony may be the only direct evidence presented by the prosecution. The need for specialized knowledge extends beyond the case-in-chief and involves battling defense-oriented expert testimony that attempts to explain, excuse, or justify a defendant's actions.

Prosecutors and members of the prosecution team assigned to handle cases involving child victims and witnesses should have more in-depth training in forensic interviewing, child development, identification of abuse-related injuries, emotional and psychological impact of abuse, as well as the legal issues related to child victims and witnesses (U.S. Department of Justice, 1999). The specialized training should include a familiarity with the social service agencies that work with children. Prosecutors should also receive training on medical conditions that can be mistaken for signs of neglect or maltreatment. This training will help facilitate a better understanding of the medical and social service community in general, which, in turn, should make it easier to incorporate them into the prosecution.

Child maltreatment cases are often made more complex due to the fact that the victims or other children are necessary witnesses. Prosecutors should be experienced and have specialized training in interviewing and preparing children (who may be inarticulate and/or reluctant) for court (American Prosecutors Research Institute, 2003). The developmental stages and needs of child victims and witnesses must be recognized to ensure they are treated with sensitivity throughout the investigative and trial process (U.S. Department of Justice, 1999). As detailed in the article by Perona, Bottoms, and Sorenson (this volume), prosecutors must speak to the children in their language and make them comfortable in court. To increase their comfort level, tours and mock trials could be staged (McAuliff & Kovera, 2002). These child-sensitive techniques will help ensure that child witnesses are protected from being further traumatized by the court system and that their testimony has maximum impact. That is, children can be harmed not only as a result of maltreatment but also from systematically insensitive procedures used to address reported maltreatment, such as a particularly insensitive interview process (Kolbo & Strong, 1997). They need to be treated with compassion and professionalism by criminal justice personnel from the first response to the crime throughout the prosecution process (U.S. Department of Justice, 1999).

Early and continued involvement by the prosecutor is important during the interviews of witnesses. There is extensive research on the interviewing of child witnesses that give investigators guidance as to legally and scientifically sound interviewing techniques (Perona, Bottoms, & Sorenson, this volume). Protocol should be followed to gather as much accurate information as is possible (Sternberg, Lamb, Orbach, Esplin, & Mitchell, 2001). Inappropriate interview techniques can compromise and contaminate children's testimony (Bruck, 1999). The prosecutors and investigators need to discuss and agree upon the manner in which the interviews are to be conducted and the method by which they will be recorded (Cook County Task Force on Intake and Interviewing, 1996).

A trained investigator or prosecutor will also have specialized knowledge in the interrogation of a suspected child abuser. There are important factors to draw out in an interview, such as the disparity in size between the victim and the suspect, the instrument used to inflict the injury, past abuse and its frequency, history of relationship, and the stated "reason" for the abusive actions, all of which will be important when the case is in court.

The prosecutor who is involved early in a case will also have the opportunity to develop a legal strategy for the case and a plan for anticipating and meeting defenses from the outset of the case. The prosecutor can assist with preparing warrants or interviewing witnesses and ensure that the collection and preservation of evidence is conducted in a manner required by law, so that the evidence will be admissible at trial (Vieth, this volume). There should also be agreement concerning the collection, preservation, and scientific analysis of physical evidence. Special consideration should be given to the collection of evidence that may be later needed and submitted for scientific testing (American Prosecutor's Research Institute, 2003).

These delicate and complex cases need the continuity provided by the same prosecutor, investigator, and victim-witness specialist. Lack of continuity can adversely impact the presentation of the case. Revolving prosecutors may have an inadequate understanding of the history of the case or of the child's family dynamics. This incomplete perspective often results in shifting legal theories or inaccurate analysis. A less-experienced prosecutor who lacks an intimate knowledge of the case may incorrectly assess the case as a lesser offense, such as second-degree murder, involuntary manslaughter, or reckless homicide. Strategically, one prosecutor may feel a child witness (victim or non-victim) is competent to testify while another may feel the witness cannot testify and file hearsay exception motions. These differences in approach may unnecessarily split the focus of the prosecution, and in some cases, convey to the judge inaccurately that there are evidentiary problems with the case. Both scenarios inevitably diminish the chances of a conviction. Vertical prosecution has proven an effective tool in combating these (and related) problems.

The prosecutor should ensure that cases involving child victims and witnesses receive priority and are handled as expeditiously as possible, minimizing unnecessary delays. The combination of case complexity, expert testimony, technical legal issues, reluctant defense attorneys, and numerous pre-trial motions all contribute to delaying disposition of these cases. A child abuse homicide case may have as many as 30 to 40 witnesses in the prosecution's case alone: law enforcement, medical personnel, forensic scientists, civilian witnesses who are unfamiliar with the criminal process and court, family members and friends of the victim and defendant who are reluctant to testify and may need convincing of the importance of their testimony, and child witnesses who are afraid and inarticulate. The longer these cases are delayed, the greater the potential for an adverse and long-term psychological impact on the victims and their families. As these cases often involve familial relationships, there is a higher likelihood that, in time, pressure will be exerted on the victims and their family members to change their testimony. Furthermore, children, like most other witnesses, testify more accurately when they testify closer in time to the offense (Perona, Bottoms, & Sorenson, this volume).

Expediting cases will also help minimize trauma to the child and the child's family, which is another goal prosecutors must strive for. Multiple, changing prosecutors threatens this goal. A change in prosecutors often breaks the lines of trust and communication with the witnesses and the family, factors that are understandably difficult to establish and often difficult to maintain in this type of victim-sensitive cases. Having multiple people deal with the children and their families over a long period of time will invariably result in a lack of trust in the justice system. Instead, the prosecutor must invest significant time with witnesses and victims to build trust and a strong relationship. The prosecutor should ensure that child victims and witnesses receive support services as they go through the criminal justice system. Failure to find prompt dispositions of child fatality cases may contribute to a poor outcome for the victim's family and the criminal justice system (North Carolina Child Advocacy Institute, 2000).

Finally, prosecutors are in the position to lead community efforts in re-affirming the value of our children. As advocates, prosecutors have the ability to prosecute offenders on a case-by-case basis. Their impact, however, can be far reaching. Prosecutors can effect changes in the development and application of laws by writing and lobbying for laws. New and improved laws could provide greater protection to children and allow prosecutors greater latitude in the use of evidence. Education efforts, both in prevention and in punishment, may reduce the incidence of child maltreatment. This, in turn, could affect societal perception of the important issues pertaining to physically abused and murdered children.

The Issues of Coordination with the Community and Other Agencies

The prosecutor should not impede the work of the other professionals involved in a case, but should actively participate in the coordination of efforts and the development of investigative and prosecutorial strategies. The process of gathering and preserving evidence, whether it is testimonial or physical, is crucial to the prosecutor's search for the truth and justice. Thus, the prosecutor should work with the police throughout the evidence gathering stage. The police can also rely on the prosecutor for legal research, arrest warrants, and search warrants. The prosecutor can then evaluate all the evidence to make decisions concerning how best to build a strategy to prove the case at trial or decide that the evidence is not sufficient to pursue criminal charges. To protect the innocent and punish the guilty, it is essential that all case facts are properly evaluated.

There must be continuity from the investigation through prosecution to ensure that guilty offenders are held accountable their actions. Without a CVU, the prosecution of offenders may suffer from the enormity of the extended criminal justice system. That is, frequently, a variety of agencies such as the local police department, child welfare, guardian's office, and/or other family court personnel will be involved in these types of cases. At times, there is a lack of communication between these various agencies and/or disputes over child protection issues, which hamper the effective prosecution of some offenders. In some situations, this lack of continuity prevents the prosecution of the most culpable offenders based on ever-evolving, yet uncommunicated factual information. The CVU would create and facilitate multi-disciplinary cooperation between various agencies and would lead to a higher percentage of successful prosecutions. Efforts to ensure coordination and continuity in these cases will not only enhance the relationship between the prosecutor and witnesses but also will increase the rapport with investigators and service providers. This methodology would create a team atmosphere in which all the participants would join together as a team with a unified goal. As each is an integral component of the prosecution team, each member consequently has a vested interest in the success of the outcome. All of the members of the team have particular responsibilities to the investigation and to their agencies. All parties should work together equally with the common goal of pursuing justice in these cases. This will be facilitated via bi-monthly meetings in a round table format to discuss investigations and to assign tasks to each member to ensure accountability and communication. Members should be available and immediately accessible to each other, similar to the child advocacy center model. Unlike many advocacy center models, the CVU prosecutor follows the case from the child advocacy center, into the courtroom, and throughout the criminal justice process.

A child's death presents unique challenges to prosecutors, doctors, and law enforcement. The available evidence is much different than that of the murder of an adult. The bodies of murdered adults usually bear obvious signs of violence such as gunshot or stab wounds (Hanson, 2000). A child who is murdered, especially an infant, may not have outward signs of injury and those injuries that do appear may be missed if doctors and investigators are not trained to understand the signs of child abuse (Parrish, 2002). In child homicide cases, emergency personnel often times have removed the victim or the defendant or other family members have "cleaned" the crime scene. Medical experts trained in forensics are crucial in reading these injuries in determining abuse. If misdiagnoses are made or suspicious injuries are not reported, the offender may not be held legally responsible for his or her actions. For example, it is very difficult to distinguish between SIDS and accidental or deliberate asphyxiation with a soft object (American Academy of Pediatrics, 2001). However, when using a multi-disciplinary approach that takes into account the case history of the child and family, it is easier to make a more accurate determination regarding the injuries and the circumstances surrounding them (American Academy of Pediatrics, 2001).

This expertise of prosecutors, investigators, and medical specialists goes beyond just the courtroom but extends into educating the public and medical employees to be aware of child abuse and develop proper techniques to ensure punishment of abusers. This includes training medical professionals to recognize the signs and injuries often associated with child abuse, how to treat these injuries, and how to document these injuries, which includes photographs. The medical community is an integral part of the prosecution team and is of crucial importance. Often times, many of these cases would go unreported if not for hospital employees, ambulance drivers, emergency medical technicians, social workers, nurses, and protective services. The expert testimony from emergency room doctors, treating physicians, forensic pediatrics, medical examiners, and other expert doctors in areas from burns to bone fractures is often the critical factor in proving the case. Early recognition, treatment, and documentation of children's injuries can save their lives.

In summary, prosecuting agencies must work hard to establish and maintain a procedural infrastructure in which prosecutors, the police, child welfare workers, doctors, medical examiners, and others involved in the investigation and the prosecution of child homicides work as a team. Working together, the prosecutor and the multidisciplinary team can evaluate the evidence, search for the truth, and find justice. The team can successfully fulfill the mission of protecting the innocent and punishing the guilty by understanding, collecting, and preserving evidence so that it can be analyzed by experts and used in the prosecution.

ESTABLISHING AN INVESTIGATIVE PROTOCOL

How, in practice, can a community establish its own CVU? The first step is establishing a protocol that specifies the role of all involved agencies. The protocol should be developed with the input of all the multidisciplinary professionals and should establish procedures and delineate responsibilities of all parties (Vieth, 1998). An initial meeting of all the parties should establish the advantages and disadvantages of forming a multidisciplinary team and set forth what each party can contribute (U.S. Department of Justice, 2000). The next meeting would focus on a mission statement that should set out the philosophical direction of the team, such as the one provided below. After this has been discussed, the team should then create a protocol, which is a working document that clearly delineates each team member's responsibilities, as well as establishes the structure and processes of the team (e.g., meetings, notifications, decision making). Uniform intake and procedural guidelines should be developed to ensure the integrity of each investigation and to ensure communication between agencies. The protocol should set forth conflict resolution procedures to minimize interagency disputes (U.S. Department of Justice, 2000).

Child advocacy centers are a great tool to be implemented with the Child Victim Unit, but the CVU is prosecutorial driven. The mission of the CVU is to investigate and prosecute these cases using a multi-disciplinary approach combined with vertical prosecution.

An example of a protocol is given next.

PROPOSED PROTOCOL FOR SPECIALIZED UNIT: MURDER AND PHYSICAL ABUSE OF CHILDREN UNDER THE AGE OF 13

Mission Statement

This Unit (herein referred to as the "Child Victim Unit" or "CVU") will strive to provide the most effective and efficient prosecution of offenders who intentionally inflict serious injuries upon children entrusted to their care. The Child Victim Unit will prosecute these offenders to the fullest extent under the law, while attempting to make the criminal justice system less traumatic and impersonal to the victims and their families who have suffered at the hands of these offenders.

Goals of the Child Victim Unit

The Child Victim Unit is designed to accomplish its mission by:

- Establishing and maintaining a multidisciplinary team approach by creating a cohesive infrastructure within the prosecutor's office and between related law enforcement and social service agencies to ensure that cases do not get lost in the system, that the innocent do not get punished, and that the guilty do not escape prosecution.
- Coordinating prosecution efforts and liaisons with child abuse teams at advocacy centers, local hospitals, and social service agencies.
- Establishing the best possible rapport with child victims and their families.
- Providing greater continuity for cases throughout the legal process. This would be accomplished through vertical prosecution: having the same prosecutor handle the case from overseeing the investigation through sentencing.
- Prosecuting cases as expeditiously as possible.
- Educating the community, child advocacy groups, and law enforcement agencies on criminal prosecution of child abuse.
- Proposing and lobbying for legislation to strengthen the prosecution of child abuse.
- Becoming national leaders and a resource center in the area of child abuse prosecutions.

Case Acceptance Policy

The criteria for the cases handled by the Child Victim Unit would be very specific. This would allow for the best allocation of limited prosecutorial resources to ensure the most efficient and effective prosecutions.

1. *The Victim:* The unit would handle only cases involving victims of a certain age. This would provide the unit with a focus for those victims who are in the greatest need of the specialization provided by the unit. The age requirement should be directed by the law of the jurisdiction. In the State of Illinois, for example, the statues set the age of 13 years or less as an element of particular crimes such as aggravated battery of a child. Thus, a CVU in Illinois would handle cases involving children 13 years of age or younger.

2. *The Crime:* The unit would prosecute only crimes involving physical abuse or gross maltreatment of a child. These offenses would include and would be specifically limited to the following:

    a. Murder
    b. Attempted Murder
    c. Aggravated Battery to a Child
    d. Heinous Battery
    e. Child Endangerment
    f. Long Term Abuse of a Dependent

3. *The Offender:* The unit would focus on cases in which the child was the target of intentional physical abuse and/or gross maltreatment by an individual who:

    a. Is an adult under the laws of the jurisdiction
    b. Has a relationship with the child in which the offender was responsible for the care or custody of the child, including but not limited to:
        i. Family member, such as natural father, mother, sibling, stepparent, etc.
        ii. Caretaker, including paramour, baby-sitter, camp leader, coach or other child care personnel.

4. Focusing the CVU on these types of cases would allow the resources of the Unit to be maximized toward the cases that are the most serious and, consequently, the most in need of additional time and attention.

Structure of the Proposed Unit

The CVU would handle cases currently assigned to prosecutors in regular felony trial courts. The proposed CVU could work within the normal felony trial division or be a part of a special prosecutions division.

Staffing. Initially, the Child Victim Unit is envisioned as being staffed by experienced prosecutors who would be primarily responsible for trying all of the cases. At some point, their work could be supplemented with less experienced prosecutors who could work in the CVU for a designated period of time as part of a rotation through the juvenile court system. This would allow young prosecutors exposure to the felony court system while allowing the trial prosecutors an opportunity to focus on preparing their cases for trial.

Additional Services. The CVU would be aided by internal support from the prosecutor's office internal investigative and victim support units. Designated victim/witness personnel and designated investigators, specially trained, would facilitate the progress of these cases through the legal system and ensure that victims and their cases are adequately served. This unit could also coordinate with a local child advocacy center for interviewing and/or supportive services. Therapeutic resources and other referrals would be provided upon request or via a needs assessment.

BARRIERS TO THE CREATION OF A CVU

The creation of a CVU may be impeded by several factors. There may be reluctance to share responsibilities and decision-making processes with other agencies. Some prosecutors are also reluctant to open up their internal processes by aligning themselves with investigators, medical personnel, and child protection services. To some, the team approach may appear to be a loss of control over the process, or an admission of prior failings. Some may fear breaches of confidentiality and lack the level of trust needed to establish partnerships. Some prosecutors fear that specialization is limitation; they might feel that the needs of their offices are best served by general practice prosecutors who can be deployed on a variety of cases. Contrary to these fears, however, the powers of the prosecutor's office are not ceded to affiliated agencies through a CVU. Nor are the powers of other agencies ceded to the prosecutor's office. Statutory duties and responsibilities are retained. As issues become more complex, greater flexibility is required of prosecutors, both at the investigative and prosecution stages. The establishment of a CVU is a case management strategy that enables prosecutors to fulfill their primary duty: the search for justice. Members of a CVU team must find ways to come together and build the trust necessary to allay fears that will preclude establishing a unit that could promote justice for children and their families.

FUNDING FOR THE PROPOSED UNIT

In many cases, the greatest impediment to the implementation of a CVU is a lack of funding. Prosecuting offices run on tight budgets and are constrained by the budgets of local and state governments. Despite the financial limitations of already strained budgets, sources of funds are available to support CVUs.

Ideally, this unit would be funded, in part or in whole, through state and federal grant money that is available for criminal justice programs that focus on prosecuting offenders in cases where the victims are children who have been physically abused. There are federal funds allocated to increase the number of communities working on developing a multidisciplinary team approach to child abuse (National Children's Alliance, 2003). Private institutions and corporations could be additional sources of funding. Matching grants from city and county sources could be obtained to assist in financing the Child Victim Unit. Community outreach efforts may also generate supportive funds. Cost could be minimized by borrowing or using the resources of local hospitals, child advocacy centers and social services, as well as resources already allocated to the prosecutor's office (office supplies, investigators, support staff, etc.).

CONCLUSION

The murder and severe physical abuse of children are among the most important cases handled by our criminal justice system. These cases deserve the highest priority. The influence of the prosecutor's office in these cases goes beyond the courtroom, reaching the medical establishment, advocacy groups, and the public at large. These complex cases demand an understanding of both technical medical evidence and legal issues. It is all of the prosecutor's responsibility to ensure that these cases are handled with compassion and understanding by appropriately trained attorneys.

Unfortunately, due to the constraints of an overburdened criminal justice system, these child victim cases do not currently receive the amount of time, resources, or attention needed. We, as prosecutors, need to take the lead in this area by creating specialized units that will efficiently and effectively prosecute these serious offenders and bring justice for our children and our community.

REFERENCES

American Academy of Pediatrics. (2001). Distinguishing sudden infant death syndrome from child abuse fatalities. *Pediatrics, 107*(2), 437-441.
American Prosecutors Research Institute. (2003). *Finding words: Half a nation by 2010: Interviewing children and preparing for court.* Alexandria, VA: Author.

Bruck, M. (1999). A summary of an affidavit prepared for the *Commonwealth of Massachusetts v. Cheryl Amirault Lefave. Applied Developmental Science, 3,* 110-127.

Cook County Task Force on Intake and Interviewing. (1996). *Cook County procedural manual for criminal child abuse intake and forensic interviewing for children's advocacy centers and victim sensitive intervention programs.* Chicago, IL: Author.

Delany-Shabazz, R., & Vieth, V. (2001, August). *OJJDP Fact Sheet #33.* Washington DC: The National Center for the Prosecution of Child Abuse.

Finkelhor, D., & Ormrod, R. (1999). *The homicides of children and youth.* Washington DC: U.S. Department of Justice.

Hanson, J. (2000, April 23). The forgotten children: Justice undone: Bungled investigations let killers off. *Atlanta Journal-Constitution,* p. A1.

Kilpatrick, D., & Saunders, B. (1997). *Prevalence and consequences of child victimization.* Washington DC: National Institute of Justice.

Kolbo, J., & Strong, E. (1997). Multidisciplinary team approaches to the investigation and resolution of child abuse and neglect: A national survey. *Child Maltreatment, 2,* 61-72.

McAuliff, B., & Kovera, M. (2002). The status of evidentiary and procedural innovations in child abuse proceedings. In B. Bottoms, M. Kovera, & B. McAuliff (Eds.), *Children, social science and the law* (pp. 412-445). Cambridge: Cambridge University Press.

National Children's Alliance. (2003). *Request for proposals: grants for the establishment and expansion of children's advocacy centers.* Washington DC: Author.

North Carolina Child Advocacy Institute. (2000). *Not invisible . . . in vain, child maltreatment fatalities: Guidelines for response.* Raleigh, NC: Author.

Perona, A., Bottoms, B. L., & Sorenson, E. (2006). Research-based guidelines for child forensic interviews. *Journal of Aggression, Maltreatment & Trauma, 12*(3/4).

San Diego Regional Child Victim-Witness Task Force. (1991). *Child victim-witness protocol.* San Diego, CA: Author.

Scarnberg, K. (2002, June 27). The quiet horror. *Chicago Tribune,* Tempo Section, p.1.

Sternberg, K., Lamb, M., Orbach, Y., Esplin, P., & Mitchell, S. (2001). Use of a structured investigative protocol enhances young children's responses to free-recall prompts in the course of forensic interviews. *Journal of Applied Psychology, 86*(5), 997-1005.

U.S. Department of Justice. (1994). *National assessment program survey results.* Washington, DC: Author.

U.S. Department of Justice. (1999). *Breaking the cycle of violence: Recommendations to improve the criminal justice response to child victims and witnesses.* Washington, DC: Author.

U.S. Department of Justice. (2000). *Children as victims.* Washington, DC: Author.

Vieth, V. (1998). In my neighbor's house: A proposal to address child abuse in rural America. *Hamline Law Review, 22,* 143.

Vieth, V. (2006). Unto the third generation: A call to end child abuse in America within 120 years. *Journal of Aggression, Maltreatment & Trauma, 12*(3/4).

APPENDIX

Other Useful References Not Cited Above

Alexander, R., & Kleinman, P. (1997). *Diagnostic imaging of child abuse.* Washington, DC: U.S. Department of Justice.

American College of Obstetricians and Gynecologists National Fetal and Infant Mortality Review and Child Fatality Review. (2000). *Fetal and infant mortality review and child fatality review: opportunities for local collaboration.* Washington, DC: U.S. Department of Health and Human Services.

American Prosecutors Research Institute. (1998). *Selected case law: Child homicide and physical abuse.* Arlington, VA: Author.

Bottoms, B., Kovera, M., & McAuliff, B. (2002). *Children, social science and the law.* Cambridge: Cambridge University Press.

DerOhannesian, P. *Legal and trial issues in child homicide.* Albany, NY: Office of the District Attorney.

Durfee, M., Durfree, D. T., & West, P. (2002). Child fatality review, an international movement. *Child Abuse and Neglect, 26,* 619-636.

Ells, M. (2000). *Forming a multidisciplinary team to investigate child abuse.* Washington, DC: U.S. Department of Justice.

Farley, R., & Reece, R. (1997). *Recognizing when a child's injury or illness is caused by abuse.* Washington, DC: U.S. Department of Justice.

Holmes, L., & Sellars, I. (1997). *A guide for child protective services, law enforcement, and county attorney's in Minnesota.* MN: Author.

National MCH Center for Child Death Review and Child Death Review Program Leaders and Advocates. (2003). *A child death review program manual: Strategies to better understand why children die and taking action to prevent child deaths.* Okemos, MI: Michigan Public Health Institute.

National Medicolegal Review Panel. (1997). *National guidelines for death investigations.* Washington, DC: U.S. Department of Justice.

National District Attorneys Association and the U.S. Department of Justice. (1998). *Memorandum of understanding between the National District Attorneys Association and the Department of Justice.* Washington, DC: Author.

Rosenberg, D. (1997). *Child neglect and Munchhausen syndrome by proxy.* Washington, DC: U.S. Department of Justice.

Runyan, D. K. (1993). The emotional impact of societal intervention into child abuse. In G. S. Goodman & B. L. Bottoms (Eds.), *Child victims, child witnesses: Understanding and improving children's testimony* (pp. 263-277). New York: Guilford.

Webster, R., Schnitzer, P., Jenny, C., Ewigman, B., & Alario, A. (2003). Child death review: The state of the nation. *American Journal of Preventive Medicine, 25*(1), 58-64.

U.S. Department of Justice. (2000). *Forming a multidisciplinary team to investigate child abuse*. Washington, DC: Author.

The Master of Arts in Child Advocacy:
A Contribution to an Emerging Discipline

Robert D. McCormick

SUMMARY. Recent heinous examples of child neglect and abuse in the State of New Jersey have called into question how public child welfare workers are trained. The author, in collaboration with the Division of Youth and Family Services (DYFS) and other experts in the field of child welfare, worked on the development of a new degree that would more appropriately educate these workers. This paper discusses the development of the Master of Arts of Child Advocacy and its optional Concentration in Public Child Welfare and offers its curriculum as an alternative to the Master of Arts of Social Work (MSW). Child Advocacy is also explored as a new and emerging discipline. *[Article copies available for a fee from The Haworth Document Delivery Service: 1-800-HAWORTH. E-mail address: <docdelivery@haworthpress.com> Website: <http://www.HaworthPress. com> © 2006 by The Haworth Press, Inc. All rights reserved.]*

Address correspondence to: Robert D. McCormick, PhD, Director, Center for Child Advocacy, Montclair State University, Montclair, NJ 07043.

The author extends his appreciation to an extraordinary faculty: Joseph Del Russo, Assistant Prosecutor for Sex Abuse Crimes in Passaic County, NJ; and Dr. Christine Baker, Clinical and Forensic Psychologist. The author would also like to thank Professor Francine Raguso for her significant work on the curriculum and her endless mentoring, and Joan Kanner, Program Assistant, whose dedication and commitment to all of us has been invaluable. Special appreciation to Victor Vieth for his many helpful suggestions on this article.

[Haworth co-indexing entry note]: "The Master of Arts in Child Advocacy: A Contribution to an Emerging Discipline." McCormick, Robert D. Co-published simultaneously in *Journal of Aggression, Maltreatment & Trauma* (The Haworth Maltreatment & Trauma Press, an imprint of The Haworth Press, Inc.) Vol. 12, No. 3/4, 2006; and: *Ending Child Abuse: New Efforts in Prevention, Investigation, and Training* (ed: Victor I. Vieth, Bette L. Bottoms, and Alison R. Perona) The Haworth Maltreatment & Trauma Press, an imprint of The Haworth Press, Inc., 2006. Single or multiple copies of this article are available for a fee from The Haworth Document Delivery Service [1-800-HAWORTH, 9:00 a.m. - 5:00 p.m. (EST). E-mail address: docdelivery@haworthpress.com].

doi:10.1300/J146v12n03_06

KEYWORDS. Child advocacy, public child welfare, Division of Youth and Family Services, Post-BA Certificate in Child Advocacy, Montclair State University

It is well documented that many undergraduate and graduate programs in the United States are not providing current and future law enforcement officers, social workers, psychologists, medical professionals, child protection attorneys, and other professionals with the skills necessary to handle cases of child protection competently.[1] Frontline child protection professionals are increasingly vocal in calling on universities to provide better training.[2]

In recognition of this fact, the United States Congress appropriated funds to create the National Child Protection Training Center (NCPTC).[3] A primary purpose of the NCPTC is to assist in developing and promoting model child protection curricula at institutions of higher education.[4] Good examples of such innovative curricula can be found at Montclair State University (MSU)[5] in New Jersey. To address the need for better child protection training at the undergraduate and graduate levels, MSU has implemented a series of educational innovations. First, the MSU faculty created an undergraduate concentration in child advocacy within its multidisciplinary Justice Studies major (it is also open to students from other majors). Second, MSU faculty members designated six courses for child protection professionals who are already in the field. Upon completion of the courses, professionals in the field receive a post-baccalaureate certificate in child advocacy. Finally, MSU faculty most recently developed a master's degree program in child advocacy to meet the needs of social workers and other professionals desiring a career primarily, if not exclusively, in the field of child protection.

In this paper, I provide an overview of each of these MSU curricula, in hopes it will prove useful as other universities revise or develop undergraduate and graduate courses in the field of child protection.

MONTCLAIR STATE UNIVERSITY: UNDERGRADUATE CONCENTRATION IN CHILD ADVOCACY

In 1999, MSU began offering a major in Justice Studies with concentrations in Paralegal Studies, Justice Systems and Child Advocacy.[6]

This latter concentration was designed to prepare students to advocate for children in a variety of settings. The program presently has over five hundred students and draws its resources from the participating departments of legal studies, sociology, and psychology.

POST-BA CERTIFICATE

The undergraduate program provided a platform from which to address the needs of professionals already in the field. Many of New Jersey's child protection professionals are employed by the Division of Youth and Family Services (DYFS). DYFS workers could have degrees in virtually any area of academic study. In 1999, there were no formal credentials or training programs in child advocacy in the State of New Jersey. With the help of experts in the field, a Post-BA Certificate in Child Advocacy was developed. This was the first professional credential in the state that recognized child advocacy as a field requiring specific training. The Division of Youth and Family Services funded this program and each certificate bore DYFS' imprimatur: "Approved by the Division of Youth and Family Services."

To earn the certificate, students must complete five courses: (a) Introduction to Child Advocacy, (b) Children and Justice, (c) Child Abuse and Neglect, (d) Interviewing Skills for the Child Advocate, and (e) Current Social Issues in Child Advocacy. The course offering of the Post-BA Certificate in Child Advocacy, similar to their undergraduate counterparts, were intended to reflect the multidisciplinary nature and content of the field itself. Experts in the field of child advocacy praised the program. The Director of the Division of Youth and Family Services hailed the program as "innovative, creative, and perfectly suited for DYFS workers." It is significant that MSU faculty worked closely with DYFS from the beginning. Student response to the certificate program was equally positive. In addition to providing child welfare professionals with appropriate content in courses that were relevant to what they did, the Post-BA Certificate "experience," that is, the relationship that developed between faculty and student, served to improve markedly the morale at work.[7]

In addition to covering full tuition, New Jersey's Division of Youth and Family Services allowed employees to leave work early on class days. There were also a number of non-DYFS child protection professionals enrolled in the program. The program allows seasoned DYFS workers to mix with newly minted graduate students. Students' backgrounds also differed remarkably with graduates from a myriad under-graduate majors and/or professional fields. This created a wonderful cross-pollination of the learning experience.

MASTER'S DEGREE IN CHILD ADVOCACY

In developing an undergraduate program and the post-BA certificate in child advocacy, it became clear that to work in the "system," it was necessary to collapse disciplinary boundaries. Child advocacy research makes it obvious that the field demands a multidisciplinary approach to child protection.[8]

It is within this philosophical perspective that Montclair State University developed its Master of Arts in Child Advocacy[9] along with its optional concentration in Public Child Welfare.[10] The process was a lengthy one. Nevertheless, the journey was rich in learning, the dialogue energizing and passionate, and the resulting degree relevant to what child advocates do.

While the post-BA certificate in child advocacy offered DYFS workers and others a unique opportunity to broaden their understanding of the public child welfare system, it also stimulated thinking among MSU faculty about a more academic degree. Presently, the most advanced degree for professionals working in the system is the Master of Social Work (MSW) degree. The post-BA certificate had proven that a program of study could be developed that would enhance the knowledge of DYFS workers. The faculty believed that a professional degree could be developed that would offer a curriculum optimally suited for the child protection worker. Therefore, the faculty embarked on developing a new degree for the field, the Master of Arts in Child Advocacy, with an optional concentration in public child welfare. This was designed to offer a viable, cost-efficient alternative to the MSW, one that would focus exclusively on the child welfare system, enabling graduates to begin work without the further training required of MSWs who begin work at DYFS upon graduation.

The first challenge facing MSU faculty was the absence of practical models for the concept of a graduate degree in child advocacy. In most states, the degree of choice for working in the Public Child Welfare system and other related fields within child advocacy is the MSW. While a perfectly fine degree, the faculty of Montclair State University observed subtle, and in some programs, not so subtle, shifts in the MSW curriculum. Over the past two decades, perhaps as a result of gaining licensure requirements,[11] many MSW programs appear to be less concerned with teaching students to work directly with families influenced by child abuse and neglect, poverty, and domestic violence, and more concerned with preparing students for private practice or administration. Although this might be a general trend, it appears to be particularly true in this region of the country where social workers often have lucrative private practices.

MSU faculty discussions with DYFS personnel confirmed there was a wide chasm between the education offered in an MSW program and the needs of the Division. Newly hired MSW graduates along with many entry-level employees had to be (re)trained. Not only was this costly for DYFS but it also delayed the use of these personnel until they were adequately educated. To address this situation, MSU sought to develop a program from which students would proceed seamlessly from classroom to actual work. To achieve this goal, MSU urged DYFS to participate actively in designing the curriculum. What follows is an outline of this process along with comments that allow the reader to understand what exactly this new MA contributes to the field of child advocacy.

FOCUS GROUPS

During the summer of 2002 the faculty of Montclair State University's Center for Child Advocacy ran focus groups to garner input regarding the potential content of a Master of Arts in Child Advocacy. The groups included experts in the field of child advocacy with an emphasis on public child welfare. Attorneys, DYFS workers at various levels of employment, Court Appointed Special Advocates (CASA), clinical psychologists, social workers, and sociologists all attended lengthy meetings, engaged in lively and productive dialogue and helped to frame this program.

CURRICULUM

Although some members of the focus groups identified child advocacy as essentially a field to help neglected and abused children, MSU adopted the view of the majority of the working group members for a more inclusive definition and developed a degree to reflect this view. The result was the development of the Master of Arts in Child Advocacy with an optional concentration in Public Child Welfare. MSU faculty concluded that the general MA would allow for the creation of additional "concentrations" or certificate programs under its aegis, while the Public Child Welfare Concentration would address specifically the educational needs of those working for DYFS, CASA, and similar agencies. Both state and national consultants praised the program. Barbara Bonner, an internationally respected expert in child advocacy, stated that the " . . . MA in Child Advocacy appears to represent an opportunity for MSU to not only provide a valuable academic experience for students in New Jersey, but to become a model program for other universities nationwide. . . . It is well designed, has superb faculty, and meets the state's need for highly trained personnel in the field of child welfare."[12]

The curriculum provides a unique learning experience for students. It combines both theoretical and applied components. Beyond a 33-credit course of study, students may elect to write a research thesis or take an additional class. To complement this more academic aspect of the program, students take either a Practicum in Child Advocacy or, in the Concentration in Public Child Welfare, both a Practicum and an Externship. Students receive experience in a myriad of settings including the Juvenile Justice System, CASA (Court Appointed Special Advocates), Residential Treatment Facilities, Child Advocacy Centers, and the Division of Youth and Family Services.

The curriculum reflects the multidisciplinary nature of child advocacy. Each and every course contains aspects of several disciplines that are necessary to ensure appropriate training. For example, in a course such as Interviewing Skills for the Child Advocate, students are taught how to perform a clinical interview with children (psychology) along with whatever restrictions may be placed on their interviewing (law). The curriculum is infused with this multidisciplinary perspective and each course has been crafted to reflect this approach, one that MSU faculty members believe best represents the field of child advocacy.

MASTER OF SOCIAL WORK VS. THE MASTER OF ARTS IN CHILD ADVOCACY

The MA in Child Advocacy is an alternative degree to the more familiar Master of Social Work degree. While the MSW is a recognized and relevant credential in the field of public child welfare, the MA in Child Advocacy offers at least four advantages.

First, the MA in Child Advocacy was developed directly with the individuals who know public child welfare best: DYFS workers, professional staff, CASA personnel, attorneys, and psychologists who work in the field. It is not a generic degree, but rather one that focuses specifically and exclusively on child advocacy.

Second, unlike most MSW degrees, the MA in Child Advocacy is a multidisciplinary program. The courses, the practicum, the externship, and the thesis adhere to this orientation.

Third, MSW curricula often reflect student interest in private practice. The MA in Child Advocacy focuses exclusively on relevant course content for those interested in working as child advocates within the public child welfare system. Developed by experts in the field, the content validity of the MA in Child Advocacy curriculum is high. Students graduating with this degree will need little, if any, on-the-job training.

Fourth, the MA in Child Advocacy provides direct and intense experience in the field through practicum and externship experiences. Both of these experiences are accompanied by on-site supervision and a weekly graduate class that offers additional off-site supervision.

THE FUTURE

Montclair State University has a broad view of child advocacy. Although the Concentration in Public Child Welfare is primarily focused on child abuse and neglect, it achieves this through a multidisciplinary and therefore a broad perspective. The Master of Arts in Child Advocacy allows for even broader definitions. In the future, MSU plans to offer additional concentrations and/or certificate programs in Special Education Advocacy, Parenting Advocacy, and other programs developed by it's Center for Child Advocacy[13] devoted to such topics as first-time fathers, parents of adolescents, or other topics that impact directly on the well-being of children.

CONCLUSION

It is necessary to raise the bar on educating the child advocate. The Master of Social Work, the present degree of choice in the field, covers too much academic material and lacks an exclusive focus on child advocacy. MSU's Master of Arts in Child Advocacy is not a degree for the private practitioner. It is for the individual who wishes to devote his/her professional career to working in the system. Often, new disciplines emerge from the mixture of old ones, such as psychology, which emerged in toward the end of the 19th century from philosophy, psychophysics, and physiology. The Master of Arts in Child Advocacy represents such a blending of disciplines. This degree offers professionals and students an innovative curriculum seen through a multidisciplinary template and a course of study more compatible with the work of the child advocate.

The Master of Arts in Child Advocacy validates child advocacy as an emerging discipline. Presently, most courses and/or programs in child advocacy are found in departments such as justice studies, sociology, and psychology. The faculty of MSU feels strongly that child advocacy represents a way of thinking about children that is unique. Although child advocacy courses may exist in psychology or sociology, for example, our faculty contends that the discipline-specific perspective of that particular field limits these courses. To be a child advocate implies a knowledge of many areas of inquiry and several domains of knowledge and, together, these form a whole much greater than the sum of their parts.

NOTES

1. *See* Victor Vieth, *Unto the Third Generation: A Call to End Child Abuse in the United States Within 120 Years*, (this volume) notes 35-43, 68-90, and accompanying text.

2. *See* Maja Beckstrom, *Good guy vs. bad guys*, St. Paul Pioneer Press at 1F (May 23, 2004) (article noting the enthusiastic reaction of an audience of child protection professionals to a call to reform the undergraduate and graduate training these professionals receive and quoting one social worker as claiming "Everyone knows it's on the job training").

3. *Gutnecht: WSU to get DOJ Grant*, Winona Daily News at 1A (article discussing the announcement by United States Congressman Gil Gutnecht that the U.S. Department of Justice awarded the NCPTC federal funds to "develop a model college curriculum" for child protection professionals). In a December 12, 2003 press release, United States Senator Mark Dayton announced the 2003 omnibus bill included funds for the NCPTC for the purpose of developing a model child protection curriculum. This press

release can be accessed at:
http://dayton.senate.gov/~dayton/releases/2003/12/2003 c12445.html

4. Victor I. Vieth, *The National Child Protection Training Center: A Partnership Between APRI and Winona State University*, 38(1) The Prosecutor 33 (January/February 2004).

5. Montclair State University is a four-year liberal arts college located in Montclair, New Jersey.

6. To graduate from MSU with a major in Justice Studies and a concentration in Child Advocacy, students must complete the following nine courses: Perspectives on Justice Studies I, Perspectives on Justice Studies II, Research in Justice Studies: Social Science Perspective, Foundations of Legal Research, Child Psychology, Children's Rights and Child Advocacy, Forensic Psychology, Contemporary Issues in Child Advocacy, and an externship. Students must also complete at least two of the following courses: Adolescent Psychology, Psychology of Aggression, Mental Health Issues of Hispanic Americans, Psychology of the Black Experience, the Black Family, Psychology and Law, or Introduction to Community Psychology. Finally, students must take at least two of the following courses: Family Law, Mediation Process and its Applications, State and Local Government, or Psychology of Women. For more information about these courses, visit the MSU web site at <http://www.montclair.edu>.

7. Exit interviews with students emphasized positive feelings toward the certificate and improved morale at work. Graduates attributed this to their educational experience at MSU that included course work, faculty and the student-friendly environment.

8. *See generally, The Benefits of Working as a Multidisciplinary Team*, published in Investigation and Prosecution of Child Abuse Third Edition xxix-xliv (2004) (SAGE, Thousand Oaks, CA).

9. To receive the Master of Arts in Child Advocacy, students must complete the following courses: Introduction to Applied Child Advocacy, Child Abuse and Neglect, Current Social Issues in Child Advocacy, Children and Justice, Theoretical and Applied Models of Interviewing Children, Selected Topics in Child Advocacy, and a practicum. Students must also take at least one of the following courses: Adolescents in the System, Substance Abuse and Families in Crisis, Family Empowerment Models, Child Protective Service Investigation, Child Welfare Policy. Finally, students must take at least two of the following courses: Counseling the Alcoholic and the Substance Abuser, Multicultural Counseling, Mentally Impaired and Chemically Addicted Client, Counseling the Family, Selected Problems in Counseling Handicapped Persons, Evidence, Juvenile Law, Education Law, Child in the Family, Intercultural Study of the Family.

10. To complete the MA in Child Advocacy with a concentration in Public Child Welfare, students must complete the following courses: Introduction to Applied Child Advocacy, Child Abuse and Neglect, Current Social Issues in Child Advocacy, Children and Justice, and Theoretical and Applied Models for Interviewing Children. Students must also select three courses from the following: Adolescents in the System, Substance Abuse and Families in Crisis, Family Empowerment Models, Child Protective Service Investigation, Permanency Planning, Child Welfare Policy. Finally, students must complete the course "Selected Topics in Child Advocacy" as well as complete a practicum and an Externship in Public Child Welfare.

11. *See* Victor Vieth, *Unto the Third Generation: A Call to End Child Abuse in the United States Within 120 Years* (this volume) notes 37-38 and accompanying text (noting the Council on Social Work education, the organization that accredits undergradu-

ate social work programs discourages concentration in specific fields such as child protection).

12. Barbara Bonner, *Consultant's Report on a New Academic Program: Master of Arts Degree in Child Advocacy*, November 4, 2003 (the original of this document is on file at Montclair State University).

13. Further information about the Center for Child Advocacy at MSU is available at: <http://chss2.montcliar.edu/cca/>.

CONCLUSION

Ending Child Abuse

David L. Chadwick

The authors of this remarkable work speak of ending child abuse not as a platitude but as an attainable goal for our country. For the first time in our history, we are presented with a blueprint for accomplishing the goal of ending child abuse and are given an estimate of the time required. The authors propose transformation of professional education in social, legal and health fields, much more complete reporting of abuse by professionals, hugely improved management of suspected and recognized cases, research-based forensic interviewing, vertical prosecution of all cases of child abuse, better treatment, better punishment, perfected prevention and ongoing training and technical assistance for civil, as well as criminal child protection professionals.

The authors point out the encouraging beginnings that have been made in many of the areas of professional competence that transformed child protection in the twentieth century, and led to the hope of ending abuse. Their proposals for change are very substantial. So much so that

Address correspondence to: David L. Chadwick, MD, Primary Children's Medical Center, Safe and Healthy Families, 100 North Medical Drive, Salt Lake City, UT 84113.

[Haworth co-indexing entry note]: "Ending Child Abuse." Chadwick, David L. Co-published simultaneously in *Journal of Aggression, Maltreatment & Trauma* (The Haworth Maltreatment & Trauma Press, an imprint of The Haworth Press, Inc.) Vol. 12, No. 3/4, 2006; and: *Ending Child Abuse: New Efforts in Prevention, Investigation, and Training* (ed: Victor I. Vieth, Bette L. Bottoms, and Alison R. Perona) The Haworth Maltreatment & Trauma Press, an imprint of The Haworth Press, Inc., 2006. Single or multiple copies of this article are available for a fee from The Haworth Document Delivery Service [1-800-HAWORTH, 9:00 a.m. - 5:00 p.m. (EST). E-mail address: docdelivery@haworthpress.com].

doi:10.1300/J146v12n03_07

they will dwarf present efforts, and require a societal commitment greater than the war on cancer and comparable in cost to the exploration of space.

DEVELOPING THE POLITICAL WILL TO END CHILD ABUSE

Initiating efforts of this scope requires strong political will, especially when an honest appraisal of our past efforts does not guarantee success of our future ones. Still, no guarantee of success preceded the effort to go to the moon. It did require a reasonable prospect of success and considerable political courage. With respect to child abuse, there is a reasonable prospect that we can end maltreatment and, as reflected in the foreword to this publication, there are at least some members of Congress courageous enough to advocate for children. Unfortunately, most elected leaders, just like most Americans, do not have the needs of maltreated children on their radar screen.

Why do we not have the political will to end child abuse? How is it that behaviors that are intolerable to most people are widely prevalent in a society? How can we understand the persistent, silent, acceptance of child abuse for millennia?

The silence about child abuse appears to be an absolute social requirement in all cultures. Perhaps the human mind cannot accommodate the moral dissonance between the accepted imperatives of child nurture and the realities of the lives of many children. The dilemma is solved by silence. If no one believes they have the power to stop abuse, we must keep it out of sight and out of mind.

To break this silence, and develop the political will to end child abuse, the authors of this volume suggest, beginning in college, teaching child protection professionals the art and science of advocating for children not only in our nation's courtrooms but in front of county boards, state legislatures, and in the halls on Congress. This advocacy is critically important simply because many of these children cannot advocate for themselves. A lot of the worst maltreatment affects infants and very young children who will *never* be able to speak about it.

Although child victims cannot advocate for themselves, many adult survivors of maltreatment can. If the voices of adult survivors are added to the voices of child advocates, the prospect of meaningful reform increases.

The price we pay for our silent tolerance of child abuse is high. It is probably greatest in the unmeasurable, unfulfilled human achievement potential of the infants and children affected by neglect. But each form of abuse adds to the likelihood of lifelong physical or mental health problems. Taken together, they impose an enormous burden on the health of millions.

UNANSWERED QUESTIONS

In the struggle to end child abuse, there are many unanswered questions. How we define child abuse will impact on how we measure our success in reducing maltreatment. We must develop new definitions that describe things that we can actually measure that are correlated with the incidence and prevalence of abuse.

In terms of prevention, we know more about what does not work than what does. As noted in one of the articles in this volume, some of the most widespread prevention efforts, such as teaching children personal safety, have been called into question. Even prevention efforts that have measurable success, such as risk-based prevention programs, may be criticized as stigmatizing.

We also need to understand why many boys evolve into men that want to have sex with children. Interventions that might reduce the likelihood of men growing up with this desire have not been adequately developed. A better understanding of sexual development is needed, and this requires a willingness to speak openly about the subject.

A MEANINGFUL FRAMEWORK

Perhaps the most remarkable aspect of this volume is that it does not pretend to have the answer to all the questions that can arise when boldly speaking about ending child abuse. Instead, the authors offer numerous reforms that nearly all child advocates can agree with. Equally important, the authors offer a framework in which to address the myriad unanswered questions.

It is good to hear from authors who will write about ending child abuse, and no one can be faulted for being a generation or so off the mark in either direction. It will surely take some time. We may already be moving in the right direction. The present volume contains numerous helpful recommendations. If they all come to pass, we will be on the right path.

Index

Abuse
  child. *See* Child abuse
  physical. *See* Physically abused
    children
  sexual. *See* Sexual abuse
Abuser(s), child. *See* Child abusers
Aeschylus, 6
American Professional Society on the
    Abuse of Children (APSAC),
    16,91
American Prosecutors Research
    Institute (APRI), xviii,15
  NCPCA of, 16
American Psychological Association
    (APA), 12,66
Americans With Disabilities Act, 112
APA. *See* American Psychological
    Association (APA)
APRI. *See* American Prosecutors
    Research Institute (APRI)
APSAC. *See* American Professional
    Society on the Abuse of
    Children (APSAC)
*APSAC Handbook on Child
    Maltreatment*, 121

Baltimore City Commission for
    Children and Youth, 71
Battered child syndrome, 8,72
Batterman-Faunce, J.M., 87
Boardman, H., xv
Bonhoeffer, D., 28
Boston College Law School, xvi
Bottoms, B.L., 1,2,81,90,136
"Broken Windows" theory, 35
Burnout, 19

CAPTA. *See* Child Abuse Prevention
    and Treatment Act (CAPTA)
CBFRS program. *See*
    Community-Based Family
    Resource and Support
    (CBFRS) program
Center for Child Advocacy, xv
Chadwick Center for Children and
    Families, xv
Chadwick, D.L., xv,3,7,13,159
Chicago Children's Advocacy Center,
    xvi
Child abuse
  clear concept of, developing of,
    58-64
  defined, 58
  ending of
    within 120 years, 5-54
    battle plan for, 14-21
    developing political will for,
      160-161
    last full measure of, 36-39
    law schools role in, 21
    meaningful framework for, 161
    medical schools role in, 21-22
    obstacles to, 9-14
    prevention efforts in
      local running of, 28-30
      tailored to local needs, 28-30
    timeline for, 31-36
      2001-2040, 31-33
      2040-2120, 33-36
    unanswered questions related to,
      161
    understanding one's role in
      history, 31
  fight against, history of, 8-9
  legal handling of, history of, 23-24
  prevention of, 55-80

Child sexual abuse, defined, 59
Child victim(s)
adolescents, interviewing of,
107-110
with disabilities, interviewing after,
110-114
individual differences among,
104-116
of physical abuse, interviewing of,
114-116
pre-adolescents, interviewing of,
107-110
pre-school-aged child, interviewing
of, 105-107
Child Victim Unit (CVU), 134,141
case acceptance policy of, 142-143
creation of, barriers to, 144
funding for, 144-145
goals of, 142
mission statement of, 141
protocol for, 141-144
structure of, 143-144
Children
murdered, vertical prosecution of
cases involving, national
model for, 131-148. *See also*
Murdered children, vertical
prosecution of cases
involving
physically abused, vertical
prosecution of cases
involving, national model for,
131-148. *See also* Physically
abused children, vertical
prosecution of cases
involving
Children, Social Science, and the Law,
121
Children's Advocacy Centers (CACs),
xvii
Children's Hospital of San Diego, xv
Children's Testimony: *A Handbook of
Psychological Research and
Forensic Practice*, 121

Cincinnati Children's Hospital Medical
Center, 16
Closed questions, 87
Cognitive Interview, 91
Collin, C.C., 69
Community-Based Family Resource
and Support (CBFRS)
program, 72,73
Connelly, A.C., 7
CornerHouse, 16,17
Council on Social Work Education
(CSWE), 11-12
CPS. *See* Child protection system
(CPS)
Cramer, R.E., Jr., xv,xvi
Criminal Justice Department, of
University of Illinois at
Chicago, xvi
CSWE. *See* Council on Social Work
Education (CSWE)
CVU. *See* Child Victim Unit (CVU)

Daro, D., 29,30,64
Davis, M.K., 65
Davis, S.L., 90
Disability(ies), children with, abuse of,
interviewing after, 110-114
Disclosure process, described, in child
forensic interviews, 100
Division of Youth and Family Services
(DYFS), xv,149,151
Donnelly, A.C., 29,30
"Double-barreled" questions, in child
forensic interviews, 88-89
DYFS. *See* Division of Youth and
Family Services (DYFS)

Eckenrode, J., 69
Emery, R.E., 63

Faith-based community, child
protection professionals
enlisting support of, 26-28

BOOK ORDER FORM!

Order a copy of this book with this form or online at:
http://www.HaworthPress.com/store/product.asp?sku=5638

Ending Child Abuse
New Efforts in Prevention, Investigation, and Training

_____ in softbound at $24.95 ISBN-13: 978-0-7890-2968-3 / ISBN-10: 0-7890-2968-5.
_____ in hardbound at $39.95 ISBN-13: 978-0-7890-2967-6 / ISBN-10: 0-7890-2967-7.

COST OF BOOKS _____

POSTAGE & HANDLING _____
US: $4.00 for first book & $1.50
for each additional book
Outside US: $5.00 for first book
& $2.00 for each additional book.

SUBTOTAL _____

In Canada: add 7% GST. _____

STATE TAX _____
CA, IL, IN, MN, NJ, NY, OH, PA & SD residents
please add appropriate local sales tax.

FINAL TOTAL _____
If paying in Canadian funds, convert
using the current exchange rate,
UNESCO coupons welcome.

❑ BILL ME LATER:
Bill-me option is good on US/Canada/
Mexico orders only; not good to jobbers,
wholesalers, or subscription agencies.

❑ Signature _____

❑ Payment Enclosed: $ _____

❑ PLEASE CHARGE TO MY CREDIT CARD:

❑ Visa ❑ MasterCard ❑ AmEx ❑ Discover
❑ Diner's Club ❑ Eurocard ❑ JCB

Account # _____

Exp Date _____

Signature _____
(Prices in US dollars and subject to change without notice.)

PLEASE PRINT ALL INFORMATION OR ATTACH YOUR BUSINESS CARD
Name
Address
City   State/Province   Zip/Postal Code
Country
Tel   Fax
E-Mail

May we use your e-mail address for confirmations and other types of information? ❑ Yes ❑ No We appreciate receiving
your e-mail address. Haworth would like to e-mail special discount offers to you, as a preferred customer.
We will never share, rent, or exchange your e-mail address. We regard such actions as an invasion of your privacy.

Order from your **local bookstore** or directly from
The Haworth Press, Inc. 10 Alice Street, Binghamton, New York 13904-1580 • USA
Call our toll-free number (1-800-429-6784) / Outside US/Canada: (607) 722-5857
Fax: 1-800-895-0582 / Outside US/Canada: (607) 771-0012
E-mail your order to us: orders@HaworthPress.com

For orders outside US and Canada, you may wish to order through your local
sales representative, distributor, or bookseller.
For information, see http://HaworthPress.com/distributors

(Discounts are available for individual orders in US and Canada only, not booksellers/distributors.)

Please photocopy this form for your personal use.
www.HaworthPress.com

BOF05